PENGUIN BOOKS

ENGLISH ECCENTRICS

Dame Edith Sitwell was born in Scarborough, the sister of Sir Osbert and Sacheverell Sitwell, and educated privately. In 1916 she became the editor of *Wheels*, an annual anthology of modern verse. She received honorary degrees for her poetry from many universities, including Oxford, Sheffield, and Durham, and she was an honorary associate of the American Institute of Arts and Letters. In 1951 she was the Visiting Professor at the Institute of Contemporary Arts and in 1958 she was the Vice-President of the Royal Society of Literature. In 1963 she was made a Companion of Literature.

Among Dame Edith's other publications are her *Collected Poems* (latest edition 1957), *Alexander Pope* (1930), *Aspects of Modern Poetry* (1934), *Victoria of England* (1936), *A Poet's Notebook* (1943), *Fanfare for Elizabeth* (1946), *The Canticle of the Rose* (1949), and *The Outcasts* (poems, 1962).

Dame Edith, whose greatest pleasures were listening to music and silence, died in 1964. Her *Selected Letters* are shortly to be published.

D0193206

English Eccentrics

Edith Sitwell

Penguin Books

Penguin Books Ltd, Harmondsworth, Middlesex, England
Penguin Books Australia Ltd, Ringwood, Victoria, Australia

—

First published by Faber & Faber 1933
Revised and enlarged edition first published in
Great Britain by Dobson Books 1958
Published in Penguin Books 1971

—

Copyright © Edith Sitwell, 1958

—

Made and printed in Great Britain
by Richard Clay (The Chaucer Press) Ltd,
Bungay, Suffolk
Set in Linotype Granjon

To

"Sirius"

From

"Judy"

25/4/72.

Author's Note

THE author would like to express her indebtedness to the biographers of her Eccentrics, and to those other collectors of Eccentricity whose works she has had an opportunity of consulting. Acknowledgements to the many titles have been made in the text wherever possible.

Contents

Pasquier, in his *Recherches sur la France*, is giving an account of the Queen of Scotland's execution; he says, the night before, knowing her body must be stripped for her shroud, she would have her feet washed, because she used ointment to one of them that was sore. I believe I have told you, that in a very old trial of her, which I bought from Lord Oxford's collection, it is said that she was a large lame woman. Take sentiments out of their pantoufles, and reduce them to the infirmities of mortality, what a falling off there is!

HORACE WALPOLE *to* GEORGE MONTAGU
18 May 1749

I

'Goose-Weather'

IN this strange 'goose-weather', when even the snow and the black-fringed clouds seem like old theatrical properties, dead players' cast-off rags, 'the complexion of a murderer in a bandbox, consisting of a large piece of burnt cork, and a coal-black Peruke', and when the wind is so cold that it seems like an empty theatre's 'Sea, consisting of a dozen large waves, the tenth a little bigger than ordinary, and a little damaged',[1] I thought of those medicines that were advised for Melancholy, in the Anatomy of this disease, of mummies made medicine, and of the profits of Dust-sifting.

Each tenth wave of the wind blew old memories like melting snowflakes in my face. 'The Battlebridge Dust and Cinder-Heap', it is said, existed since the Great Plague and the Great Fire of London. This mountain of filth and cinders afforded food for hundreds of pigs. Russia, hearing in some way of the enormous dust-heap, purchased it for the purpose of rebuilding Moscow after it had been burned. The side of the mountain of dust is now covered by thoroughfares whose names were derived from the popular ministers of that day. And again: 'Descending the hill, you will find yourself at Battlebridge, among a people as characteristic and looking as local as if the spot had been made for them, and they for the spot. At a glance you will perceive what are the distinctions which make the difference between them and the population you have just passed through. . .'

Here comes another memory, colder still, and melting like the snow. 'The ground on which the Battlebridge Dust-Heap stood, was sold to the Pandemonium Theatre

1. 'List of Theatrical Properties', *Tatler*, No 42.

Company. They built a theatre, where that cloud-kissing dust-heap had been. Come, I'll enter. The interior is somewhat fantastic, but light and pretty too; and filled with Battlebridge beaux and belles. There was no trace of any dustman there.'

There have, too, been humbler profits from the dust. An old woman named Mary Collins, a dust-sifter, giving evidence before a judge, answered when he expressed surprise that she should possess so much property: 'Oh, your worship, that's nothing . . . we find them among the dust. It is dustman's law. I have raised houses from my profits made among the dust.'

Whether the inhabitants of those thoroughfares near the dust-heap, from which those who believe in the destiny of mankind were to rebuild Moscow, listened, in the early dawn, to the far-off sounds of what songs the sirens sang, I know not. Perhaps, instead, they listened to the little hopeful articulations rising from the dust – the lip-clicks of the earthworms which are, it may be, amongst the earliest origins of our language. 'The clicking noises made by earthworms recently discovered by the physiologist, O. Mangold, do not concern us,' we are told by Herr Georg Schwidetzky, in a profoundly interesting recent book,[2] 'for though the ancient race of earthworms can claim kinship with us, our own wormlike ancestors were water animals, and at present we know nothing of their noises. Still, there is a possibility that certain lip-clicks were derived from the noises made by worms.'

Shall we find our cure for Melancholy in this thought of the origin of the kiss between loved one and loved one, mother and child, or in that other statement made in the same book: 'The Latin word "Aurora" (dawn) can without difficulty be derived from an earlier "ur-ur", supple-

2. *Do You Speak Chimpanzee?* published by Messrs Routledge.

mented in two places by A. The changes are, of course, always later editions. Now, phonetically "ur-ur" is the remains of a lemur word, and is a sound characteristic of the whole genus. When we seek information about the lives of these lemurs (who live, today, in the tropics, and especially in Madagascar), we learn to our surprise that they indulge in a kind of morning worship. They sit with raised hands, their bodies in the same position as that of the famous Greek praying boy, warming themselves in the sun. . . . It is therefore not unwarrantable to assume that Aurora, the Roman goddess of dawn, has her ultimate origin in the morning exercise of a lemur.'

We may find some cure for Melancholy in the contemplation of this, or in the reason given by some scientist for distinguishing Man from Beast. 'Man's anatomical preeminence', we are told, 'mainly consists in degree rather than in kind, the differences are not absolute. His brain is larger and more complex, and his teeth resemble those of animals in number and pattern, but are smaller, and form a continuous series, and, in some cases, differ in order of succession.'

We have, indeed, many causes for pride and congratulation, and amongst these is the new and friendly interest that is shown between nations. 'Richard L. Garner' (again I quote from Herr Schwidetzky) 'went to the Congo in order to observe gorillas and chimpanzees in their natural surroundings, and to investigate their language. He took a wire cage with him, which he set up in the jungle and from which he watched the apes.' Unfortunately, the wire cage, chosen for its practical invisibility to imaginative and idealistic minds, always exists during these experiments. 'Garner, however, tried to teach human words to a little chimpanzee. The position of the lips for the word Mamma was correctly imitated, but no sound came.' This is interesting, because a recent psycho-analyst has claimed that the reason for the present state of unrest in Europe is that every man wishes to be the only son of a widow. We can see, therefore, that if imbued with a few of the doctrines and speeches of civilization, the innocent, pastoral, and backward nations of the Apes will become as advanced, as 'civilized', as the rest of us. Who knows that they may not even come to construct cannon?

To go further in our search for some antidote against Melancholy, we may seek in our dust-heap for some rigid, and even splendid, attitude of Death, some exaggeration of the attitudes common to Life. This attitude, rigidity, protest, or explanation, has been called eccentricity by those whose bones are too pliant. But these mummies cast shadows that do not lie in their proper geometrical proportions, and from these distortions dusty laughter may arise.

Eccentricity exists particularly in the English, and partly, I think, because of that peculiar and satisfactory knowledge of infallibility that is the hallmark and birthright of the British nation.

This eccentricity, this rigidity, takes many forms. It may even, indeed, be the Ordinary carried to a high degree of pictorial perfection, as in the case I am about to relate.

On the 26th of May, 1788, Mary Clark, aged twenty-six, and the mother of six children, was delivered of a child in Carlisle Dispensary. I will not enter into the medical details, but it seems that this interesting infant was 'full grown, and seemed in perfect health. Her limbs were plump, fine and well proportioned, and she moved them with apparent agility. It appeared to the doctors that her head presented a curious appearance, but this did not trouble them much, for the child behaved in the usual manner, and it was not until the evidence of its death became undeniable, at the age of five days, that these gentlemen discovered that there was not the least indication of either cerebrum, cerebellum, or any medullary substance whatever.'

Mr Kirby, from whose pages I have culled this story, and who seems to have been one of those happy persons who never look about them, but who, when confronted with an indubitable fact, are astonished very easily, concludes with this pregnant sentence: 'Among the inferences deduced by Dr Heysham from this extraordinary conformation, but advanced with modest diffidence, is this: that the living principle, the nerves of the trunk and extremities, sensation and motion, may exist independent of a brain.' This is the supreme case of Ordinariness, carried to such a high degree of perfection that it becomes eccentricity. Again, any dumb but pregnant comment on life, any criticism of the world's arrangement, if expressed by only one gesture, and that of sufficient contortion, becomes eccentricity.

Thus, Miss Beswick, who belongs to the former order of eccentrics, did not resemble the child who was born without brains, whose supreme ordinariness and resemblance to other human beings was proved by the fact that it did not know that it was alive. Miss Beswick's ordinariness lay in the fact that she could not realize that she was dead, and, as a result, the cold dark shadow of her mummy hung over Manchester in the middle of the eighteenth century. If she was buried in the earth, reasoned Miss Beswick, her death might prove to be only an illusion, a dreamless sleep. . . . She left, therefore, a large sum of money to Dr Charles White and his two children, Miss Rosa White and her sister, with their cousin Captain White, on condition that the doctor should pay her a visit every morning, after what appeared, to uninstructed persons, to be her death, in order that he might be assured of the reality of this. When her last breath ceased, therefore, this motionless old lady, with her white staring face, black menacing eyes, and thick black eyebrows, was embalmed and laid in the dust of the attic, in the house where she had passed nearly eighty years. Dr White lived below, and the silence and dust of the house was disturbed, from time to time, by the scuttling of his ghostlike children, and every morning by the voice of the Doctor as he examined his mute and watchful patient.

When the Doctor died, the mummified Miss Beswick, that candidate for immortality, was removed to the Lying-in Hospital.

Another eccentric, of quite a different order, was Major Peter Labellière. Described as a Christian patriot and Citizen of the World, he expressed his criticism of the conduct of that planet, by leaving in his will the direction to bury him head downwards, in order, he explained, that 'as the world was turned topsyturvy, it was fit that he should be so buried that he might be right at last'. He died on June the 6th, 1800, and was buried at Box Hill.

We have, too, Richard Brothers, the sailor, a courageous and tragic figure, who did, in reality, become mad in later life, as a result of the privations he endured for conscience' sake. This poor humble and bewildered saint resigned his commission because, according to his own statement, he 'conceived the military life to be totally repugnant to the duties of Christianity, and he could not conscientiously receive the wages of plunder, bloodshed, and murder'. Mr Timbs remarks that 'this step reduced him to great poverty, and he appears to have suffered much in consequence. His mind was already shaken, and his privations and solitary reflections seem, at length, to have entirely overthrown it. The first instance of his madness appears to have been his belief that he could restore sight to the blind.' This pitiful hallucination, on the part of Richard Brothers, was called madness. But, according to the writer I have just quoted, the same illusions or hallucinations, in other and more fortunate minds, have been, even if disregarded by those minds, held to be a proof of genius. He says, gravely: 'It would be easy to mention many examples of illustrious men who have been subject to hallucinations without them having in any way influenced their conduct. Thus, Malebranche declared he heard the voice of God distinctly within him. Descartes, after long confinement, was followed by an invisible person, calling upon him to pursue the search of truth.'

But it is not this unregarded voice alone which, if heeded, would bring us to paradise. Might I not, indeed, write of those persons who, beset by the physical wants of this unsatisfactory world, can, by the force of their belief, satisfy those wants through the medium of the heaven they have created for that purpose. In this heaven, anything may happen; it is a heaven built upon earth, yet subject to no natural laws. It is true that it is invisible to all but its fortunate inhabitants, and that all material needs are gratified spiritually; but this state may be better than to have no heaven at all. Among these heaven-inhabitants were the Shakers, and the foundress of this particular heaven was Ann Lee, who was born at Manchester in 1736. Eventually, the Shakers settled in America, where their fervour, and particularly their tenets, caused a good deal of astonishment, and, in some cases, resentment. The reason for both astonishment and resentment was this: Mrs Lee had received the intimation, straight from heaven, that the outward manifestation of love between the sexes was at the root of this world's downfall; and, according to some rebels against this theory, matters had come to a pretty pass; since the choice lay between the downfall of the world, and the complete discontinuation of life on that planet. They preferred the downfall, they said – every time! Even Mr Lee, who had at first been frightened by Mrs Lee into respecting the results of this message from heaven, and who for some time followed her about hoping that she might receive counter-orders of some sort, in the end plumped for the downfall, and disappeared, when the Shakers reached America, in the company of a female Shaker whom he had converted to his heresy. Mrs Ray Strachey, in her delightful book *Religious Fanaticism* (Faber & Faber), gives a pleasing picture of the fervour and practices of these virtuous persons, quoted from the writings of a contemporary member. 'Heaven', he writes, 'is a Shaker Community on a very large scale. Everything in it is spiritual. Jesus Christ is the Head Elder, and Mother Ann the Head Eldress. The buildings are large and splendid, being all of white marble. There are large orchards with all kinds of fruit . . . *but all is spiritual*' (the italics are mine). Mother Ann, when not in heaven, worked hard as a laundress, so that those large and splendid mansions, those large orchards with all kinds of fruit, must have been a comfort to that worn body, that kind heart. 'At one of the meetings', the narrative continues, 'it was revealed to us that Mother Ann was present, and that she had brought a dozen baskets of spiritual fruit for her children, upon which the Elder invited us all to go forth to the baskets in the centre of the floor, and help ourselves. Accordingly, all stepped forth and went through the motions of taking fruit and eating it. You will wonder if I helped myself to fruit like the rest. No; I had not faith enough to see the baskets or the fruit; and you may think perhaps that I laughed at the scene; but in truth I was so much affected by the general gravity and the solemn faces I saw around me that it was impossible to laugh.'

Other things as well as fruit were sometimes sent as presents, such as spiritual golden spectacles. These heavenly ornaments came in the same way as the fruit, and just as much could be seen of them. We are told that 'On the second Sunday I spent with the Shakers there was a curious exhibition. After dinner, all the members assembled in the hall and sang two songs. Then the Elder informed them that it was a "gift" for them to march in procession, with their golden instruments playing as they marched to the holy fountain, and wash away all the stains they had contracted by sinful thoughts and feelings; for Mother Ann was pleased to see her children pure and holy. I looked for musical instruments, but as they were spiritual I could not see them. The procession marched two and two into the yard, and round the square, and came to a halt in the centre. During the march, each one made a sound with the mouth, to please him or herself, and at the same time went through the motions of playing on some particular instrument, such as the clarinet, French horn, bass drum, etc.; and such a noise was made that I felt as if I had got among a band of lunatics. Most of the brethren then commenced going through the motions of washing face and hands, but finally some of them tumbled themselves in all over; that is, they rolled on the grass, and went through comical and fantastic capers.

'During my whole time with the Shakers a revival was going on among the spirits in the invisible world, and much of the members' time was spent in such performances. It appeared to me that whenever any of the brethren or sisters wanted some fun they "got possessed of spirits".'

This, indeed, was a less concrete heaven than that modern paradise, that cloud-high world of paper erected by Ivar Kreuger, a heaven which, though it was made of paper, he succeeded in making untransparent, so that none of the financiers who were its saints could catch any glimpse, through those glistening walls, of the rotting physical and spiritual slums beyond it. Indeed, in the little shallow hell which was its foundation, he built the most modern and convenient of all heavens, wherein, instead of Mother Ann's unheard voice, he had his dummy telephone.

Let us leave the thought of that shallow hell, and turn, for a medicine for our Melancholy, to one case where no heaven, but a complete world whose glory enters, usually, through the medium of five senses, was received through the medium of four senses alone. This conqueror of the material world was named Margaret McAvoy, and she was born at Liverpool on the 28th June, 1800. After she had become totally blind at the age of sixteen, she could distinguish colours by the touch of her fingers. This power of touch, it seemed, varied very materially with circumstances. When her hands were cold, she declared that the faculty was altogether lost, and that it was exhausted, also, by long and unremitting efforts. In these days of the triumph of that great and noble woman Helen Keller, the minor and rather elementary triumphs of Margaret McAvoy may not seem significant: but I append some notes about her experiences, taken down by a committee of doctors and other scientists who examined her, for the reason that education – the mind – played no part in these triumphs. They are due to physical sensibility alone. As against this, we must acknowledge that the description given to the doctors must have been less difficult in her case than in the case of one who was born blind.

'The red rays of the solar spectrum being thrown upon her hand, she said it appeared as gold. All the colours being thrown on the back of her hand, she distinctly described the different parts of her hand. She marked the moments when the colours became faint, and again vivid, by the occasional passing of a cloud, without being desired to do so. The prismatic colours afforded her the greatest pleasure that she had experienced since her blindness. She never saw a prism in her life. She felt the spectrum warm – the violet rays were the least pleasant. She observed that the red rays appeared warmer and more pleasant than the violet, which opinion coincides with that of Herschel, who proved the great differences of heat-content among the different prismatic rays.

Question: "What sensation did you feel when you first were asked and told the colour of my coat?"

Answer: "At first it was a sensation of astonishment and then of pleasure."

Question: "Do you prefer any colour?"

Answer: "I prefer the lightest colours, as they give a pleasurable feeling; a sort of glow to my fingers, indeed, all through me. Black gives me rather a shuddering feel."

Question: "Is the feeling similar when they are enclosed in a phial bottle, or when you feel them through the plain glass?"

Answer: "It is similar, but not exactly so, if the bottle is cold."

Question: "Do you feel the colour equally well if the glasses are placed before an object?"

Answer: "If the glasses are very close to each other, as if there were only one glass, I feel the colour, but it appears more faint; but if they are placed at a distance from each other, I do not feel the object."

Question: "If coloured glasses are given to you, what sensation do you feel?"

Answer: "Much the same as when silks are put into my hand."

Question: "How do you tell glass from stones?"

Answer: "The stones feel harder and more solid, and the glass softer."

Question: "Did you not recently feel a seal which you declared was neither stone nor glass?"

Answer: "Yes, I did say so, and it felt softer than glass."

Question : "In what way was the impression made upon the fingers, when you felt the figures reflected from the mirror through the plain glass?"

Answer : "I feel the figures as an image upon each finger."

Question : "How do figures or letters feel through the glass?"

Answer : "As if they were raised up to the finger."

Question : "What is the feeling you have of different fluids?"

Answer : "Similar to my feeling of silks."

Question : "How do you know the difference between water and spirits of wine?"

Answer : "By the spirits of wine feeling warmer than water."

Question : "How do you know that a person is putting out his hand, or nodding to you?"

Answer : "If anyone puts out his hand on entering, or going out of the room, I feel as if air, or wind, was wafted towards me, and I put out mine. If a nod is made pretty near to my face, a similar sensation is felt, but if a finger is pointed at me, or a hand held before me in a gentle manner, I do not feel it unless I am about to read or tell colours, and then I very soon tell if there be any obstruction between the mouth, the nostrils, and the object."

Question : "How do you calculate the height of persons entering the room?"

Answer : "By feeling, as if less or more wind were wafted towards me, according to the height of the person."

Question : "If a person passes you quickly, do you feel any additional sensation?"

Answer : "Yes, I feel a greater sense of heat, according to the quickness with which a person passes me, or comes into the room." '

*

From reflecting on this triumph over the material world, we may turn to the thoughts of that heaven of love that survives material death, and of the angels of that heaven. Such an angel appeared in the painted, half-mad guise of poor Sarah Whitehead, known as the Bank Nun.

This solitary and destitute creature, once so happy and rich, not in material comforts only, but in love, was a girl of seventeen when her brother, who was employed at the Bank, took her to live with him. His house was luxurious, for he was living far beyond his means, and Sarah had carriages, and as many dresses as she could want. Nobody knew where he procured his money, but the truth was that he had been speculating like a madman, for, having begun the life of luxury, he did not know how to withdraw from it. Indeed, his most valued friendships, excepting that of one family, who come into the story later, depended upon that luxury; for nothing, as we know, causes a deeper pain (and a greater shrinking from pain) than the sight of a friend suffering from need. When the Bank knew of his speculations, the governors warned him kindly and delicately that gambling on the part of those employed was against the rules of the Bank, and that in the end, if he did not stop speculating, he must be dismissed. Whereupon he lost his temper and, in spite of all that could be said to dissuade him, resigned his situation.

His sister never knew that he had left the Bank, and the luxuries in the house continued; but she did notice that many of the guests who came to their daily dinner-parties were not of the same kind as those who came in former days. They were noisier and were dressed more flashily. Her brother, too, seemed changed. His face was dulled and pale, as if he were starved with cold, although it was burning summer weather; and it seemed, too, as if he were listening, not to what was being said to him, but for some knock upon the door. After a while the dinner-parties ceased. The carriages disappeared. 'Want', Messrs Wilson and Caulfield tell us, 'planted a withering finger where, before, luxury had revelled. Despair seized him and, harried on by his friends, he associated himself with the notorious Roberts, who raised heavy sums of money among the Hebrew tribes of London by representing himself as the heir of the Duke of Northumberland, and he absolutely effected a mortgage on the Duke's estate, with many other expert forgeries, which, however, could not be proved in a legal way.' But though *he* could not be punished by the law, the poor foolish creature whom he had used as a cat's-paw must die.

Young Whitehead left the house, for the last time, one dawn, before his sister was awake, and without leaving one word of farewell for her, since he hoped to spare her the knowledge of his fate. She waited for him all day, and then, as the evening fell and he did not come, a feeling of mortal illness stole over her, and she crouched near the door, listening for his footstep. But time went by, and still he did not come. . . . At last, just as the light was fading, some friends came to the house; but they did not seem surprised to find her crouching near the door. They spoke in a queer muttering voice, and their faces were sickly and pale, but they explained that they had not been well. Besides, the light was strange, and this might explain their look. Her brother, they said, had sent a message asking her to go with them to their house in Wine Court, for he could not return home that evening or the next.

Three mornings afterwards, Sarah Whitehead, in that distant street, did not hear the bell of St Sepulchre's Church tolling for the death of the man who had been hanged for forgery, only three days after he was condemned to death, whilst the man who was guilty went free.

The days passed, and Sarah Whitehead's friends begged

her to stay with them still, for her brother could not return home yet, they said. But his long absence, so strange, so unexplained, with not a word, not a sign to her, preyed upon her spirits. Perhaps, she thought, he had married and forgotten his sister. So at last, unknown to her friends, she left their house and made her way to the Bank, and a young and foolish clerk, taken aback at her appearance, blurted out the whole story of that day which she had spent alone, and the three days that followed. She neither spoke nor wept, but stood looking at the man, whose voice, before that look, died away till it was nothing but a whisper. She stood there, for a very long time, looking at that silent white-faced young man. Then, very slowly, walking on such heavy feet as the dead might use if, after many years of waiting, of numbed, dumb and anguished pain, they might return to us to watch the little details of our life, Sarah Whitehead, aged in this life less than twenty years, gathered up her broken dust, her blood that had turned to stone and, in the space of some hours, those remains of ruin found themselves once more in the home of her friends.

In the days and nights that followed, those wrecked and jagged pieces left by ruin, were drawn together until they formed some kind of despairing prison for a huge world of primitive chaos wherein no form existed, only a period of huge clots of darkness followed by an universe of mad and chattering light that had once been empty waiting sunlight. Then, slowly, her whole being would be invaded by some huge and formless bulk, growing vaster as it loomed out of the blackness and the light, until both blackness and light were blotted out. Then after an aeon that existed not in time, that huge bulk would shrink until it was nothing but a small helpless creature, emitting a terrible broken crying, a hopeless, helpless whimpering as it was torn to pieces. But no sound from that crying reached the world beyond, for the prison that entombed it was too strong, and that prison longed to break, but could not. Yet I have heard that sound raising itself, amid the little tumults of the dust, the lip-clicks of worms that are soon to transform themselves into the speech, and the kiss of mankind; although the busy dusty world is too deafened by the sound of the machines that it has made for the trapping and murdering of time to listen to those sounds that are clear as the songs of angels.

At eight o'clock every morning, Sarah Whitehead would make her way to the Bank, to wait for her brother. She had been left as destitute as any scarecrow in the fields, but she never knew this; for Alderman Birch, we are told, 'was a true friend to her, and allowed her a small annuity, which was regularly paid to her every week by a lady in the city, who kindly undertook the office to save her the trouble of going out of the city to the house of her benefactor. Her existence depended entirely on the bounty of friends. In a dress of sable, with painted face, and head enveloped with a sort of coronet fancifully decked out with streamers of black crape, and a reticule hung on her arm, she daily attended at the Bank, where she continued loitering about for hours, waiting for her brother, under the belief that he was still employed in the establishment.'

The Governors of the Bank, overcome with pity for her misery, and knowing her condition would have been destitute were it not for the compassion of Alderman Birch and one or two other friends, very frequently gave her money; and so did everyone else who worked at the Bank; but at last, owing to this kindness on their part, her unhappy mad brain conceived the idea that they were trying to keep her out of immense sums of money. She began to make scenes at the Bank, and these, taking place in business hours, became in the end so painful that the authorities were obliged to forbid her to come to the Bank for a time. They did this very unwillingly, since they were full of pity for her; and, as soon as she had promised to be quieter in her behaviour, she was allowed to come again, and could be seen haunting the Bank as before. Only once did she forget her promise, and that was when, walking up to the Lord Rothschild of that time, in the Stock Exchange, she accused him violently of trying to rob one so forlorn as herself and, declaring that he had defrauded her of her whole fortune, she demanded the £2,000 which he had stolen from her. Looking at her with compassion, Lord Rothschild took a half-crown from his pocket, and said, gently, 'There, then, take that, and don't bother me now; I'll give you the other half tomorrow.' She thanked him quietly and gratefully, and went away without another word.

Every day, for twenty-five years, this ghost might have been seen waiting for that other and beloved ghost, at one or another of the chop-houses near the Bank, for, although he was long in returning, he must come to her soon, she thought. If one, richer than herself, offered her a glass of brandy, she would accept it with a grateful look, but silently; then, having drunk the brandy she would creep out again into Threadneedle Street, to wait for her brother there. For twenty-five years this life of hope continued, but then the appearance of the Bank Nun began to change. Perhaps some ray of dreadful piercing light had pierced the inner darkness of her mind. In any case, though she was now only between fifty-five and sixty years of age, she broke very fast. One day, some time before her death, she did not go to the Bank as usual; and from that time, until she was laid in her grave, her brother, had he come to the Bank to meet her, would have found no faithful loving ghost awaiting him. Something in that ghost had broken, was lost.

This was one of the tales of heaven, hidden in the guise of despair, that I heard rising from the dust, and broken or muffled by that deadness. Who knows, that some strange gesture, some remembered look, may not recall the soul to these mummies lying under the ruins of time, though the dust mutters: 'Egyptian ingenuity was more unsatisfied, continuing their bodies in sweet consistencies to assist the return of their souls. But all was vanity, feeding the wind, and folly. Egyptian mummies, which Cambyses or time hath spared, avarice now consumeth. Mummy is become merchandise, Mizraim cureth wounds, and Pharaoh is sold for balsam.'

Ancients and Ornamental Hermits

'MUMMIES were of several kinds,' we learn, 'and all were of great use in magnetic medicines. Paracelsus enumerates six kinds of mummies: the first four, only differing in the composition used by different peoples for preserving their dead, are the Egyptian, Arabian, Hirasphatos, and Libyan. The fifth mummy of peculiar power was made from criminals that had been hanged, for from such there is a gentle siccedion, that expungeth the watery humours without destroying the oil and spirituall which is cherished by the heavenly luminaries, and strengthened continually by the affluence and impulses of the celestial spirits, whence it may be called by the name of constellated or celestial mummy. The sixth kind of mummy was made of corpuscles or spiritual effluences radiated from the living body; though we cannot get very clear ideas on this head, respecting the manner in which they were caught.' (Medicine, Disuetatica, or Sympathetica, from Paracelsus.) Our first spiritual effluences, our first mummy-made medicine, shall be physic made from those who showed their eccentricity by their unnatural persistence in retaining the appearance of life, and from those who, whilst in this life, mimic'd mortality.

Of these two strongly opposed races of the Dead, the first was deeply affected by the moon. At every waxing or waning of the moon over the countryside, a faint whispering as of drowsy complaining nightingales might be heard, for the ancients were dying under the strange influence of the moonlight. Some were brightening into eternal glory with the full moon, others were waning and being born again with the new moon, whilst their ancient dust sank into a mossy green

fresh grave. For the planet has a strange influence. Ambrose
Paré believed that the danger of contagion from the plague
is nearer to all men at the time of the full moon, whilst,
according to Pliny, the fourth day of the moon determines
the wind of the month. The growth of the moon, if we may
believe Gellius, enlarges the eyes of cats, and onions bud at
the decrease of the moon, and wither whilst she grows –
a sinister and unnatural vegetation which induced the people
of Pelusium to avoid their use. Ants, we are told by Pliny,
never perform their work whilst the moon is about to
change. Aristotle is convinced that the time for earthquakes
is when the new moon is born, and that under the strange
and drowsy influence of this light (which is nourished by
the sound and the ripples of rivers, as the sun draws its
strength from the sea), those sleepers who lie beneath its
beams grow drowsier still, whilst the moon corrupts all slain
carcases she shines upon. He is confirmed in this matter by
Van Helmont, who assures us that a wound inflicted by
moonlight is most difficult to heal. Shepherds must pray to
the moon, for according to Galen 'all animals that are born
when the moon is falciform, or at the half-quarter, are weak,
feeble, and short-lived, whereas those that are dropped at the
full moon are healthy and vigorous'.

In the house in the wood, where the moonlight shines
green through the leaves, and there is no sound excepting for
the little drowsy household noises dying away into silence,
the cook will warn you that meat hung in the moonlight
soon becomes rotten. Far away, amongst other and very
different trees, wild races, the Arabs and the Egyptians and
the Negroes in the West Indies, fear sleeping in the moonlight. Many a careless Negro, if we may believe Lieutenant
Burton, after sleeping under the light of the full moon, has
risen to find that one half of his face is by no means the
same colour as the other half of his face; nor does this strange

metamorphosis fade with the moon; on the contrary, many months must pass before both sides of that dark face are of the same colour once more. With these records of the moon's evil influence in our mind, we cannot be surprised that the researches of a certain Dr Moseley led him to the conclusion that persons in extreme old age wane into death at the time of the full or the new moon.

Amongst other aged quivering nightingale-like voices complaining from the white nodding cottages on this drowsy night of the full moon, we may hear the ghosts of the bones of old Mr John de la Smet, who died, aged one hundred and thirty years, in 1766; of Mr George King, aged also one hundred and thirty years, who died at the same time; of Mr John Taylor, whose age was the same, and who died in 1767; of Mr William Beattie whose death took place in 1774; Mr John Watson who died in 1778; Mr Robert MacCride, who died in 1780; and Mr William Ellis who trembled into dust in 1780. All these ancient persons reached the age of one hundred and thirty years, and then sank into a greenish dust under the light of the full moon, whilst Mr Peter Garden lived to the age of one hundred and thirty-one, and died in 1775. Mrs Elizabeth Merchant died at the age of one hundred and thirty-three, in 1761; Mrs Catherine Noon, white and ghostlike, faded in 1763, at the age of one hundred and thirty-six. Mr William Leland, and the ancient Countess of Desmond, died in 1732, aged one hundred and forty, and old Mrs Louisa Trusco beat the lot by crumbling into dust at the age of one hundred and seventy-five, in the year 1780.

I am told that the eighteenth century was remarkable for the age and darkness of the full-leaved shady mulberry trees and fig trees, and it may be that this century was fortunate also in bringing its ancients into a sleepy plenitude of time. But there was an earlier shady old person named Thomas

Parr, who was, I believe, painted by Rubens when he was a hundred and forty years old, whose age and prowess was celebrated in verse by John Taylor, the water poet, and who died on the 15th of November, 1635, at the age of one hundred and fifty-two. In spite of the unsuitable sprightliness of his later years, he was buried in Westminster Abbey.

John Taylor tells us that 'the Right Hon. Thomas Earl of Arundel and Surrey, Earl Marshal of England, etc., being lately in Shropshire to visit some lands and manors which his lordship holds in that country, or for some other occasions of importance, the report of this aged man was certified to his honour, who, hearing of so remarkable a Piece of Antiquity, his lordship was pleased to see him, and in his innate, noble and Christian piety, he took him into his charitable tuition and protection; commanding a litter and two horses (for the more easy carriage of a man so enfeebled and worn with age) to be provided for him; also, that a daughter-in-law of his (named Lucy) should likewise attend him, and have a horse of her own riding with him; and to cheer up the old man, and make him merry, there was an antique-faced fellow, called Jack, or John the Fool, with a high and mighty no-beard, that had also a horse for his carriage. These were all to be brought out of the country to London by easie journeys, the charges being allowed by his lordship; and likewise one of his honour's own servants, named Brian Kelly, to ride on horseback with them, and to attend and defray all manner of reckoning and expenses; all which was done accordingly.'

The journey was not by any means devoid of incident, for the 'rabble' was so intent on seeing the Piece of Antiquity that he was nearly smothered. We hear that 'at Coventry he was most opprest; for they came in such multitudes to see the old man, that those who defended him were almost quite tyred and spent, and the aged man in danger to have been stifled'. However, after several excitements of this kind, the cortège reached London.

Mr Parr married for the first time when he was eighty; and marriage after that became a habit with him, though there was an occasion when, owing no doubt to an oversight, he was made to do public penance, at the age of one hundred and five, for omitting this ceremony. The ghostlike Piece of Antiquity, fading like the moon in summer daylight stood, on this occasion, wrapped in a white sheet at the church door. But I am afraid the ancient and rattling-boned gallant rather gloried in this fall from grace, for he certainly boasted about it to King Charles I. Afterwards, he married again, this time at the age of a hundred and twenty, and his wife, whose maiden name was Catherine Milton, presented him with a child. He was, at that time of his life, 'employed in threshing and other husbandry work', and his portrait shows a rather noble windformed head and beard – the face, indeed, of a sylvan Jupiter, wrinkled and brown like the trunk of a fig tree.

Two other remarkable ancients were the Countess of Desmond, whose death, at the age of one hundred and forty years, seems to have been less the result of age, or even of the full moon, than the result of climbing an apple tree – and falling from this, amidst a shower of glistening apples; and Mr Henry Jenkins, who died in 1670, at the age of one hundred and sixty-nine.

In spite of his remarkable career, Mr Jenkins had, perhaps from fatigue, elected to die, humbly on the day of the new moon, instead of surrounded by the splendours of the full moon. Mrs Anne Saville, of Bolton, Yorkshire, who knew him well, remembered that one day when this venerable person came to beg from her, he confided in her that he remembered the Battle of Flodden Field with great distinctness. King Henry VIII was not there, he informed the tongue-tied Mrs Saville, for he was in France; the Earl of Surrey was General. When Mrs Saville recovered from the not unnatural astonishment into which she was thrown by this confidence on the part of Mr Jenkins, she asked for more details about Flodden Field and Mr Jenkins' age at the time of the battle. 'I was between ten and twelve,' that remarkable old gentleman assured her, 'for I was sent to Northallerton with a horse-load of arrows, but they sent a bigger boy from thence to the army with them.'

As the battle of Flodden Field was fought on September the ninth, 1513, and Mr Jenkins was now approaching his death, which took place on December the eighth, 1670, Mrs Saville felt she would like to inquire into the truth of Mr Jenkins' memories. Might they not, indeed, have been born from some trance of age, some sleep like death? But, in the course of her inquiries, she discovered that four or five ancient men of the same period, all of whom were over a hundred years of age, remembered Mr Jenkins when they were boys of a bird's-nesting age; and he was already an extremely aged person when they knew him first. Mr Jenkins' activities, it seemed, were many: he was, for instance, an extremely lively and garrulous witness in a law case between Messrs. Smithson and Anthony Clark at Kettering in the year 1665, when he, Mr Jenkins, was a labourer of the age of one hundred and fifty-seven years. And his biographer tells us, in an ecstasy of admiration, that this vivacious old person spent the last century of his life as a fisherman, and might frequently have been seen swimming in the rivers, with his beard spreading like weeds among the ripples.

These, then, are our 'mummies made medicine', who now are dying, nodding away into nothingness, in the calm light of the full moon. No longer can they be soothed into sleep, or lulled into an ever more peaceful dream, by medicines more ancient than themselves – such as the thousand-year-old Arabian draught,[1] made of 'Cinnamon, common pepper, juice of poppies, dried roses, water germander, rape seed, Illyrian iris, agaric, opobalsam, myrrh, saffron, ginger, rhaponticum, cinquefoil, calamint, horehound, stone parsley, cassidary, costus, white and long pepper, dittany, flowers of sweet rush, male frankincense, turpentine, mastrich, black cassia, spikenard, flowers of poley, storax, parsley seed, shepherd's pouch, bishopsweed, ground pine, juice of hypocristus, Indian leaf, spignel, gentian, anise, Jenvel seed, Lemmian earth, roasted calchetis, amomum, sweet flag, balsamum, Pontic valerian, St John's wort, acacia, carrot seed, galbanum, sagapen, bitumen, aposonax, castor, centaury, clematis, attic honey, and Falernian wine'. Even this recipe, nearly as long as the years they had passed, could not save them, nor could they be cured of the Melancholy and the Falling Evil by the use of figs, so strongly recommended by Dr Boleyn, that relative of the late Queen Anne Boleyn, who practised in the reign of Queen Mary and advocated the use of these fruits in his Book of Simples. For the ancients were as mummy-like as the sweet, overripe, and shrunken figs, and their sinews, shrunken by age, could not have their strength renewed by this prescription, given in the *Book of Knowledge* (1687): 'Take young swallows out of their nests, by number twelve, rosemary tops, bay leaves, lavender tops, strawberry leaves, of each a handful : cut off the long feathers of the swallows' wings and tails, put them into a stone mortar, and lay the herbs upon them, and beat them into pieces, guts, feathers, bones and all; then mix them with three pounds of hogs' grease, and set it in the sun a month together, then boil it up and strain it and keep the ointment, and anoint the place grieved.' In vain, too, had these ancient persons eaten swallows, which according to the

1. See Dr Russell's *History of Medicine*.

Pharmacopoeia of 1654 clear the sight like fresh dew falling upon the eyes.

These remedies were useless to them, and so were the remedies administered to their Saxon grandfathers a thousand years ago, for such disabilities as 'wens at a man's heart', which were cured by cucumbers and radish, and the small rape, and garlic and southernweed, and cinquefoil and pepper, and honey unsodden; or 'warty eruptions', which were cured by the following recipes: according to the first prescription you must 'make several little wafers, such as a man offereth with, and write these names on each wafer: "Maximanus, Malchus, Johannes, Martianus, Dionysius, Constantinus, Serefian"; then again, one must sing to charm, which is hereinafter mentioned, first into the left ear, then into the right ear, then above the man's poll; then let one who is a maiden go to him and hang it upon his neck, do so for three days, it will soon be well with him.' If you were unconvinced by the efficacy of this prescription, you might 'wring the nethermost part of cowslip and of hollow fumitory into the nostrils, and make the man lie on his back for a good while'.

These remedies were of no use to Mr Jenkins and Mr Parr and those other ancients who had passed a century of life. But still, in dark caves in the forests, and small white cottages amidst a world of orchard leaves, simple-gatherers are compounding remedies for those rare cases where women grow dumb from any cause but death – taking pennyroyal and rubbing it into dust, winding it into wool and laying it under the woman; whilst, for dim eyes, they took green rue, pounded it small, washed it with 'dumbledores'' (humble-bees') honey, and lay it on the eyes. As for those unfortunate persons who suffered from 'ill humours on the neck', the wise women took halswort and woodmarch, the wild chervil and strawberry plants, and stitchwort and tree holly, and broad bishopsweed and brown wort, all these were gathered for three nights 'before summer came to town; of each one equally much', then, according to the directions, the patient must 'work them to a drink in foreign ale', and then, on the night when summer comes to town, he 'having stayed awake all night' (for reasons known to the inventor of this recipe alone) 'may drink the first draught, and the second, as he heard the first cock crow'. He must then remain in a state of suspense, and, I presume, wakefulness, for a day and a half, and 'on the blessed rising of the sun' take a third dose. After that, we are told, 'let him rest himself'.

It was, as we may see, a strenuous matter to preserve health and life to the age of a hundred and fifty years in the midst of such prescriptions as these, and such country dangers as those brought about by birds, who, at any moment, might fly into your window, seize a golden or a silver hair from your head, and build a nest from this. Anything might happen as a consequence of this theft, for ill fortune was the inevitable result and death a frequent result.

Nor were birds, or wens, or humours on the neck, and unaccountable dumbness in women, the only dangers which must be avoided, the only disorders which must be cured, for groundsel, is seems, would put the gout to flight, even if it raged like a fire, whilst peony was an infallible cure for lunacy. Wood chervil, again, proved very useful if an evil man, through spite, had enchanted another; whilst the herb heraclea, should one wish to make a long journey through dark woods, averted any danger of an attack of robbers.

In the lonely houses on the edge of the forests, the housekeeper and the chattering maids were chanting the following spell against thieves, whilst the household noises died down, and there was no light but one fluttering candle:

39

Tho sains the house the night,
They that sains it ilk or might.
Saint Bryde and her brate,
Saint Colne and his hat,
Saint Michael and his spear,
Keep the house from the weir;
From running thief,
And burning thief;
And from a' ill rea
That be the gate can gae.
And from an ill wight
That be the gate can light,
Nine reeds about the house
Keep it all the night.
What is that what I see
So red, so bright, beyond the sea?
'Tis He was piercèd through the hands,
Through the feet, through the throat,
Through the tongue,
Through the liver and the lung;
Well is them that may
Fast on Good Friday.[2]

Strangely enough, whilst the virtuous inhabitants of the houses in the wood were quaking and saying their prayers, the very robbers, against whose depredations they were interceding, were holding a prayer-meeting of their own on the moors, for they believed that they, too, were created for their own purpose, and had as much right to a well-fed life, as have wolves, or company-promoters, or any other living beings who are dependent upon their own efforts and the sweet trustfulness of sheep.

The prayer they chanted was this:

2. 'Sains' means preserves, 'brate' means apron, 'rea' means plunder, 'reeds' means roods, or Holy horses.

He that ordains us to be born
Send us more meat for the morn;
Part of t' right and part of t' wrong,
God never let us fast over long.
God be thanked, and our Lady,
All is done that we had ready.

Whilst these persons of varying respectability were trying, in their several ways, to preserve their lives, others, equally, or more, praiseworthy, were trying to escape the consequences of being alive. And, in aid of this praiseworthy desire, certain noblemen and country squires were advertising for Ornamental Hermits. Nothing, it was felt, could give such delight to the eye, as the spectacle of an aged person with a long grey beard, and a goatish rough robe, doddering about amongst the discomforts and pleasures of Nature.

The Honble Charles Hamilton, whose estate was at Pains' Hall, near Cobham, Surrey, and who lived in the reign of King George II, was one of these admirers of singularity and silence, and, having advertised for a hermit, he built a retreat for this ornamental but retiring person on a steep mound in his estate.

This hermitage annoyed Mr Horace Walpole, who announced that it was ridiculous to set aside a quarter of one's garden to be melancholy in : and, indeed, the retreat seems to have been remarkable more for its discomfort than for its beauty, for we learn that there was 'an upper appartment, supported in part by contorted legs and roots of trees, which formed the entrance to the cell'. Still, Mr Hamilton seems to have found no difficulty in procuring the hermit; and in any case, a professional discomfort was only to be expected by the hermit, who, according to the terms of the agreement, must 'continue in the hermitage seven years, where he should be provided with a Bible, optical glasses, a mat for his feet, a hassock for his pillow, an hourglass for his timepiece, water for his beverage, and food from the house. He must wear a camlet robe, and never, under any circumstances, must he cut his hair, beard, or nails, stray beyond the limits of Mr Hamilton's grounds, or exchange one word with the servant.' If he remained without breaking one of these conditions, in the grounds of Mr Hamilton for seven years, he was to receive, as a proof of Mr Hamilton's admiration and satisfaction, the sum of seven hundred pounds. But if, driven to madness by the intolerable tickling of the beard, or the scratching of the camlet robe, he broke any of the conditions laid down, he was not to receive a penny! It is a melancholy fact that the Ornamental Hermit stayed in his retreat for exactly three weeks!

But a gentleman living near Preston, Lancashire, had better luck with his hermit. He had advertised in the papers, offering a salary of £50 a year for life, to any man who would live for seven years underground, without seeing any human being, and without cutting his hair, beard, toe-nails, or finger-nails. The advertisement was answered immediately, and the happy advertiser prepared an apartment underground which, as Mr Timbs assures us, was 'very commodious, with a cold bath, a chamber organ, as many books as the occupier pleases, and provisions served from the gentleman's own table'. The ornamental occupant bloomed, unseen, in this retreat for the space of four years. But, unseen as he was, it is a little difficult to guess what pleasure his employer can have got out of the matter.

The aged were not alone in answering these advertisements, or inserting advertisements of their own; for the following notice appeared in the *Courier* for January the eleventh, 1810: 'A young man, who wishes to retire from the world and live as a hermit, in some convenient spot in England, is willing to engage with any nobleman or gentleman who may be desirous of having one. Any letter directed to S. Laurence (post paid), to be left at Mr Otton's, No. 6 Coleman Lane, Plymouth, mentioning what gratuity will be given, and all other particulars, will be duly attended.'

The mention of the gratuity sounds a little mercenary, and I do not know what answers Mr S. Laurence received. Nor do I know what was the social position of an Ornamental Hermit. But I *do* know that in *Blackwood's Magazine* for April, 1830, Mr Christopher North, in the 'Noctes Ambrosianae', informs us (I dare not think in what spirit or for what reasons) that the editor of a certain other magazine had been 'for fourteen years hermit to Lord Hill's father, and sat in a cave in that worthy baronet's grounds with an hour-glass in his hand, and a beard belonging to an old goat, from sunrise to sunset, with orders to accept no half-crowns from visitors, but to behave like Giordano Bruno'.

It is not, I am sorry to say, impossible that this inspiration on the part of Mr North arose from reading the correspondence in *Notes and Queries* for 1810, wherein a gentleman relates that, on visiting Sir Richard Hill's country seat at Hawkstone, he had been shown the hermitage there, inhabited by a stuffed figure dressed in the proper professional robe of an Ornamental Hermit, the whole scene being illuminated by the dimmest of lights.

But this is a painful subject, and it is pleasant to turn to a certain unpaid Ornamental Hermit, an aged person whose name is unknown, but who might have been seen tottering about his garden, in the village of Newton Burgsland, near Ashby de la Zouch, Leicestershire, any day during the year 1863, and for fifteen years previously. This Ornamental Hermit was not a professional, but an amateur; he was his own master, and, I regret to say, lived comfortably, enjoyed a good dinner, a glass of beer, and a pipe; yet, in spite of these blots on his character as a hermit, he claimed that he was entitled to the name, as 'True Hermits, throughout the

ages, have been the abettors of freedom'; and it must be said
that he conformed to the hermit ideal in sporting a very
venerable appearance, and a long white beard. This ancient
body was incurably interested in symbolization, and carried
this interest so far that he possessed twenty hats, and twelve
suits of clothes, in order that each might 'bear a strange
device'.

These suits and hats were all addressed, with proper
respect, by names bestowed upon them by their owner, and I
cannot do better than give the reader a few examples of both
names and emblems.

NO.	NAME	EMBLEM OR MOTTO
1	*Odd Fellows*	Without money, without friends, without credit
5	*Bellows*	Blow the flames of freedom with God's word of truth
7	*Helmet*	Will fight for the birthright of conscience, love, life, property, and national independence
13	*Patent Teapot*	To draw out the flavour of the tea best – Union and goodwill
17	*Wash-Basin of Reform*	White-washed face and collyed heart
20	*Bee-Hive*	The toils of industry are sweet; a wise people live at peace

The shapes of the hats were intended to mirror, to express,
to symbolize, not only the proper names of the hats, but the
Eternal Truths contained in the Emblems or Mottoes. The
Suits of Clothes were not less important than the Hats. 'Odd
Fellows', for instance, was of white cotton or linen, and was
not tight-fitting; it hung loosely on the contrary, excepting
where it was bound rather tightly round the waist with a
white girdle which was tied in front. The left breast of this
remarkable confection was adorned with a heart-shaped

badge, inscribed with the motto 'Liberty of Conscience'. It must not be supposed, for a moment, that the hat 'Odd Fellows' may be confounded with this dress. The hat worn with the dress 'Odd Fellows' was nearly white, and its actual *shape* did not arouse excitement, for attention had to be drawn to the Mottoes, which were not one, but four, and bound with black ribbon. The first device bore the words 'Bless feed', the second 'Good Allowance', the third 'Well Clothed', the fourth 'All Working Men'.

You may imagine the sensation aroused by these aspirations expressed in millinery.

Other hats and costumes worn by this old gentleman were equally startling, though less improving to the character of the beholder. The costume 'Foresters', for instance, was undertaken in the lightest spirit, and was 'expressed', as dressmakers put it, in soft brown leather, slightly embroidered with braid. The shape was more or less like that of a frock coat, and this confection was closed down the front with white buttons, bound round the waist with a white girdle, and fastened with a white buckle. With this costume, the old gentleman wore a hat which bore some slight resemblance to a turban, and was divided into black and white stripes, chasing each other in a wilderness of ever-diminishing tiny circles – until they reached nothingness.

This ancient and respectable person did not confine his advertisements of the Virtues, and to quote Mr Timbs' rather unsympathetic summing up of the matter, 'mania for symbolisation', to his dress. No, his garden, which was his most treasured possession, was one mass of these advertisements and symbols. Again I find myself quoting from Mr Timbs, for the reason that it would be impossible to express the state of the garden in terms more concise than his:

'The passage leading into the garden', Mr Timbs tells us, 'was the "Three Seats of Self-Enquiry", each inscribed with one of these questions: "Am I vile?" "Am I a Hypocrite?" "Am I a Christian?" Among the emblems and mottoes which were marked by different-coloured pebbles or flowers were these: "The Vessels of the Tabernacle", "The Christian's Armour – Olive Branch, Baptismal Font, Breastplate of Righteousness, Shield of Faith, etc.", "Mount Pishap", a circle enclosing the motto "Eternal Love has wed my Soul", "a Bee-Hive", "A Church", "Sacred Urn", "Universal Grave", "Bed of Diamonds", "A Heart enclosing the Rose of Sharon", etc. All the implements included in Gardening: "The Two Hearts", "Bowers", "The Lover's Prayer", "Conjugal Bliss", "The Hermit's Coat of Arms", "Gossip's Court" – with motto, "Don't tell Anybody". "The Kitchen Walk" contained representation of culinary utensils, with mottoes – "Feast Square", "Venison Pasty", "Round of Beef", etc.; whilst "The Odd Fellows Square" sported "The Henpecked Husband put on Water Gruel", and "The Oratory" contained such mottoes as "The Orchestry", "God save our Noble Queen", "Britons never shall be Slaves", "The Sand Glass of Time", "The Assembly Room", "The Wedding Walk", "The Holy Mount", "Noah's Ark", "Rainbow", "Jacob's Ladder", "The Bank of Faith", "The Saloon", "The Enchanted Ground", "The Exit".'

I must confess that I find the description of this virtuous old gentleman's garden as bewildering as his ideals; but it seems certain that he wished to give pleasure as well as moral instruction. Amiable and charitable, there was but one person on earth whom he disliked, and that was the Pope. His garden, therefore, was adorned not only by the arbours and mottoes that I have mentioned, and by images of the Apostles, but, as well, by 'representations of the Inquisition and Purgatory, and mounds covered by sweet-smelling flowers in memory of the Graves of Protestant Martyrs and

Reformers'. In the centre of these exhortations to religious meditation, the Hermit had placed a large tub with a very odd-looking desk just before it which served him as pulpit and lectern. It is not surprising, on the whole, that his aspect and views attracted a certain amount of respectful attention, and a large crowd; and, when the crowd was large enough, the centre of attention would climb, in a sprightly manner into the pulpit, and would address the multitude on such subjects as the Pope, who, according to the speaker, was Antichrist and the enemy of humanity. Indeed, he went so far as to raise a mock gallows in his garden, adorned by an image of the Pope, dressed in a queer garb, and dangling amongst many books advocating Popery.

Far away in this strange garden, with its wildernesses of darkness, and mad dazzling hour-long summer lights masquerading as flowers, the Hermit passed his days. But alas, in the end, he grew poor, his career as an Ornamental Hermit was over, and he fades from our sight. So we must pass to another Ornamental Hermit, and one who was even less professional than the last.

The Hermit in question was Mr Matthew Robinson, afterwards Lord Rokeby, and he became famous for his amphibious habits, and for possessing benevolence and a beard. This gentleman of long life and virtuous habits, who was born in 1712, was the son of Mr Septimus Robinson, a gentleman-usher to King George II, and was the brother of the enchanting Mrs Elizabeth Montagu and Mrs Sarah Scott. He seems to have had only one fault – the vice of reciting to visitors in the most voluminous manner.

Lord Rokeby's character differed very widely from that of his sisters. Lord Rokeby was an Ornamental Hermit, adorning Nature. Mrs Montagu and Mrs Scott adorned Society. Lord Rokeby enjoyed watching birds floating freely in his woods and parks; Mrs Montagu, though she loved all birds and animals when they were living, liked, too, to see the feathers of these birds, bright, light, and glancing as her own wits, adorning her drawing-room. Peacocks, pheasants and jays, parrots and macaws, the feathers of these, woven into tapestries, adorned her room, and were the subject of a poem by Cowper. Lord Rokeby's friends were the beasts and birds on his estate, and thoughts of the Liberty of Man; Mrs Montagu's friends were Horace Walpole (who liked her at moments), Burke, Lord Bath, Mrs Vesey and the other blue-stockings, the Garricks, and Dr Johnson, who permitted no liberty – at least in the conversation of others. Lord Rokeby enjoyed the country; Mrs Montagu did *not* enjoy the company of country gentlemen. 'Our collection of men', she wrote, 'is very antique, they stand in my list thus. A man of sense, a little rusty, a beau a good deal the worse for wearing, a coxcomb extremely shattered, a pretty gentleman very insipid, a baronet very solemn, a squire very fat, a fop much affected, a barrister learned in *Coke upon Littleton*, but who knows nothing of 'long ways for marry as will', an heir apparent, very awkward; which of these will cast a favourable eye upon me I don't know.' Lord Rokeby enjoyed quiet and meditation; Mrs Fidget Montagu could never keep still. 'Why', she inquired, 'shall a table that stands still require so many legs when I can fidget on two?' and, most remarkable difference of all, whilst Lord Rokeby was celebrated for his beard, Mrs Montagu could not abide a beard: indeed, she was forced to tell her father that she could not draw the heads of Socrates and Seneca because of these appendages. 'When I told him', she informed the Duchess of Portland, 'I found those great beards difficult to draw, he gave me St John's head on a charger, so as to avoid the speculation of dismal faces.'

Lord Rokeby, in his early youth, having been a Fellow of Trinity College, Cambridge, elected suddenly to pay a visit to Aix-la-Chapelle, which, as Mr Kirby, one of his several biographers, hastens to explain to us, is 'a city distinguished for its baths'. This visit seems to have changed the whole tenor of Lord Rokeby's existence and, from that time onwards, an authority equal to that of the Archbishop of Armagh, or Prince William of Gloucester, had to be exerted before Lord Rokeby would come out of the water. The habit of eternal baths grew gradually, however, and was preceded by the equally remarkable growth of a long beard. This phenomenon appears to have arisen at about the time when Lord Rokeby was released, by death, from paternal authority, and succeeded to the family estate at Mount Morris, in Kent. Mr Kirby, who felt very strongly on the subject, said, with commendable restraint: 'Beards were once considered as marks of respectability, particularly among the ancients.' With regard to this article, however, opinion is now reversed, and it is, at least, regarded as an indubitable token of eccentricity. Why it was adopted by his Lordship is not known; reasons for such a conduct are not easily discovered; it bids defiance to conjecture, and baffles all sagacity. So much is certain, that he was for many years remarkable for this appendage, whose length, for it reached nearly to his waist, proclaimed it of no recent date. Lord Rokeby was, it seems, 'much visited on account of the singularity of his manners, and the shrewdness of his remarks'; and in order, I suppose, that strangers might gaze upon his beard; and these phenomena, taken in conjunction, 'never failed', according to Mr Kirby, 'to excite uncommon sensations'. The uncommon sensations were, a little later, excited still further by the amphibious habits to which I have referred, and which were, as I have hinted already, contracted during his visit to Aix-la-Chapelle. He erected a little hut on the sands at Hythe, about three miles from Mount Morris, and from this hut would dive, with commendable firmness, into the sea, remaining in this with the uttermost persistence, until he fainted and had to be withdrawn forcibly from the water.

Every day Lord Rokeby, whose appearance was very much like that of a benevolent troll, and whose back was bent as if he carried the weight of his winter forests, transformed into faggots, upon it, walked very slowly, carrying his hat under his arm, to the sands of Hythe. He was followed on these expeditions by a carriage and by a favourite servant, dressed in very elaborate livery, who, when he had trailed despondently for a mile or two in the wake of his master, would be hoisted into the carriage, and so transferred to the scene of action. If it rained, the servant travelled the whole way in the carriage, for Lord Rokeby would warn him that he was gaudily dressed, and not inured to wet, and might therefore spoil his clothes and occasion an illness. In the end, to the disappointment of the onlookers, but the relief of the servant, Lord Rokeby built a bath close to the house, which was 'so constructed as to be rendered tepid by the rays of the sun only'. 'The frequency of his ablutions', we are assured by Mr Kirby, who seems to have been much bewildered by the behaviour of this amphibious old person, 'was astonishing.' And listen to the testimony of an eye-witness of the behaviour in question, a gentleman who had 'resolved to procure a sight of this extraordinary character'. 'On my way, at the summit of the hill above Hythe, which affords a most delightful prospect, I perceived a fountain of pure water, overrunning a basin which had been placed for it by his lordship. I was informed that there were many such on the same road, and that he was accustomed to bestow a few half-crown pieces, plenty of which he always left loose in a side pocket, for any water-drinkers he might happen to find partaking of his favourite beverage, which he never failed to recommend with peculiar force and persuasion. On my approach, I stopped for some time to examine the mansion. It is a good, plain, gentleman's seat; the grounds were abundantly stocked with black cattle, and I could perceive a horse or two on the steps of the principal entrance. After the necessary enquiries, I was conducted by a servant to a little grove on entering which, a building with a glass covering, that at first might appear to be a greenhouse, presented itself. The man who accompanied me opened a little wicket and, on looking in, I perceived immediately under the glass a bath, with a current of water supplied from a pond behind. On approaching the door, the handsome spaniels and the faithful guardians denied me access, till soothed by the well-known accents of the domestic. We then proceeded and, gently passing along a wooden floor, saw his lordship stretched on his face at the farther end. He had just come out of the water, and was dressed in an old blue woollen coat, and pantaloons of the same colour. The upper part of his head was bald, but the hair of his chin, which could not be concealed even by the posture he had assumed, made its appearance between his arms on each side. I immediately retired, and waited at a little distance until he awoke; when rising, he opened the door, darted through the thicket, accompanied by his dogs, and made directly for the house, while some workmen employed in cutting timber, and whose tongues only I had heard before, now made the wood resound again with their voices.'

Even the majestic style of the passage quoted above cannot hide from us the awe felt by the 'gentleman who had resolved to procure a sight of the above extraordinary character', on being brought face to face with both bath and beard.

In spite of certain sinister rumours that I shall mention later, Lord Rokeby's diet consisted mainly of beef tea, while he 'discouraged the consumption of exotics of every description, from an idea that the productions of our island were competent to the support of its inhabitants'. It must be said, however, that he relented on the occasion when he was obliged to leave his bath in order to receive Prince William of Gloucester at dinner. On this occasion, though the beard was still in evidence, Lord Rokeby's other characteristics were not; the food was luxurious, and the choice of wines large, while the Prince's dessert was accompanied by a particularly precious Tokay, which had been in the cellar for fifty years or more. Lord Rokeby was not, however, so courtierlike on all occasions; and once, when he had presented the Canterbury address to the new King, his sister, Fidget Montagu, told her husband: 'I am glad he has gone into the country, but he has made a most astonishing appearance at Court with the Canterbury address. Morris says he hears of nothing else. I wish the beefeaters had not let him pass the door. Lord Harry Beauclerk, on the buzz his appearance occasioned, desired the people to be quiet, for that he had never seen the gentleman so well dressed before.' His unaccountable behaviour was, indeed, a source of constant anxiety to the enchanting Fidget, who lived in terror, as we can see from this letter to her sister, that their brother might exhibit his amphibious and carnivorous habits at Bath, during one of her visits there. 'I hope the Horton Gentleman', she wrote, 'will not change his journey to Spa for a visit to the Bath. I shall never be able to stand the joke of a gentleman's bathing with a roast loin of veal floating at his elbows, all the Belles and Beaux of the Pump Room looking on and admiring. Our guide who did not know our relation said to be sure the Quality did make a great wonderment at it, but it was nice veal and he gave what he did not eat of it to her and some others; to be sure he was the particularest gentleman as ever she heard of, but he was very good-natured.'

This amphibious habit was not the only shadow cast on Mrs Montagu's mind by her brother, for she was, as well, overshadowed by the Beard, and by the length of Lord Rokeby's hair; she was, therefore, extremely relieved when these were explained away – smoothed over, as it were, by a series of pamphlets attacking Lord North's policy. She refers to these in a letter: 'Julius Caesar', she explained, 'exercised his valour in early youth, that he might hide the defect of baldness under the conqueror's wreath. I think Mr Robinson's [Lord Rokeby's] hair wants an honourable cover as much as any baldness can do, and I am glad he has covered it with bays. There is no man in the world to whom such a proof of talents is more important. If a man shows genius, people think all his oddities are the excrescences of genius. I have sent to London for the pamphlet.'

Lord Rokeby's hair and beard were not the only products of nature which were left to run wild; for in his parks and woods – I cannot do better than quote Mr Kirby in this connection, once again, since his style is perfectly suited to the subject – 'Nature was not, in any respect, checked by art, and the animals of every class were left in the same state of perfect freedom, and were seen bounding through his pastures with uncommon spirit and energy'; whilst the venerable owner might, at moments, I imagine, be seen leaping through the same pastures with an equal freedom, in virtuous pursuit of some fleeting female form, since 'he was, in his youth, a great admirer of the fair sex, and even in his old age is said to have been a great admirer of female beauty'. 'Among the women, none more sprightly, none more ready to join in innocent mirth, or to be the subject of it,' exclaimed Messrs Wilson and Caulfield in a burst of uncontrollable enthusiasm. But then comes a darker note, for we learn that certain persons, whose susceptibilities had been offended by the beard, believed him to live on raw flesh, whilst others claimed that he was a cannibal!

It remains to be said that Lord Rokeby 'delighted much in

the air, without any other canopy than the heavens, whilst in winter his windows were generally open', and that he disapproved of medicine, and once, when threatened with a paroxysm, 'told his nephew that, should he stay, he was welcome'; but that if, out of a false humanity, he called in medical assistance, Lord Rokeby, if he remained by some strange chance unslaughtered by the doctor, hoped to retain sufficient use of his hands and senses to make a new will and disinherit his errant nephew.

Lord Rokeby had a peculiar dislike, too, of going to church, and 'this singularity', as Messrs Wilson and Caulfield gravely assure us, 'in abstaining from places of religious worship arose, partly from the exalted view which he entertained of the nature of the Deity, whose altars, he used to say emphatically, were on earth, sea, and skies; from the little regard he paid to the clerical or ministerial character, and from the disgust in his mind at the stress laid by divines upon trifles, their illiberality in wishing everyone to rely upon them, for their faith, their frequent persecution of others, and from a strong opinion of the inefficacy of their preaching'.

This exalted view of the nature of the Deity, with its accompanying train of strange opinions, led on one occasion to a magnificent exhibition of Lord Rokeby's courtesy and his resource in dealing with an awkward situation. 'The Archbishop of Armagh', said Lord Rokeby to an admirer, 'told me that he would dine with me on Saturday. I gave orders for dinner and so forth for my cousin the Archbishop; but I never thought, till he came, that the next day was Sunday. What was I to do? Here was my cousin the Archbishop, and he must go to church, and there was no way to the church, and the chancel door had been locked up for these thirty years; and my pew was certainly not fit for my cousin the Archbishop. I sent off immediately to Hythe for the carpenter and the joiners, and the drapers, and into the village for the labourers, the mowers, and the gravel-carters. All went to work, the path was mowed, the gravel was thrown down and rolled, and a gate made for the churchyard, the chancel door opened and cleaned, a new pew set up, well lined and stuffed and cushioned; and the next day I walked by the side of my cousin the Archbishop to church, who found everything right and proper; but I have not been to church since, I assure you.'

Lord Rokeby's life, indeed, was not devoid of excitement, and of such incidents as that when, aged eighty-three, he stayed at the Chequers Inn, at Lenham, for the purpose of voting in the general election of 1796, and was there surrounded by an admiring crowd, consisting of all the inhabitants of the countryside, who had conceived the idea that he was a Turk. From this scene of animation and curiosity, we are told, he proceeded to the polling-booth, and voted for his old friend Filmer Honeywood.

We are assured, finally, that in spite of the beard, which in his old age reached to his knees, and in spite of his amphibious habits, he 'possessed virtues by which his defects were abundantly overbalanced'. Particularly remarkable among these virtues were his ardent love of freedom and hatred of oppression. He never ceased to clamour on behalf of the one and against the other, 'speaking his mind freely on all occasions, and drawing from his enemies expressions of admiration. Intent on the diffusion of happiness, he uniformly studied, though in his own peculiar manner, the welfare and prosperity of his own country.'

Venerable and admired, he died at his seat in Kent in the month of December, 1800, in the eighty-eighth year of his age.

It is melancholy, but instructive, to turn from Lord Rokeby, with his habit of eternal baths, to the case of that other Ornamental Hermit, Mrs Celestina Collins, who left a large fortune, and died in her house in St Peter's Street, Coventry, at the age of seventy. Of this not entirely pleasing old lady, Mr Cyrus Redding said, with commendable restraint, that 'her disposition was eccentric, and when she once adopted an idea, nothing could induce her to abandon it'.

Among other ideas adopted by Mrs Celestina Collins was that of inviting thirty fowls to sleep in her bed, or, alternately, amongst the kitchen furniture. Her favourite, amongst these bustling and restless companions, was an immense cock, whose spurs, as the result of age, had grown to the length of three inches. This cock shared her affections with a huge rat, and these two inseparable companions were present at all her meals, which were miserly in the extreme, and which were, I am afraid, tempered by the nature and habits of the two familiars. This state of affairs lasted until, in the end, grown savage because of the shortness of the rations, the rat flew into a rage with the cock, and Mrs Collins in her turn flew into a temper with the rat, striking him a blow which, to her great remorse, killed him.

Mr Redding's restraint is shown, once more, in this pregnant sentence: 'So much was she attached to vermin, obnoxious to all other persons, that a nest of mice was found in her bed.'

Mrs Celestina Collins was not the only person whose bed held surprises for the unwary, as we shall see when we come to the chapter on 'Misers'. But meanwhile, let us dip into the nest of another Ornamental Hermit.

This gentleman, equally Ornamental, was to be found, about eighty years ago, a few miles from Stevenage, where a happy correspondent of the *Wolverhampton Chronicle* was privileged to interview him, and to tell his readers: 'Time, that destroyer of all things, had done its work here ... no cheering voice is heard within these walls, only the noise of rats and vermin.... With difficulty, by the faint rays of light, admitted into the loathsome den, I could trace a human form, clothed only in a horse-rug, leaving his arms, legs, and feet perfectly bare. Already eleven weary winters had he passed in this dreary abode, his only bed being two sheep-skins and his sole companions the rats, which may be seen passing to and fro with all the ease of perfect safety. During the whole of his seclusion he has strictly abstained from ablution. Consequently his countenance is perfectly black. How much it is to be regretted that a man, as gifted as this hermit is known to be, should spend his days in dirt and seclusion.'

3

Quacks and Alchemists

HERE come those who would cure the ills of this world.

Notice how strange and birdlike are the voices of these quarrelsome, bird-flapping gentlemen. Mr John Ashton, in his *Waifs of the Eighteenth Century*, tells us that 'the name of quack, or quacksalver', does not seem to have been much used before the seventeenth century; and its derivation has not been distinctly settled. In *The Antiquities of Egypt,* by William Osburn, Junior, published in 1847, the author says that 'the idea of a physician is frequently represented by a species of duck; the name of which is Chini'. But neither Pierret, in his *Vocabulaire Hiéroglyphique*, nor Bunsen in *Egypt's Place in Universal History*, endorses this statement. Still, the Egyptian equivalent for cackling or the noise of a goose was Ka Ka, and in Coptic, 'Quok', pronounced very much like Quack.

The first to come flapping and bird-screaming from the dust is the strange creature from whom the title 'Merry Andrew' is derived, Mr Andrew Boorde, the physician in chief to King Henry VIII. Undisturbed and undismayed by the black, thick diseases from which the King apparently suffered, his physician wrote such works as *The Breviary of Health*, *The Tales of the Madness of Gotham*, and *The Introduction of Knowledge*, 'the whych doth teach a man to speak all manner of languages and to know the usage and fashion of all manner of countries'. This work was dedicated to the Right Honourable and gracious Lady Mary, daughter of King Henry VIII. The name of 'Merry Andrew' was bestowed upon Mr Boorde by his grateful patients, because of his pleasantries. In his other and shadier years, however, he eschewed those pleasantries, and became a Monk in the Charterhouse, London. Alternately cackling with a shrill birdlike mirth, cawing gravely and blackly like a rook, this ghost took no notice of another queer doddering old ghost who crept round a corner of Salisbury Square – the place where this had lived, and died from old age – wearing the scarlet coat, flap waistcoat and frilled sleeves of the last quack doctor.

Meanwhile, fussy, self-important, pompous Sir Kenelm Digby, the husband of the beautiful Venetia Digby, is very busy preparing and selling his Sympathetic Powder, and committing to memory a paper that he has written, and is about to recite to a Learned Society at Montpellier. The paper relates the history of one of those successful cures that invariably crowned the efforts of the Sympathetic Powder.

A certain gentleman named Howell, it seems, found two friends engaged in a duel. Benevolent and officious, he stepped between the two combatants and met with the immediate fate of all peacemakers, inasmuch as he was severely wounded by both swords. As it happened, both wounds were on the hand. Seeing the mischief that had been done, both the combatants were overcome with remorse, bound up Mr Howell's hand with a garter, and took the sufferer home. Mr Howell's importance was such that the King sent his own physician to treat the wounds, but this gentleman was unable to deal with the matter; the wound seemed ready to mortify, and Mr Howell's friends prophesied the amputation of the arm. Then Sir Kenelm stepped in. Calm and assured, he faced the sufferer. 'I asked him', he told the Learned Society, 'for anything that had blood upon it, so he presently sent for his garter, wherewith his hand was first bound, and as I called for a basin of water as if I would wash my hands, I took a handful of powder of vitriol, which I had in my study and presently dissolved it. As soon as the bloody garter was brought me, I put it in the basin, observing, in the interim, what Mr Howell did, who stood talking in the corner of my chamber, not at all regarding what I was doing. He started suddenly as if he had found some strange alteration in himself. I asked him what he ailed? "I know not what ails me, but I feel no more pain. Methinks that a pleasing kind of freshness, as it were a wet cold napkin, did spread over my hand; which hath taken away the inflammation that tormented it before."

'I replied, "Since, then, you feel already so much good of my medicament, I advise you to cast away all your plasters; only keep the wound clean, and in a moderate temper, between heat and cold."

'This was presently reported to the Duke of Buckingham, and, a little after, to the King, who were both very curious to know the circumstances of the business; which was, that after dinner I took the garter out of the water and put it to dry before a great fire. It was scarce dry before Mr Howell's servant came running, and said that his master felt as much burning as ever he had done, if not more; for the heat was such as if his hand were betwixt coals of fire! I answered that although that had happened at present, yet he should find ease in a short time; for I knew the reason of this new accident, and would provide accordingly; for his master should be free from that inflammation; it might be, before he could possibly return to him; but in case he found no ease, I wished him to presently come back again; if not, he might forbear coming, whereupon he went, and at the instant, I did put the garter again into the water, thereupon he found his master without any pain at all. To be brief, there was no sense of pain afterwards; but within five or six days the wounds were cicatrized and entirely healed.'

Thrusting both these gentlemen aside – and one is too old and too frail to resist this new, businesslike force – comes

Don Lopus, the Illustrious Spanish Doctor, a mountebank
who was accompanied by his zany and assistants, for a zany
was necessary to a Spanish Doctor in the seventeenth century. His appearance and methods remind one of this strange
poem from a long work named *Bird Actors*. In this poem,
Mr Sacheverell Sitwell described how:

> That splendid charlatan Sebastian Mondor,
> Sets up his quivering trestles,
> Across the crowd they stretch
> Their twisted arches, splendider
> Than the slow palaces of air
> That screen the sun's slow stare,
> Or, when he moves in state,
> With dropped wine, sweet exhalations
> Smooth the gay arch he traverses,
> Two feathers in their hair,
> Comedians strut the sheer edge
> Above the foaming crowd
> Loose sleeves and trousers flapping with the wind
> Through the crowd
> The tremors of their movements run;
> Till the furthest feel,
> Dashed in their faces
> The fierce blossoms of each whistling parrot-cry.

Don Lopus, the illustrious Spanish Doctor, was a mountebank such as this. Mounting the trestles above the crowd, he
cried: 'Most noble gentlemen and especially beautiful and
virtuous Ladies, with the rest of my friends and auditors.
Behold your humble and most officious servant Lopus, who
has come on purpose to make you a present of his Physical
and Chymical arts to your fair acceptance, and especially
his most inestimable Vegetable and highly valued Oil, which
I protest I and my six servants are not able to make so fast
as it is fetched away from my Lodging by Gentlemen of your

City. Strangers of the terra firma, and worshipful merchants, ever since my arrival have detained me to their uses by their splendid liberalities and worthily. For what avails your rich man to have his magazines stufft with peccadilloes of the purest grape, when his physicians prescribe him, on pain of death, to drink nothing but water cooked with aniseeds?

'O Health, Health, the blessing of the Rich, the Riches of the Poor. Who can buy thee at too dear a Rate, since there is no enjoying this world without thee. Be not so sparing of your purses, honourable gentlemen, I entreat ye, as to abridge the natural course of Life.

'This is the Physician. This the Medicine. This counsels. This cures. This works the effect; and in uniting both together may be term'd an abstract of the Theorick and Practick in the Aesculapian Art.

'Now, Zan Fritado, prithee sing a verse extempore in honour of it.'

THE ZANY'S SONG

Had old Hippocrates or Galen
(That to their books put medicine all in)
But known this Secret, they had never
(Of which they will be guilty ever)
Been murderers of so much paper
Or wasted many a hurtless taper;
No Indian drug had e'er been famed
Tobacco, Sassafras, not named;
Nor yet of Guaiacum one small stick, Sir,
Nor Raymond Lully's Great Elixir.
Nor had been known the Danish Gonswart,
Or Paracelsus, with his long sword.

'No more, zany,' said the Doctor, with a wave of his hand.

'Well, Gentlemen, I am in a humour (at this time) to make a present of the small quantity my coffer contains, to the Rich in courtesy and to the Poor for God's sake. Come, you shall not give me the price of six shillings, nor five, nor four, nor three, nor two, nor one. Sixpence it will cost you, *or Six Hundred Pounds*.

'Except no lower price by the Banner of my Front. I will not bate a Bagatine. That, I will have only as a Pledge of your Love, to show I am not contemn'd by you.

'Therefore now, toss your handkerchief cheerfully, and be advertised, that the first heroick spirit that deigns to grace me with a handkerchief I will give it a little remembrance of something besides shall please it better than if I had presented it with a double Pistolet.

'O, thank you Lady.... Here is a Powder concealed in this paper. I will only tell you, it is the Powder that made Venus a goddess (given her by Apollo), that kept her perpetually young, cleared her wrinkles, firmed her gums, fill'd her skin, colour'd her hair, from her derived to Helen and the sack of Troy! Unfortunately lost till now, in this our age it was as happily recovered by a studious antiquary out of some Ruins of Asia, who sent a moiety of it to the Court of France, wherewith ladies there now colour their hair; the rest (at this present) remains with me, extracted to a Quintessence, so that wherever it but touches in youth it perpetually preserves, in age restores the complexion, seats your teeth till they dance like virginal Jacks, firm as a wall, and makes them white as ivory that were black as hell.'

Those benefactors of humanity seemed as numerous as the feathers of the birds they resembled so strangely. New diseases were found, which, though they were not apparent, must be cured. A Seventh Daughter, who advertised from The Sign of the Blew Ball at the upper end of Laborious Vain Street, near Shadwell New Market, that she would resolve all manner of Questions and interpret Dreams; a book published late in the seventeenth century, called *The Woman's Prophecy, or the Rare and Wonderful Doctress,* undertook to cure 'the most desperate diseases of the Female Sex, as the Glimm'ning of the Gizzard, the Quavering of the Kidneys, the Wambling Trot, etc.' A gentleman who lived at the Three Compasses, in Maiden Lane, issued a handbill offering to cure several strange disorders, which though not as yet known to the world, he would 'plainly demonstrate to any Ingenious Artist to be the greatest Causes of the most common Distempers, Incident to the Body of Man. The names of which are as follows: "The Strong Fives, the Marthambles, the Moon-Pall, the Hockogrockle".'

Though the Hockogrockle and the Wambling Trot were beyond the aid of family remedies, in this century, it seems that the homely ailment known as wind was dealt with in the home circle – sometimes, it may be, a little too firmly.

This led to Sir Charles Hall, that famous physician of the seventeenth century, becoming the centre of a scene as animated as it was remarkable. The windows of every house in the village to which he had been called, the grass-grown streets, and especially the village green outside the house of Mr Thomas Gobsill, 'a lean man, aged about twenty-six or twenty-seven', were swarming with excited yokels, as Sir Charles, calling for a ladder, and setting this against Mr Gobsill's house, bound that gentleman head downwards upon the ladder, and shook it violently.

The reason for this remarkable energy and enterprise, on the part of Sir Charles, was that Mr Gobsill, who suffered from wind, had, for some time past been in the habit – on the advice of 'a friend' – of swallowing round white pebbles, in order to quell this disorder. At first, the prescription acted admirably, and Mr Gobsill was, in the due course of nature, delivered of both pebbles and wind; but some time afterwards the wind returned to him, and Mr Gobsill returned to the pebbles, and both wind and pebbles clung to Mr Gobsill and would not be parted from him. Mr Gobsill concluded very naturally, that the best plan would be to repeat the dose, and this he did, until, instead of the original dose of nine pebbles, he had swallowed two hundred. Mr Gobsill's two hundred pebbles had remained clamped in the inner recesses of his being for the space of two years and a half, when he noticed that his appetite had gone, and that he was suffering from indigestion. He therefore consulted Sir Charles who, on examining the patient, found that if Mr Gobsill were severely shaken, the stones could be heard rattling as if they were in a bag. When the scene which I have described was enacted, the stones made a slight, slow, noisy journey in the direction of Mr Gobsill's mouth, but immediately he was reversed, and placed upon his feet once more, the surrounding multitude were gratified by the sound of the two hundred stones falling, one after another, into their original resting-place.

I do not know what was his eventual fate, or if he went to an early grave, accompanied by these faithful minerals; but his biographer, Mr Kirby, assures us, with an owlish gravity, that 'when he lay in bed, the stones would sometimes get up almost to his heart, and give him great uneasiness: at such times he was obliged to rise upon his knees, or stand upright, when he could hear them drop, and he always reckoned above one hundred'.

Imaginary invalids were, I imagine, in the sixteenth, seventeenth, and eighteenth centuries, rarer than they are now. For it was scarcely safe to be ill. The sufferer was apt to be given such restoratives and remedies as 'Live Hog Lice, Burnt Coke quenched in Agna Vitae, Red Coral, New Gathered Earth Worms, Live Toads, Black Tips of Crabs' Claws, Man's Skull, Elks' Hoofs, Leaves of Gold, Man's Bones Calcined, Inward Skin of a Capon's Gizzard, Goose Dung gathered in the Spring Time, Dry'd in the Sun, the Stone of a Carp's Head, Unicorn's Horn, Boar's Tooth, Jaw of a Pike, Sea Horse Tooth rasp'd, Frogs' livers, white dung of a Peacock Dry'd, and Toads and Vipers' flesh'. In such a manner was illness warned away, or, if it ignored the warning, expelled. To add to the other horrors attendant upon smallpox, the invalid was forced to take Pulver's Aethiopicus, the Black Powder – which was compounded of thirty or forty toads, burnt in a new pot to black cinders or ashes, and made into a fine powder. Jaundice, again, was no light matter, for the remedies in that case were either goose-dung dried in the sun, finely powdered and then mixed with the best saffron and some sugar-candy, and taken twice a day in Rhenish for six days together, or else roots of tumerick, white tartar, earthworms and choice rhubarb, taken in a little glass of white wine. Indeed, one learned physician was in the habit of routing the illness by mixing both preparations together, so that the invalid got the benefit of both.

But worst of all, Intemperance, that favourite pastime of the day, was not merely a disgrace, it was a positive danger; while lowness of spirits, whether resulting from this Intemperance, or from some other cause, was not encouraged either, as we shall see from this advertisement: 'Whereas the Viper has been a Medicine approv'd by the Physicians of all nations; there is now prepared the Volatile Spirit Compound of it, a Preparation altogether new, not only exceeding all Volatiles and Cordials whatsoever, but all the preparations of the Viper itself, being the Receipt of a late Physician, and prepar'd only by a Relation. It is the most Sovereign Remedy against all Faintings, Sweatings, Lowness of Spirits, etc., as in all Habits of Body or Disorders proceeding from Intemperance, eating of Fruit, drinking of bad Wine, or any other poysonous or crude Liquors, and is good to take off the ill effects or Remains of the Bath of Jesuits' Powder.'

In short, the intemperate not only *saw* snakes, they were forced to swallow them!

These were the remedies prescribed by the real physicians, and I cannot believe that any worse were inflicted by such gentlemen as Dr Seneschall, or Dr Anodyne, who lived in the time of King Charles II, and whose fame was not due, alone, to his habit of wearing a fur coat beneath the rays of the dog-star, in the very height of summer, but also to his skill in alchemy. Dr Anodyne was the industrious gentleman who invented necklaces (made of nutmegs) to cure children of teething troubles, and who, according to Bains, 'informs us gratis, that all the woodcocks and cuckoos go annually to the moon'.

John Wilmot, Earl of Rochester, joined this noble company of quacks, on one of the occasions when he was banished from Court. According to both Bishop Barnet and de Grammont, he carried on his business in Tower Street, next door to the Sign of the Black Swan, and worked under the name of 'Alexander Bends, new come from Germany'. It seems to have been important for a quack doctor to be a foreigner, though I do not quite know why. A famous mountebank speech of Lord Rochester's, existing in broadsheets, is to be found among the Jests of the seventeenth century. The speech contains the following passages:

'The knowledge of these secrets I gathered in my travels abroad, where I have spent my time since I was fifteen years old, to this, my twenty-ninth year, in France and Italy. Those that have travelled in Italy will tell you what a miracle of art does there assist nature in the preservation of beauty; how women of forty bear the same countenance with them of fifteen; ages are in no way distinguished by faces; whereas here in England, look a horse in the mouth and a woman in the face, you presently know their ages to a year. I will therefore give you such remedies that, without destroying your complexion (as most of your paints and daubings do) shall render them perfectly fair, clearing and preserving them from all spots, freckles, heats, pimples, and marks of the small pox, or any other accidental ones, so that the face be not seamed or scarred.

'I will also cleanse, and preserve your teeth white and round as pearls, fastening them that are loose; your gums shall be kept entire, as red as coral; your lips of the same colour, and soft as you could wish your lawful kisses.'

Lord Rochester, in the disguise of Fr Bends, understood the psychology of servants very well, and succeeded in gathering a cloud of these round him; they, in their turn, telling their masters and mistresses about the mysterious and gifted foreigner, so that, very soon, he had a large, and for the most part, secretive practice. Miss Jennings, the sister of the great and terrible Duchess of Marlborough, went to consult him on one occasion, with the beautiful Miss Price, disguised as orange girls; but they did not consult him with a view to gilding the lily, but to foretelling the future. I do not know how much dangerous information Lord Rochester succeeded in extracting from them in the course of their unwary conversation, between birdlike flights of giggles; but it seems that their visit would never have been known had they not met with 'a disagreeable adventure with a gentleman named Brounker, who was a Gentleman of the Chamber to the Duke of York, and brother to Viscount Brounker, President of the Royal Society'.

The quacks of this time were occupied as much with improving Beauty, as with curing disorders. Thus, Dr Thomas Rands, who had set up his stage in Moorfields, would inquire:

'Is there any old woman amongst you troubled with the Pimple Pamplins, whose skin is too short for their bodies? See, here is my "Anti-Pamphastich Powder" or my "Sovereign Carminick", which discharges Ventiferous

Humours, of what kind soever, and will reduce you to soundness of body in the twinkling of a Hobby-Horse.

'Then see here is my Balsamum Stobule Swordum, or an Ointment that's good against all cuts, green or canker'd wounds.

'Now suppose any honest man amongst you has hurt or cut himself with either sword, gun, or musket, spit, Jack, or gridiron, glass bottles or pint pot; by the help and application of this, my celebrated Balsam, they are immediately cured without giving themselves the trouble of sending for a surgeon. ... Then, gentlemen, see, here is my "Pirandos Tanhapon Tolos" that is to say, in the Austrian language, the wonder-working Pills, the excellent quality of which is hardly even known to myself. They purgeth the brain from all Crassick, Cloudifying Humours, which obstruct the sense of all superanuated Maids. They make the Carratich Directick and the Directick Indirectick in their lives and conversations. Then take three of these pills in a morning *jejuno stomacho*, with two quarts of Acqua Gruella. I am none of those fellows that set an extravagant value upon themselves, merely because they ride upon spotted horses, but my medicines have made themselves and me famous throughout Asia, Africa, Europe and America.'

The bird-flapping of this gentleman ceases, and here comes Mr Charles Goodal, of the Coach and Horses in Physicians' Lane, shrieking advertisements of his Superfine Bark : 'As the Colledge Tributary Dr Saffold, has well expressed it in his immortal poem : "It infallably cures the Stone, Dropsie and Gout, taken inwardly and outwardly, Rubb'd in the gums it hastens the cutting of the Teeth. It cures Convulsions, Botts, Rib'd Heels, Farcy, Chilblains, the Mange, Spasms, also Religious and Love Melancholy, Measle in Swine, Christians and Prating in Elderly Persons, and makes an admirable Beauty Water." '

Alas, the recipe is lost to us today.

The friend and brother-in-arms of this gentleman, Dr Thomas Saffold, was by profession a weaver, but announced, in advertisements, that Dr Thomas Saffold, 'an approved and Licensed Physician and Student in Astrology, who (through God's Mercy) to do good, still liveth at the Black Ball and Lilly's Head, next door to the Feather Shops that are within Black Fryers Gateway, which is over against Ludgate Church, just by Ludgate in London'.

Dr Saffold was the inventor of 'Pillulae Londinenses', or 'London Pills', which cured all imaginable and unimaginable ills. But, just at the end of the advertisement, some mood of softness seems to have invaded him, and he decided to spare certain members of the population. 'They must be freeborn,' he warns us, 'by Women with Child, otherwise they are good for any Constitution, and in any Clime. They are durable for many years, and good at Sea as well as on Land.'

Dr Saffold was much addicted to Poetry, and here is an instance of the result of his coquetting with the Muse:

> Dear Friends, let your Disease be what God will,
> Pray to Him for a Cure – try Saffold's Skill
> Who may be such a healing Instrument
> As will cure you to your Heart's Content.
> His Medicines are Cheap, and truly Good,
> Being full as safe as your daily Food,
> Saffold he can do what may be done, by
> Either Physick, or true Astrology;
> His best Pills, Rare Elizir, or Powder
> Do each Day praise him Louder and Louder.
> Dear Country-man, I pray to you so wise
> When Men back-bite him, believe not their Lyes,
> But go see him and believe your own Eyes;
> Then he will say you are Honest and Kind,
> Try before you Judge, and Speak as you Find.

But Dr Saffold died and, when he was dead, another gentle-man wrote an equally poverty-stricken poem as an Epitaph for Dr Saffold; it runs thus:

> Here lies the Corpse of Thomas Saffold,
> By Death, in spite of Physick baffled;
> Who, leaving off his Workman's loom
> Did learned Doctor soon become.
> To poetry, he made pretence,
> Too plain to any man's one sense;
> But he when living thought it sin
> To hide his talent in napkin;
> Now Death doth Doctor (poet) crowd
> Within the limits of a Shroud.

Some time later than the reign of Dr Saffold, Colonel Dalmahoy, a quack who sold love-philters and powders with which to combat every illness, and who was famous for the splendour of his deportment, and the magnificence of his wig, was celebrated in this poem:

> If you would see a noble wig
> And in that wig a man look big
> To Ludgate Hill repair, my boy,
> And Gaze on Colonel Dalmahoy.

Then, outside the Park, and peering hopefully through the bars at the fashionable ladies and gentlemen, Dr Katter-felto walked beside his huge ghostly black caravan, filled with a multitude of black cats, and, with a long flame-white finger and thumb, would flick pieces of paper that melted like snow in the dreamy sunlight. The pieces of paper bore such messages as these, culled from the *General Advertiser* of March the 26th, 1782:

'By particular desire of many of the First Nobility,

'This Present Evening and To Morrow at late Cox's Museum, Spring Gardens, A Son of the late Colonel Katterfelto of the Death's Head Hussars, belonging to the King of Prussia, is to exhibit the same variety of Performances as he did exhibit on Wednesday the 13th of March, before many Foreign Ministers, with great applause.

'Mr Katterfelto has in his travels had the honour to exhibit with great applause before the Empress of Russia, the Queen of Hungary, the Kings of Prussia, Sweden, Denmark, and Poland; and since his arrival in London he has been honoured with some of the Royal family, many Foreign Ministers and Noblemen, and a great many ladies of the first Rank.

'*Wonders, Wonders, Wonders, Wonders* are now to be seen by the help of the Sun and his new-invented Solar microscope; and such wonderful and astonishing sights of the Creation, were never seen before and may never be seen again.

'The admittance to see these wonderful works of Providence is only: Front Seats 3/-, Second Seats 2/-, Back Seats 1/-, only from 8 o'clock in the morning till 6 in the afternoon, at 22 Piccadilly, this day and every day this week.

'Mr Katterfelto's Lectures are Philosophical, Mathematical, Optical, Magnetical, Electrical, Physical, Chymical, Pneumatic, Hydraulic, Hydrostatic, Styangraphic, Palenchic, and Caprimantic Art.'

The week in question had faded many years before this summer day, but Dr Katterfelto threw several other messages into the Park.

'Mr Katterfelto has likewise, by a very long study, discovered at last such a variety of wonderful experiments in natural and experimental philosophy and mathematics as will surprise the world.

'The apparatus he has reared only a few days, and is not to be equalled in Europe, can be seen every day with his greatly admired and new Solar Microscope.

'The insects on the hedges will be seen larger than ever, and those insects which caused the late influenza will be seen as large as birds, and in a drop of water the size of a pin's head there will be seen above 30,000 insects, the same in beer, milk, vinegar, flour, blood, cheese, etc., and there will be seen many surprising insects in different vegetables and above two hundred other dead objects.

'N.B. After his evening lecture, he will discover all the various arts on dice, cards, billiards, and O.E. tables.'

Here comes another advertisement: 'Mr Katterfelto will, this and every day till the 22nd of March next, from 10 in the morning till 5 in the afternoon, show his Occult Secrets and his new improved Solar Microscope if the Sun appears, which has surprised the King and the whole Royal Family.'

About a year after the appearance of this advertisement, it seems that aspersions of an unjust nature were cast on the most favoured of all Mr Katterfelto's black cats – the Sultana, as you might say, of the Caravan – for the following notice appeared in the *General Advertiser* of May the 15th, 1783, and was duly flicked through the railings of the Park:

'COLONEL KATTERFELTO

[he seems at this point to have inherited the military title of his illustrious parent] is very sorry that many persons will have it that he and his famous Black Cat were Devils, but such suspicions only arise through his various wonderful and illustrious performances; he only purposes to be a moral and divine Philosopher, and he says that all Persons on earth live in darkness if they are able, but won't see that most enterprising, extraordinary, astonishing, wonderful, and uncommon exhibition on the Solar Microscope. He will this day, and every day of this week, show from 8 in the morning till 5 in the afternoon, his various new Occult Secrets, which have surprised the King and the whole Royal Family;

73

and his evening lecture begins this, and every night precisely at 8 o'clock – but no person will be admitted after 8; and after his lecture he will exhibit many new deceptions. His Black Cat will also make her appearance this evening at No. 24 Piccadilly. His exhibition of the Solar Microscope has caused him lately very grand houses; also his wonderful Black Cat at night. Many thousands could not receive admission lately for want of room, and Katterfelto expects to clear at least above £30,000 in a year's time, through his Solar Microscope and surprising Black Cat.'

The indefatigable Colonel-by-inheritance seems, also, to have invented a sort of lucifer match, which he claimed 'is better in a house or ship than £20,000, as many lives may be saved by it, and is more useful to the Nation than 30,000 Air Balloons. It will light 900 candles, pistols, or cannons, and never misses. He also sells the very best Solid, Liquid and Powder Phosphorous, Phosphorous Matches, Diamond Beetles, etc.'

The ghostly Mr Katterfelto paused for a moment, and then, with a fading gesture, threw this advertisement through the railings of the Parks:

'The King of Prussia has given orders, that 100,000 men of his best troops are to hold themselves in readiness to march at twenty-four hours' notice, and if so, we are to expect that the noted philosopher Mr Katterfelto, as he belongs to the "Death's Head Hussars", will be obliged to depart from England sooner than he expected. Before he goes abroad, he exhibits once more before the Royal Family.'

Mr Katterfelto's gesture was fading into the sunlight, but now arose a little wind, sounding like the noise of drums and fifes among the leaves, or like the sound of the high double-edged dew-shrill voices of cats, and at this regimental sound, Mr Katterfelto, the huge ghostly black caravan, and the multitude of cats, retreated into the distance, with a kind of mechanical hypnotized precision. Mr Katterfelto and his regiment of cats were, in short, marching to war. They were never heard of again.

Before the sound of this ghostly cat-shrill march, played by the little wind, had died down, another ghost appeared – an even earlier spectre, who might have been seen riding in the Row in the years between 1770 and 1780. This ghost bore the name of Dr Martin Van Butchell, and he wore a long grey beard, carried a large white bone, and was mounted upon a white pony painted with purple spots of the size of a peony.

This kindly and perfectly innocent old gentleman had placed the following advertisement in the *St James's Chronicle* – 'Real or Artificial Teeth from one to an entire set, with superlative gold pivots or springs, also gums, sockets and palate formed, fitted, finished and fixed, without drawing stumps or causing pain.'

This system had, before now, brought death in the wake of its superlative gold spring. Indeed death was a familiar of Mr Van Butchell, but the aspirants for teeth had been few and far between, until Dr Van Butchell's wife died in January 1775, and he, unable to bear the thought of parting from her, had her body embalmed by Dr William Hunter and Mr Cruickshank, the surgeons. When embalmed, the mummy of Mrs Van Butchell was laid reverently in a case with a glass lid, and curtains, and was introduced to visitors as 'My dear departed'.

Those who courted death became so many, as a result of curiosity, that Dr Van Butchell was obliged to insert this advertisement in the *St James's Chronicle* of 31st October, 1775:

'Van Butchell, not wishing to be unpleasantly circumstanced, and wishing to convince some good minds they have been misinformed, acquaints the Curious, no stranger can see his embalmed wife unless (by a friend personally) introduced by himself, any day between nine and one, Sundays excepted.'

Eventually, Mr Van Butchell took unto himself another, and a more wakeful wife, and the perpetual presence of the first Mrs Van Butchell became a source of dissension, and of household strife, so that she was banished from the presence of her husband, and dust was only dust.

Another quack of a different kind was Dr Graham, owner of The Temple of Health and the Hymeneal Temple. This singularly unpleasant old gentleman published several books in praise of himself, and one, called *Medical Transactions of the Temple of Health in London*, gave lists of the cures wrought, during the years 1781 and 1782, by his Electrical Aether, Nervous Aetherial Balsam, Imperial Pills, Liquid Amber, and his Restorative Balsam. He adds: 'The bottles, marked and formerly sold at one guinea, may now be had at half a guinea; the half-guinea bottles at five shillings and three pence; the five-shilling bottles at two shillings and six pence, and the two-shilling-and-sixpence bottles at one shilling and three pence.'

Dr Graham aroused such feelings of gratitude, according to his own account, that various ladies wrote poems in praise of him, and he gives us the following specimen of the art which he inspired.

AN ACROSTIC BY A LADY
Deign to accept the tribute which I owe,
One grateful, joyful tear permit to flow;
Can I be silent when good health is given,
That first – that best – that richest gift of Heaven,
O Muse, descend in most exalted lays,
Replete with softest notes, attune his praise.

Gen'rous by nature, matchless in thy skill,
Rich in the God-like art – the ease – to heal,
All bless thy gifts – the sick – the lame – the blind,
Hail thee with rapture for the cure they find,
Arm'd by the Deity with power divine,
Mortals revue His attributes in thine.

The Temple of Health and Hymen contained a Celestial
Bed, which, according to Dr Graham, had cost him £60,000.
And the effects of sleeping upon this bed were so beneficial
that those hiring it for one night – at the small charge of
£100 – though they had hitherto been childless, became prolific. The Temple contained other beds, which were not
celestial, but Magneto-Electric, and the hire of one of these
was a mere £50 per night, because, although they undoubtedly wrought cures, excepting in the most obstinate
cases, the results could not be guaranteed as in the case of the
more lucrative Celestial Bed.

This very odd old gentleman, in his enthusiasm for the
Celestial Bed, produced this title page for a Pamphlet on the
nature of his Establishment:

'Il Convito Amoroso,
Or A Seria—Comico—Philosophical
Lecture
on the
Causes, Nature, and Effects of Love and Beauty at the Dif-
ferent Periods of Human Life, in Persons and Personages,
Male, Female, and Demi-Caractère; and in Praise of the
Genial and Prolific Influences of the Celestial Bed.
As delivered by Hebe Vesteria
The Rosy Goddess of Youth and of Health
from the
Electrical Throne, in the Great Apollo Chamber at the
Temple of Hymen, in London.

'Before a glowing and brilliant Audience of near three hundred Ladies and Gentlemen, who were commanded by Venus, Cupid, and Hymen, to assist, in joyous assembly, at the Feast of Very Fat Things, which was held at their Temple on Monday Evening the 25th November, 1782, but which was interrupted by the rude and unexpected arrival of his Worship Mida Neutersex Esq, just as the dessert was about to be served up.

'Published at the earnest desire of many of the Company and to gratify the impatient and very intense longings of thousands of adepts, Hibernicen and British; of the Cognoscenti; et de les Amateurs des délices exquises de Vénus.'

To which is subjoined a description of the Stupendous Nature and Effects of the Celebrated Celestial Bed.

The presiding goddess of the Celestial Bed was, suitably enough, Emma Lyons, afterwards Lady Hamilton and the mistress of Nelson.

Such were the gentlemen who attempted to cure the physical ills of the world; and now these, too, sank into the giant dust-heap of the world, and were lost; and up sprang those who would cure by the spirit.

These were, for the most part, less gaudy in attire; but they, too, flapped their unfledged wings, their black dust-muffled sleeves, crowed for a while, and then were gone.

Here comes poor Jack Adams in his long nightgown like a shroud, with his ventriloquist voice, with a tobacco pipe in his girdle. Now he stands at a table, on which lies a torn book and *Poor Robin's Almanac*. On one shelf is a single row of books; and on another, several boys' playthings, particularly tops, marbles, and a small drum. Before him is a man genteelly dressed, presenting five pieces; from his mouth proceeds a label thus inscribed: 'Is she a Princess?' This is meant for Carleton, who married the pretended German Princess. Behind him is a ragged, slatternly woman, who has also a label in her mouth, with these words, 'Sir, can you tell my fortune?'

Jack Adams, the astrologer and conjuror, has made himself a name for ever, and is thus defined in Grose's *Dictionary of the Vulgar Tongue*: 'Jack Adams, a fool. Jack Adams' parish, Clerkenwell.' The astrologer Partridge, who calculated poor Jack Adams' nativity, says that he was born at eleven o'clock at night on December the 3rd, 1625, and that he was so great a simpleton, or natural, that he was obliged perforce to wear long coats, with sleeves covering his hands, that he might not hurt himself, whilst the parish not only maintained him, but allowed him a nurse, so that he might come to no harm. The Poor Rate's Book of 1661, in a list of Pensioners – or those persons who received outdoor relief – mentions 'John Adams', as receiving a pension of 16/- a month.

Jack Adams was once taken, long gown and all, to the Red Bull Theatre, in Red Bull Yard, which is now called Woodbridge Street; and a pamphlet called *The Wits, or Sport upon Sport*, says: 'In Simpleton the Smith, in which the incomparable Robert Cox appeared with a large piece of bread and butter, I have known several of the female spectators and auditors long for it, and once that well-known natural simpleton Jack Adams of Clerkenwell, seeing him with bread and butter on the stage, and knowing him, cryed out "Coz, Coz, give me some, give me some", to the great pleasure of the audience.'

Jack Adams was a conjuror and astrologer, and is described in the supplement to Granger's *Biographical Dictionary* in these unsympathetic terms: 'Jack Adams, Professor of the Celestial Sciences at Clerkenwell Green, was a blind buzzard, who pretended to have the eyes of an eagle. He was chiefly employed in horary questions, relative to love and marriage; and knew, upon proper occasions, how to soothe and flatter the expectations of those who consulted him, as a man might have much better fortune from him for five guineas than for the same number of shillings. He affected a singular dress and cast horoscopes with great solemnity. When he failed in his predictions, he declared that the stars did not actually force, but powerfully incline, and threw the blame on wayward and perverse fate. He assumed the character of a learned and cunning man; but was no otherwise cunning than as he knew how to overreach those credulous mortals who were as willing to be cheated as he was to cheat them, and who relied implicitly upon his art.'

The Jesuit missionary Paleotti, who wrote a treatise proving that the American aborigines were eternally damned without hope of redemption, because they were the offspring of the Devil and one of Noah's daughters – he, alas, helpful as he was, cannot be numbered among our heroes. And of Baxter, who wrote *Hooks and Eyes for Believers' Breeches*, I know nothing. But another gentleman of the same nature was Mr T. Spence, who lived at the beginning of the nineteenth century, and whose ostensible trade was that of an itinerant bookseller. He formed a sect, small in number, but ardent in following their beliefs, whose creed was that 'all human beings are equal by Nature and before the law, and have a continual and inalienable property in earth and its natural productions'. In consequence, 'every man, woman, and child, whether born in wedlock or not (for Nature and Justice know nothing of illegitimacy), is entitled quarterly to an equal share of the rents of the parish where they have settled'. Mr Spence, in addition to these doctrines, advocated that a Sabbath should be held every fifth day; though he enjoined that this should be set apart for rest and amusement, not for the boredom and gloom which was then held to be an indispensable part of reverence. The result of these teachings was, that this delightful and benign, if rather too childlike character was severely punished; for, in 1801, a horrified magistrate sentenced him to pay £50 and to serve a year's imprisonment for publishing the 'seditious libel' which inculcated these doctrines. This 'seditious libel' was called *Spence's Restoration of Society*. The author died in October, 1814.

Mr William Huntington, the coal-heaver Preacher, born in 1774, the son of a day labourer, was a gentleman of quite another kind, for he made a childlike trust into a paying proposition. With him it was an investment, and a gilt-edged one at that. He announced that he 'found God's promises to be the Christian's banknotes; and a living faith will always draw on the divine Banker; yea, and the spirit of prayer, and a deep sense of want, will give an heir of promise a filial boldness at the inexhaustible Bank of Heaven.'

The Bank, indeed, seems to have possessed inexhaustible funds, and Mr Huntington was not slow to draw upon them. Mr Timbs, who cannot be numbered among his admirers, states that: 'He lived in this manner seven or eight years, not, indeed, taking no thought for the morrow, but making no other provision for it than by letting the specific object of his prayers and their general tendency always be understood, where a word to the unwise was sufficient. Being now in much request, and having many doors open to him for preaching the Gospel very wide apart, he began to want a horse, then to wish, and lastly to pray, for one. "I used my prayers," he says, "as gunners use their swivels, turning them every day, as various cases required"; and before the day was over he was presented with a horse, which had been purchased for him by subscription. The horse was to be maintained by his own means, but what of it? "I told God", says he, "that I had more work for my faith now than heretofore; for the horse would cost half as much to keep as my whole family. In answer to which this Scripture came to my mind with power and comfort, 'Dwell in the land, and do good, and verily thou shalt be fed.' This was a bank-note put into the hand of my faith, which, when I got poor, I pleaded before God, and he answered it; so that I lived and cleared my way just as well when I had my horse to keep as I did before." '

Huntington was no ordinary man. The remarkable circumstance which occurred concerning a certain part of his dress has been told in various books.

'Having now', says Huntington, 'had my horse for some time, and riding a great deal every week, I soon wore my breeches out, as they were not fit to ride in. I hope the reader will excuse my mentioning the word breeches, which I should have avoided, had not this passage of Scripture obtruded into my mind, just as I had revolved in my own thoughts not to mention this kind providence of God. "And thou shalt make them linen breeches to cover their nakedness; from the loins even unto the thighs they shall reach : and they shall be upon Aaron, and upon his sons, when they come . . . near unto the altar to minister in the holy place; that they bear not iniquity, and die : it shall be a statute for ever unto him and his seed after him." Exod. xxviii, 42, 43. By which, and three others, namely, Lev. vi, 10; xvi, 4; and Ezek. xliv, 18, I saw that it was no crime to mention the word breeches, nor the way in which God sent them to me; Aaron and his sons being clothed entirely by Providence; and as God himself condescended to give orders what they should be made of, and how they should be cut. And I believe the same God ordered mine, as I trust will appear in the following history.

'The Scripture tells us to call no man master; for one is our master, even Christ. I therefore told my most bountiful and ever-adored Master what I wanted; and he, who stripped

Adam and Eve of their fig-leaved aprons, and made coats of skin, and clothed them; and who clothes the grass of the field, which today is and tomorrow is cast into the oven, must clothe us, or we shall go naked; and as Israel found it, when God took away his wool and his flax, which he gave to cover their nakedness, and which they prepared for Baal; for which iniquity were their skirts discovered and their heels made bare. Jer. xiii, 22.

'I often made very free in my prayers with my invaluable Master for this favour; but he still kept me so amazingly poor that I could not get them at any rate. At last I determined to go to a friend of mine at Kingston, who is of that branch of business, to bespeak a pair; and to get him to trust me until my Master sent me the money to pay him. I was that day going to London, fully determined to bespeak them as I rode through the town. However, when I passed the shop, I forgot it; but when I came to London, I called on Mr Croucher, a shoemaker in Shepherd's Market, who told me a parcel was left there for me, but what it was he knew not. I opened it, and behold there was a pair of leather breeches, with a note in them, the substance of which was, to the best of my remembrance, as follows: "Sir, I have sent you a pair of breeches, and hope they will fit. I beg your acceptance of them; and if they want any alteration, leave in a note what the alteration is, and I will call in a few days and alter them. I.S."

'I tried them on, and they fitted as well as if I had been measured for them; at which I was amazed, having never been measured by any leather-breeches maker in London. I wrote an answer to the note to this effect:

' "Sir, I received your present and thank you for it. I was going to order a pair of leather breeches to be made, because I did not know till now that my Master had bespoke them of you. They fit very well, which fully convinces me that the same God who moved thy heart to give, guided thy hand to cut; because He perfectly knows my size, having clothed me in a miraculous manner for near five years. When you are in trouble, Sir, I hope you will tell my Master of this, and what you have done for me, and He will repay you with honour.''

'This is as near as I am able to relate it, and I added: "I cannot make out I.S., unless I put I. for Israelite indeed, and S. for sincerity; because you did not sound a trumpet before you, as the hypocrites do." '

The plan of purveying for himself by prayer, with the help of hints in proper place and season, answered so well, that Huntington soon obtained by the same means a new bed, a rug, a pair of new blankets, doeskin gloves, and a horseman's coat; and, as often as he wanted new clothes, some chosen almoner of the Bank of Faith was found to supply him. His wife was instructed to provide for her own wants by the same easy and approved means. Gowns came as they were wanted, hampers of bacon and cheese, now and then a large ham, and now and then a guinea, all which things Huntington called precious answers to prayer.

Some awkward disclosures were now made, and he became weary of Thames Ditton and, having a well-timed vision, he secretly wished that God would remove him from that place; and as London was the place where he might reasonably expect to work less and feed better, it was 'suddenly impressed on his mind to leave Thames Ditton, and take a house in the great metropolis, where hearers were more numerous, and that this was the meaning of the words spoken to him in the vision'. The great metropolis seems to have been only another branch of the Heavenly Bank, and Mr Huntington's overdraft on this included, by now, not only the goods mentioned above, but a chapel, a furnished bedroom, a mirror, a pulpit cushion, a very grand Bible, and a well-stored tea-chest.

Providence, it seems, was undoubtedly on the side of Mr Huntington; for when a certain Mrs Bull became too persistent in her religious attentions, and Mr Huntington, in reply to her far too numerous letters, told her that he did not like her head-dress, or her preposterous streamers, or her first, second, or third tier of curls, and that 'a little more furnace work would teach her to pull down her useless topsails', Providence came in strongly on his side, and Mrs Bull, who was about to write him another letter – this time of a too sour, instead of a too sweet, nature – according to her version 'happened to fall asleep by the fire as I was reading the Bible; the candle caught the lappet of my cap, and a good deal of my hair, and I own it a great mercy that I was not consumed myself, and you may be assured that you will see neither streamers, curls, nor topsails again'.

It remains to be said that Mr Huntington, according to a contemporary account, was possessed of a remarkable and disconcerting eloquence, interlarding his sermons with such exhortations as: 'Take care of your pockets! Wake that snoring sinner! Silence that noisy numskull! Turn out that drunken dog!' His contemporary adds that, 'By way of clenching his point, he would say: "Now you can't help it, it must be so, in spite of you." He does this with a most significant shake of his head, and a sort of Bedlam hauteur, with all the dignity of defiance.'

As the years rolled by, the Bank continued to pour still further and further treasures on him: a country house, a well-stocked farm, a coach and a pair of horses, the death of his first wife, and a second wife in the shape of Lady Sanderson, the widow of the Lord Mayor, who was won by his preaching. Mr and Mrs Baker, of Oxford Street, seem to have been among the principal officials of the Bank, for Mr Huntington assured his admirers that these, though 'sorely tried by various losses in business, bankruptcies and bad debts, supplied him with money whenever he required it. While the chapel was building, when money was constantly demanded, if there was one shilling in the house I was sure to have it.'

Mr Huntington died in 1813 at Tunbridge Wells, and was buried beneath this epitaph written by himself:

> Here lies the Coalheaver
> Beloved of his God, but abhorred of men;
> The Omniscient Judge
> At the Grand Assize shall rectify and
> Confirm this to the
> Confusion of many thousands;
> For England and its Metropolis shall know
> That there hath been a prophet
> Among them.

Yet though he may have been abhorred of men, it is equally certain that he was appreciated by women, who, when he died, rushed to the 'elegantly appointed Villa' which had been supplied by the beneficent, and evidently myopic, Heavenly Bank, to pay fabulous sums for any small piece of bric-à-brac which would remind them of their beloved Preacher. 'An ordinary case of spectacles', we are told, 'sold for seven guineas; an old armchair, intrinsically worth fifty shillings, actually sold for sixty guineas, and many other articles fetched equally high prices, so anxious were his besotted admirers to obtain some precious memorial of that most artful fanatic.' The late Mr Pink, describing Mr Huntington's portrait, in the *History of Clerkenwell*, says: 'He might pass, as far as appearances go, for a convict, but he looks too conceited. The vitality and strength of his constitution are fearful to behold, and it is certain that he looks better fitted for coalheaving than for religious oratory.'

Alas, that this book, which is confined, with the exception of Margaret Fuller, to English Eccentrics, may contain no eulogy of that benefactor of humanity, and supreme chaperon, Brigham Young. Into how many lonely lives did he bring romance and happiness, hallowed by the knowledge that his rather ubiquitous affection was splashed about, in this indiscriminate manner, by the commands of God. The home-life of Mr Brigham Young was purity itself, and no laxity was allowed amongst his offspring. One of his numerous daughters, Mrs Susan Young Yates (once more I cull this information from the pages of Miss Barton's and Sir Osbert Sitwell's *Sober Truth*), pays a noble tribute to that austere but happy life. 'How pleasant', she exclaims, 'were the seasons of evening prayers when ten or twelve mothers with their broods of children came from every nook and corner of the quaint, old-fashioned, roomy house at the sound of the prayer-bell.

'Sometimes, after the prayers, especially on Sunday evenings, the girls would be requested to sing and play, or would all join in a hymn. Father would kiss the children, dandle a baby on his knee with his own particular accompaniment of "link-a-toodle-ladle-iddle-oodle", surprising baby into round-eyed wonder by the odd noise; then a goodnight, and we would all separate.'

After the girls began to 'grow up', beaux naturally appeared on the scene. The long parlour, which was prayer-room, reception-room, music-room and best-room, was usually filled on Sunday evenings with a quietly gay crowd of young women and their 'beaux'. Music and laughter, jest and repartee, filled in the evening till the clock struck ten. Then promptly, if the adieux had not already been said, the young people were apt to be startled by the sudden appearance of the President, loaded with hats of all shapes and sizes; each young man would be asked, kindly and pleasantly, to select his own, and the goodnights were exchanged in the ensuing hurry and embarrassment.

'One night there happened to be about eight or ten couples, most of whom were already engaged lovers. Now, as walking in the street was out of the question, and as the parlour was the only resort, it was found to be a very unsatisfactory place for a lover, who would, if he could, whisper sweet nothings, or even venture to steal an arm about his sweetheart. I never knew who made the proposition on that particular Sunday night, but certain it was that in the course of the evening the one large lamp on the centre table was discreetly lowered a trifle, while around it in a close barricade stood a small army of books.

'Very charming, no doubt. But some stray wind carried a whiff of what was going on in the parlour to the President's ear. Less than a quarter of an hour of the happy gloom had been enjoyed before the parlour door quietly opened, and on the threshold, lighted candle in hand, stood father. Without saying a word he walked slowly and deliberately up to the first couple, holding his candle down in their faces, looked keenly at them, then to the next couple, repeating his former scrutiny, and so on, round the room. Not a word said he, but, pulling down the scandalized books, and putting them gravely in their places, he turned on the full blaze of the lamp and walked quietly out of the room.'

Mr Thomas Lake Harris and his disciple Mr Laurence Oliphant were two other gentlemen who resembled Mr Brigham Young in everything excepting his gift for overt domesticity, and his careful chaperonage.

Mr Harris, who was born in England in 1823, and taken to America by his parents at the age of five years, was particularly fortunate inasmuch as it was revealed to him, and to an equally businesslike Salvation Company-promoter, Mr J. L. Scott, that their common friend, Ira S. Hitchcock, had discovered the site of the Garden of Eden at Mountain Cove, Virginia, and that this spot alone, it seemed, would remain, with its inhabitants, untouched by those convulsions which would soon destroy the rest of the world. So Messrs Scott, Hitchcock and Harris, with over a hundred adherents, all of whom, luckily, were possessed of a little money, which their leaders had impounded 'in trust for the Lord', proceeded to form a community in this sacred place. Unfortunately, the dictates of heaven became confused in the extreme, one leader receiving one set of orders, another – commands which were in direct contradiction to these. The result was a most unspiritual series of disputes – one band of followers fighting on the side of one prophet, another on the side of his adversary, so that, in the end, as Mrs Ray Strachey remarks in her *Religious Fanaticism*, 'The Serpent scored his victory once more, and the dark cloud of death descended upon what was to have been the everlasting city.'

The Garden of Eden was broken up, and Mr Harris, who was happily not unprovided for, since he held many possessions in trust for the Lord, founded a new sect, known as Christian Spiritualism, and a new settlement at Brocton, Salem on Erie, New York. It will not be out of place to describe this gentleman, as he appeared in after life to his disciple Laurence Oliphant, who gives a portrait of him in *Masollam*.

'There was a remarkable alternation of vivacity and deliberation about the movements of Mr Masollam. His voice seemed pitched in two different keys, the effect of which was, when he changed them, to make one seem a distant echo of the other – a species of ventriloquistic phenomenon which was calculated to impart a sudden and not altogether pleasant shock to the nerves of the listeners. When he talked with what I may term his "near" voice, he was generally rapid and vivacious; when he exchanged it for his "far-off" one, he was solemn and impressive. His hair, which had once been raven black, was now streaked with grey, but it was still thick, and fell in a massive wave over his ears, and nearly to his shoulders, giving him something of a leonine aspect. His brow was overhanging and bushy, and his eyes were like revolving lights in two dark caverns, so fitfully did they seem to emit flashes, and then lose all expression. Like his voice, they too had a near and a far-off expression, which could be adjusted to the required focus like a telescope, growing smaller and smaller as though in an effort to project the sight beyond the limits of natural vision. At such times, they would be so entirely devoid of all appreciation of outward objects as to produce almost the impression of blindness, when suddenly the focus would change, the pupil expand, and rays flash from them like lightning from a thundercloud, giving an unexpected and extraordinary brilliancy to a face which seemed promptly to respond to the summons. The general cast of countenance, the upper part of which, were it not for the depth of the eye-sockets, would have been strikingly handsome, was decidedly Semitic; and in repose the general effect was almost statuesque in its calm fixedness. The mouth was partially concealed by a heavy moustache and long iron-grey beard; but the transition from repose to animation revealed an extraordinary flexibility in those muscles which had a moment before appeared so rigid, and the whole character of the countenance was altered as suddenly as the expression of the eye. It would perhaps be prying too much into the secrets of nature, or, at all events, into the secrets of Mr Massollam's nature, to enquire whether this lightening and darkening of the countenance was voluntary or not. In a lesser degree, it is a common phenomenon with us all; the effect of one class of emotions is, vulgarly speaking, to make a man look black, and of another to make him look bright. The peculiarity of Mr Masollam was, that he could look so much blacker and brighter than most people, and make the change of expression with such extraordinary rapidity and intensity, that it seemed a sort of facial legerdemain, and suggested the suspicion that it might be an acquired faculty. There was, moreover, another change which he apparently had the power of working on his countenance, which affects other people involuntarily, and which generally, especially in the case of the fair sex, does so much against their will: Mr Masollam had the faculty of looking very much older one hour than he did the next. There were moments when a careful study of his wrinkles, and of his dull faded-looking eyes, would lead you to put him down at eighty, if he was a day; and there were others when his flashing glance, expanding nostril, broad smooth brow, and mobile mouth, would make a rejuvenating combination, that would for a moment convince you that you had been at least five-and-twenty years out in your first estimate. These rapid contrasts were calculated to arrest the attention of the most casual observer, and to produce a sensation which was not altogether pleasant when first one made his acquaintance. It was not exactly mistrust – for both manners were perfectly frank and natural – so much as perplexity. He seemed to be two opposite characters rolled into one, and to be presenting undesigningly a curious moral and physiological problem for solution which had a disagreeable sort of attractiveness about it, for you almost immediately felt it to be insoluble, and yet it would not let you rest. He might be the best or the worst of men.'

This octopus-like old gentleman wrote many books, in which he succeeded in spreading a great deal of mystery round his theories and his creed. Mrs Strachey, indeed, remarks, succinctly, that 'it is impossible to distinguish their meaning'. His publishers however were, if we may believe their own words, not only conversant with the meaning of the books, but overcome with admiration for them. 'These lyrics,' they assure us, 'with their introduction, are intended to deduce some methods and processes whereby the Divine One-Twain Creator transposes the natural bodies of all such as receive and embody the Redemption Life of the Saviour–Saviouress, from the separate sex-lines of the third dimension of con-dissolving nature, to those of the reunited twain – one sex of the fourth dimension of eternal Arch-Nature, whereby Sin is abolished in the flesh, and its wages, Death, abolished in and for the body.' This remarkable book was called *The Marriage of Heaven and Earth, Triumph of Life*, by T. L. Harris, and was published by C. W. Pearce and Co., 139 Regent Street, Glasgow.

Mrs Strachey explains Mr Harris' comfortable doctrine so plainly that it would be impossible to transfer the explanation into other words, and I cannot do otherwise than quote from her:

'The belief', she writes, 'was based, as so many others have been, upon the dual sex of the Almighty. From this basis it went on to maintain that man also, being created in the image of God, was a bi-sexual creature; not, indeed, in this life, but in the fuller life towards which he must ever be striving. The necessary half needed to complete the full human being was called a counterpart, who might possibly be met on earth, and must certainly be searched for, but who would inevitably be met in heaven if missed below.

'In the Brotherhood of the New Life, however, little heed was paid to disappointments. The true counterpart could be approached through the false, and each person in whom you detected any noble and lovable quality was able to that extent to put you in touch with the real creature. Thus it was the duty of a true believer to love, and approach as close as possible to any and every other human being (if of the opposite sex), so as to be united to that part of their own counterpart which was mirrored within; and the more often the experiment was repeated (with a different partner), the more thorough the approximation would become.'

The way was clear, and the duty plain. And who more eager to follow the way of Righteousness than Mr Harris, known, by his disciples, as Father. Mr Harris had a female counterpart in heaven, whose name was Lily Queen. But I regret to say that this heavenly visitant was an extremely bad companion for him, encouraging him, indeed, to a course of conduct which, in a less spiritually minded man, might have been misunderstood. The duty of Lily Queen was to 'comfort'; and, unlike many members of her sex, she preferred ladies who were young and pretty to those who were not. There is indeed no record of her having 'comforted' any man, or any older, or plainer lady – perhaps because these had learned wisdom, and were in no need of comfort. Mrs Hannah Whitall Smith, whose papers are edited, in *Religious Fanaticism*, by her granddaughter Mrs Strachey, was told by a Miss X that 'the method of getting this consolation from Lily Queen was rather peculiar. The troubled soul was to go into Mr Harris's room and get into bed with Lily Queen.' When Miss X not unnaturally inquired what became of Father, she was told 'Oh, Lily Queen is inside of Father, and consequently he, of course, stays in the bed, and by getting into his arms we get into her arms.'

No wonder that his disciple Laurence Oliphant wrote: 'He senses the least coldness towards himself, and it stops everything. We have each of us to feel more knit into his organism than with each other. His functions are pivotal, and we in a sense meet in him; for our breath is in some mysterious way enfolded in his. All he knows of you is through the conspiration of your united breaths. It differs

from the afflatus, of which Miss – speaks so lightly, in
certain particulars, which he will explain to you some day.
But we all owe under God what we have and feel as the
breath to him; the particular quality of it which we enjoy
came first to him, and owing to our *rapport* with him we get
the same. Nor would it be possible for anyone to be in our
breath who was not first in closest *rapport* with him and then
with each other. It is the sensational bond of our union; it
binds us together mysteriously and internally.'

Whether owing to doubts about this 'internal binding',
or to certainty about the possessions impounded 'in trust
for the Lord', the relations of the beautiful and rich Miss le
Strange were strongly opposed to her marriage to Laurence
Oliphant, but in the end all opposition was overcome, the
trusteeship for the Lord was increased, and Mr Oliphant,
his wife, and his mother, returned to Father. Lady Oliphant
had passed the time of life in which Lily Queen might
have brought comfort to her, so, uncomforted, she was set
to wash the handkerchiefs of the community; Mr Oliphant –
for Father was nothing if not practical – 'was sent to sleep
in a large loft containing only empty orange-boxes and one
mattress; and he remembered arranging these articles so as to
form some semblance of a room. His earliest work was cleaning out a large cattle-shed or stable. He often, he said, re-
called in a sort of nightmare the gloomy silent labour for
days and days, wheeling barrows of dirt and rubbish in
perfect loneliness, for he was not allowed to speak to anyone;
and even his food was conveyed to him by a silent messenger, to whom he might speak no word. Often after this
rough work was ended, and he came home dead beat at nine
o'clock, he was sent out again to draw water for household
purposes till eleven o'clock, till his fingers were almost frost-
bitten.'

How strenuous was the life of the disciples of Mr Harris,

and how useful! When Mr Harris was immersed in the work of expelling devils from possessed persons, the whole community was obliged by him to sit up all night, and to watch. . . . 'For this reason,' as Mrs Oliphant tells us in her life of her cousin, 'persons were kept almost without sleep for months. One woman, in particular, for weeks was allowed to sleep from nine o'clock till twelve, all the rest of the twenty-four hours being spent in the hardest work.'

Mr Harris disapproved of any 'strong, merely natural affection', and Lily Queen made it clear that in certain marriages, separation became necessary, 'until the affection was no longer selfish'. Soon after Mr Oliphant's marriage, Mr Harris noticed that Mrs Oliphant bore a strong resemblance to Lily Queen, and he proposed therefore to take her behind the veil, whilst the selfishness of Mr Oliphant was checked, largely, I imagine, through the medium of the loft with the empty orange-boxes. How far Mr Harris and Mrs Oliphant went, I do not know, but Mrs Oliphant left the community for some time. That Father could be trying at moments, even to the most devoted of his adherents, cannot be denied. For Mr Oliphant confessed that 'Father's presence is an awful pressure, though it is a blessed one. Because he feels our states so terribly, the watchfulness over ourselves has to be unceasing. So it should be always; but somehow I am miserably finite, and I do not realize the divine presence checking me so much as the human one.'

In the end, an unseemly wrangle took place in the law courts in which Mr Harris was deprived of part of the Lord's possessions; and, after this blasphemous proceeding, the attentions of the newspaper reporters were so assiduous that he complained: 'They are especially painful, at the present moment, when, having been relieved of my various trusts for others, I have withdrawn into private life.' 'As our beloved country', he continues, 'sinks daily into deeper profligacy and corruption, and the Press becomes more and more infernal, I shrink more and more from that contact which is caused by publicity.'

Mrs Oliphant returned to England, and in a letter to her mother, dated the 1st of November, 1880, states: 'It appears there is a ball at Sandringham on the 12th, and Hamon is naturally anxious that I should be there; which I could do as well as not by taking care of myself up to that time.'

The life led by Mr and Mrs Oliphant, freed from the 'awful pressure' of Father's presence, seems to have been varied; but both Father's former disciples appear to have adopted the methods of Lily Queen; and we hear much later the reasons for this procedure.

'The experiences were so long and so extraordinary, yet many of them of a nature that could not at once become universal nor consistent with the present constitution of man, because of the excessive strain entailed by them, which confirmed the apprehension of the biune character of our being – that I know it must at best appear as a hypothetical idea for many people for a long while, or rest as a vague basis of life theories in their minds. And I believe that, whatever the clearness of my perception of the subject, nothing could have made it possible to launch it with the frail and imperfect vehicle of printed words to carry it upon the social mind, but the instinct that arose as the result of work among the weakest and most tempted of human beings, to whose salvation at this date I know no other doctrine than this could serve. It seems very hard to have to remember always in striving to call down God's fire of purity, that it streams as an atmosphere into a vacuum, towards all that is most foul and grievous in social life. But who are we that we should dare to be satisfied with surface decency, when we ought, like the light of God, to probe the darkness of caverns wherever they be? Yet, with our natural cowardice and superficiality, we dislike to remember always those very things in human earth-life that inspirations and progressions come to eradicate.'

The methods of Lily Queen were carried out in a community formed by the Oliphants in Palestine. But, as Mrs Smith remarks in *Religious Fanaticism*, 'Very remarkable things are reported to have gone on in that community, and finally it had to be closed at the instance of the Vigilance Association of London, which threatened a complete exposure if it continued.' It seems that Mrs Oliphant, in helping the Arabs towards what she and her husband called 'Sympneumata', or the union of the spiritual counterpart with the earthly one, was so forgetful of self that, in the real Lily Queen manner, she would accomplish this 'by getting into bed with these Arabs, no matter how degraded or dirty they were, and the contact of her body brought about, as she supposed, the coming of the counterpart. It was a great trial to her to do this, and she felt that she was performing a most holy mission.'

It is unnecessary to follow this unpleasing pair through all the mazes of their inspirations, doubts, and pretences. Thinking of them, I feel myself in strong sympathy with our lifelong friend Mr Henry Mouat, of Whitby, Yorkshire, whose forebears have been whaling captains, in an unbroken line since the time of Elizabeth, and who, hearing of some of the more reputable exploits of the later religious fanatics, said: 'Look at yon stars,' and then with an enormous whale-spouting sigh, continued: 'Well, Miss, if it's the same to you, I think I'll stick to the bacon and eggs.'

4

Some Sportsmen

HERE, through the bright light glancing boughs, scattering sprays of green dew-like fountains, come the sportsmen, some riding like centaurs, some driving madly, through the shade. High birdlike cries echo, the fine barouches, the landaus, fly like birds. The sportsmen are driving to a race-meeting, perhaps, or to a meeting of the Whip Club.

Here they come, thick and bright as stars in a July night, thick and bright as July roses.

Lord Hawke drives first, and then Mr Buxton and the Hon. Lincoln Stanhope, 'in yellow-bodied carriages with whips, springs and dickey-boxes; cattle of a bright bay colour, with plain silver ornaments on the harness, and rosettes to the ears'. The drivers are dressed in light drab-colour cloth coats, made full and single-breasted, with three tiers of pockets, the skirts reaching to the ankles; and these coats are held in by a mother-of-pearl button the size of a crown piece. The waistcoats have blue and yellow stripes, each an inch in depth. The small-clothes are corded with silk plush, and are made to button over the calf of the leg, with sixteen strings and rosettes to each knee. The boots are very short and finished with very broad straps, hanging over the top and down to the ankle. As for the hats, they are an inch and a half deep in the crown only, and the same depth in the brim exactly. This splendid costume is enhanced by the large bouquet pinned at the breast, 'in imitation of the coachmen of our nobility'.

In spite of the magnificence of this costume, it will soon be changed, or bettered; for when the name of the 'Whip Club' is altered to that of the 'Four-in-Hand Club', we shall read in the *Morning Post* of 3rd April, 1809 that, on the occasion of their first meet – 'so fine a cavalcade has not been witnessed in this country at any period'. The drivers wore 'a blue (single-breast) coat, with a long waist, and brass buttons, on which were engraved the words "Four-in-Hand Club"; their waistcoats were of kerseymere, ornamented with alternate stripes of blue and yellow; their small-clothes of white corduroy, made moderately high and very long over the knee, buttoning in front over the shin bone. Boots very short, with long tops, only one outside strap to each, and one to the back; the latter was employed to keep the breeches in their proper longitudinal shape. Hats with a conical crown and Allen brim' (whatever that may have been); 'a box driving coat of white drab cloth, with fifteen capes, two tiers of pockets, and an inside one for the Belcher handkerchief; cravat of white muslin spotted with black. Bouquets of myrtle, pink and yellow geraniums were worn.' But even these splendours were not sufficient, for in May of that year the Club buttons went out of fashion, and we learn that 'Lord Hawke sported yesterday, as buttons, Queen Anne's shillings; Mr Ashurst displayed crown pieces.'

These gentlemen, good sportsmen, all of them, would pay no attention to that foolish Jessamy, that four-in-hand driver of fifteen years before, Sir Robert Mackworth, who, we are assured by *The Times*, 21st January, 1794, 'appeared to be no otherwise distinguished than by the particularity of his equipage'. Sir Robert Mackworth, it appears, drove 'four horses of different colours in his phaeton, which has four wheels painted to correspond with the colours of the horses; in the midst of the badge of his distinction, the Bloody Hand, is the figure of four, which he explains in this way, four-in-hand. The motto, "This is the Tippy." ' 'If anything', *The Times* continues severely, 'can add to the folly of the whole, it is that he intends to crop four opposite ears to his horses, to make room for four monstrous roses, of different colours, to match.'

Here they come, these different sportsmen, all, with the exception of the white-faced, ghostlike, moonlike, wind-swift Colonel Mellish, red-faced as July roses, bright and shining as July stars.

Here comes the star-dust, the noisy chattering crowd of tipsters and smaller racing men. Where have we seen this smooth bright turf before? Why, we are on Brighton race-course, and we are waiting for the arrival of the Prince Regent. Lord George Germain, his brother the Duke of Dorset, and Mr Delme Radcliffe, the three best-known gentlemen riders, are waiting for their horses. They are little men, with eager eyes and obliterated faces, like most jockeys. Perhaps the wind, excited by the speed of their riding, has blown their features away. 'There was a great stir,' wrote old Mr Thomas Parker in his diary, twenty-seven years afterwards, 'and the buzz was tremendous, till Lord Foley and Mellish, the two great confederates of that day, approached the ring, and then a sudden silence ensued, as they awaited the coming of their betting books. They would come on perhaps, smiling and mysterious, without making any demonstration. At last, Mr Jerry Cloves would say, "Come, Mr Mellish, will you light the candle and set us a-going?" Then if the Master of Buckle would say, "I'll take three to one about Sir Solomon," the whole pack opened and the air resounded with every shade of odds and betting.'

The ghost of Colonel Mellish, as resplendent as ever, is driving up to the Brighton racecourse. His 'white but handsome face', so much admired by Nimrod, is no whiter than it was then, and he wears, still, the same 'style of dress, remarkable for its lightness of hue, with a neat white hat, white trousers, and white silk stockings'. He drove his barouche himself, as Nimrod is careful to tell us, and this equipage is drawn by four beautiful white horses, with two outriders as matches to them, ridden in harness bridles. In his rear was a saddle-horse groom, leading a thoroughbred hack, and at the rubbing-post on the heath was another groom, all in crimson liveries, waiting with a second hack.

Now the light bright star-dust are gathered together, to a Milky Way, for here come the racehorses. Their names are : 'Jenny, Come Bye Me', 'Kiss in a Corner', 'Jack, Come Tickle Me', 'I am Little, Pity my Condition', 'Jack is my Favourite', 'Britons, Strike Home', 'Why do You Slight Me', 'Turn About Tommy', 'Sweeter when Clothed', 'Watch Them and Catch Them', 'First Time of Asking', 'Fear Not, Victorious', and 'Hop, Step, and Jump'.

'About half an hour before the signal of departure from the Hill,' said old Mr Parker, 'the Prince himself would make his appearance in the crowd – I think I see him now, in a green jacket, a white hat and tight nankeen pantaloons, and shoes, distinguished by his highbred manner and handsome person; he was generally accompanied by the late Duke of Bedford, Lord Jersey, Charles Wyndham, Shelley, Brummel, Mr Day, Churchill, and oh, extraordinary anomaly, the little old Jew Travers, who, like the dwarf of old, followed in the train of royalty. The Downs were covered with every species of conveyance, and the Prince's German Wagon – so were barouches always called when first introduced at that time – and six bay horses, the coachman on the box and being replaced by Sir John Lade, issued out of the gates of the Great Pavilion, and, gliding up the green ascent, was stationed by the great stand, where it remained the centre of attraction for the day. At dinner-time the Pavilion was resplendent with lights, and a sumptuous banquet was served to a large party.'

But now the lights are dying down, and a cold evening wind is blowing through the branches, blowing that light bright chattering star-dust away and away. Farther and farther away sound those high hoarse bird-voices. But now and again, one horseman, one charioteer, one sportsman turns his head, and we may see his face, though it is shadowed by the branches. Some of these are men of high, some of low degree, but all seem – not so much hunters, as hunted.

Let us follow them to their lairs, watch their ordinary daily pursuits.

In the flat countryside near Doncaster, stout Mr Jemmy Hirst, the Rawcliffe tanner, who had retired from business with a large fortune, might have been seen any autumn day about the year 1840, leaving his house to go shooting. His jolly, if coarse, face was as round as the autumn sun, and shone like brightly polished leather, whilst everything about him had a strong, horsy, leathery smell. But Mr Hirst did not approve of horses excepting on the racecourse, and he went shooting mounted on the back of a bull of ample proportions and uncertain temper, whilst for pointers, he made use of the services of a crowd of vivacious and sagacious pigs, all of whom answered to their names, and did their duty irreproachably. It is said that Mr Hirst rode the bull when hunting with the Badsworth hounds. If he did, his presence must, I imagine, have lent animation to the scene, and speed to the chase. But we cannot be certain of the truth of the story.

His household staff consisted of a valet, a female general servant, a tame fox, and an otter, whilst he possessed, as well, a large stud of mules and dogs. The house itself was rendered cheerful by the presence – in the dining-room, which was redolent of leather, and was hung about with rusty agricultural instruments – of a large coffin. Mr Hirst had shown a long foresight in buying this coffin, for he was to live till the age of ninety years; but meanwhile, it proved useful as a sideboard, and Mr Hirst, when visited by his racing friends and others, would produce spirits from the inner recesses of this.

Mr Hirst's sporting activities did not stop at going shooting and hunting, mounted on a bull, for he was as well, a very well-known figure on the Doncaster racecourse, to which he drove in a very odd carriage, perched on extremely high wheels, shaped like a palanquin, and innocent of nails. His arrival was pleasant, since he was extremely popular on the racecourse, and he would swagger about the enclosure in his glossy shining waistcoat, made of drakes' feathers, from the pockets of which, when making bets, he would draw bank-notes, made by himself, and bearing the responsibility of payment to the amount of fivepence-halfpenny.

His last ride was as remarkable as any he had taken. The coffin was withdrawn from the dining-room and, the spirits having been ejected from it, and the body of the ninety-year-old Mr Hirst substituted for these, it was borne to the grave by eight stout widows, followed by a vast procession of sporting men and racing tipsters, to the accompaniment of a lively march played by a bagpipe and fiddle. Mr Hirst's wish had been to be carried to the grave by eight old maids, and he went so far as to try to bribe ladies to perform this service by the promise of a guinea each; but unluckily the bribe was not large enough to overcome the shyness habitual to the maiden state; so, in the end, Mr Hirst had to fall back upon widows, who, being more accessible, were regarded by him as not being worth more than half a crown each.

Colonel Thornton, of Thornville Royal, Yorkshire, was a less amiable type of sportsman than Mr Hirst, though his exploits were, according to himself, equally remarkable. Although he wrote a book on his sporting trips in the Highlands, the boredom of which was commented upon by that virtuoso in that quality, Sir Walter Scott, yet his imagination, when it was confined to conversation, was roving and incalculable. His nature was as cold, niggardly, and blustering as the north wind.

On one occasion, when, to the Colonel's delight, a rider fell from his horse, and somebody exclaimed that he would have a broken head, the Colonel countered this with: 'Broken head? – I am the only man in Europe, Sir, that ever had a broken head, to live after it. I was hunting near my place in Yorkshire, when my mare threw me, and I was pitched head foremost upon a scythe which had been left on the ground. When I was taken up, my head was literally found to be cut in two, and was spread over my shoulder like a pair of epaulettes – that was a broken head if you please, Sir.' It was, indeed, impossible for anybody to mention any adventure in the presence of the Colonel, without that gentleman turning royal purple and explaining, at great length, that he had endured the same trials, not once, but twice. 'Arrested? – Why, I have been arrested oftener than anyone in England, once, under the most atrocious circumstances. You must know I was lodging at Stevens', my wife was with me. One morning between seven and eight o'clock, while we were in bed, a bailiff came into the room. "I understand your business, my good fellow," said I. "Wait below, I'll get up and dress, and accompany you to my solicitor, who'll do the needful." He swore I should get up and go with him as I was. "What, in my nightshirt?" said I He insisted. I resisted, when the scoundrel went to the fireplace, drew out the poker which had been left in the fire all night, and thrust it, red as it was, in the bed between my wife and me. She, womanlike, as all women would do, jumped out of bed; not so your humble servant. There I lay, and there stood the scoundrel poking at me; and there, Sir, I would have remained had not the bedclothes taken fire.

Now I did not choose to be burnt in bed, nor would I endanger the safety of the house, in which there happened to be many lodgers at the time, so up I got and dressed myself. I resolved to carry *that* point, and I did. Now I put it to you, as men, as *gentlemen*. Did I compromise my honour by giving in at last? But observe, gentlemen, 'twas as I told you, not until the bed took fire.'

Mrs Thornton, however frightened she may have been when the bailiff set her bed on fire, seems, in other ways, to have been an intrepid lady. She was a great horsewoman, and rode in a race at York. We read in the *Morning Post*, 20th August, 1805, these particulars:

'Mrs Thornton is to ride 9st. against Mr Bromford, who is to ride 13st. over the York Course, four miles, to run the last race on Saturday in the next August meeting, for four hogsheads of Coti Roti p.p. and 2000 guineas h.ft.; and Mrs Thornton bets Mr Bromford 700 guineas to 600 guineas p.p.; the 2000 guineas h.ft. provided it is declared to the Steward four days before starting. Mrs Thornton to have her choice of four horses.

'Mr Bromford to ride Allegro, sister to Allegranti. *N.B.* Colonel Thornton or any gentleman he may name, to be permitted to follow the lady over the course, to assist her in case of any accident.'

I am sorry to say, that when it came to the point, Mr Bromford declined the race, and paid the fine. But later in the day, Mrs Thornton raced Buckle, a jockey, mounted on Allegro, and beat him by half a neck.

As for Colonel Thornton, his exploits as a sportsman were as remarkable as they were fortunate. When complimented on his reputation as a shot, he would reply: 'Ah, Sir, I shoot with a ramrod sometimes.' 'Shoot with a ramrod?' 'Why, how in the devil's name would you shoot when you are in a hurry?' 'I really don't quite understand you.' 'This

is what I mean, Sir. For example, I was going out one fine
morning, towards the latter end of October, when I saw the
London mail changing horses, as it always did within a mile
of my gates. I suddenly recollected that I had promised my
friend a basket of game. Devil a trigger had I pulled, the
coach was ready, what was to be done? I leaped over the
hedge, fired off my ramrod, and may I be damned if I did
not spit, as it were, four partridges and a brace of pheasants.
Now I should be a liar if I was to say the same thing twice,
in point of number, I mean.'

After a life of such amazing exploits and feats, such appalling dangers and accidents, one cannot be surprised that
Colonel Thornton, when he was dying in Paris, fell out of
bed and found that the floor was bristling with pins and
needles, the points upwards, so that when he arose, he was,
according to his own narrative, the picture of a hedgehog
with them, 'only the bristles were reversed, the points being
in the flesh'.

Colonel Thornton, when in other people's cups, if I may
so express myself, was in the habit of asking the whole company to dinner, in the hope of gaining that general attention
which, for some reason or another, was never as firmly fixed
upon his narratives as he could have wished. But, equally
invariably, next day some appalling disaster overtook his
household, so that he was constrained to put off the company, and the manoeuvre ended as a rule in the victorious
Colonel dining at the house of one of the disappointed guests.

How different was the career of Colonel Thornton to that
of poor generous Squire Mytton, doomed, as I suppose, before his birth, to the horrors of the death that seized him
when he was only thirty-eight years of age. This squire of
Halston, near Shrewsbury, was born on the thirtieth of
September, 1796, and was left fatherless before he was two.
When he was ten years old, according to his friend Nimrod,

he was 'a Pickle of the first order. Indeed, his neighbour, Sir Richard Puleston, with a felicity of expression peculiarly his own, christened him "Mango, the King of the Pickles", and he proved his title to the honour even to the end of his life.'

Alas, how little did Sir Richard Puleston, with a felicity of expression peculiarly his own, or any other friend of poor John Mytton, know the doom that was in store for him, the eight bottles of port a day, changing soon to scarcely less of brandy, the ruined estate, the ruined life, the debtor's prison, the death amid the horrors of delirium tremens.

Here he comes, that poor driven drunken ghost, blown by a turbulent hurricane weather. His life seemed to be spent in running like an ostrich – he walked as fast and as strongly as that bird – racing, jumping, driving, hunting, chased always by a high mad black wind.

He meant, always, to cheat that wind. Let it blow through him and eat him to the bone. He would show it how little he cared.

This half-mad hunting hunted creature never wore any but the thinnest of silk stockings, with very thin boots or shoes, so that in winter his feet were nearly always wet. His hunting breeches were unlined, he wore only one small waistcoat, and that was nearly always open. He rarely wore a hat, and in winter went shooting in white linen trousers without either a lining or drawers and, with this, a light jacket. No matter how black the frost, no matter how high and mad was the black turbulent wind in which he lived, he would wade through any water, break down the ice of any pond and trample through it, such was his impatience to have his way. He might often be seen stripped to the shirt and following wild-fowl in the snowiest weather, and once lay down in his shirt to await their arrival at dusk. And once the keepers at Woodhouse, an estate belonging to his uncle, were surprised, to say the least of it, to see Squire Mytton, stark naked, pursuing some ducks over the ice in a most determined manner.

It is a matter for wonder, indeed, that Squire Mytton reached his thirty-eighth year, for no man in a peaceful countryside ever ran more risks or had more accidents. 'How often', inquired his friend Nimrod, admiring but regretful, 'has he been run away with by gigs, how often struggling in deep water without being able to swim? How was it that he did not get torn to pieces in the countless street brawls in which he was engaged?' On one occasion he nearly was torn into two pieces, at a race-meeting in Lancashire, for one gang of thieves took it into their heads to pull Squire Mytton into a house at the very moment when a rival gang of thieves took it into *their* heads to pull him out of it. In this encounter, neither side won, because the Squire's enormous physical strength kept him stationary and, in the end, one of the gentlemen engaged in the struggle was transported to the Colonies as a reward for his violence and the attempted robbery.

The Squire was constantly riding at dangerous fences, falling off his horse when drunk, driving his tandem at a frantic speed, and paying no more attention to crossroads and corners than he did to creditors. 'There goes Squire Mytton,' the country people would say, when they saw a crazily driven tandem, rushing along like the north wind; and they would raise a cheer, for the Squire was warm-hearted and beloved. Once he galloped at full speed over a rabbit-warren, to find out if his horse would fall. He found out. Rolling over and over, after a time both horse and Squire rose to their feet unhurt.

John Mytton was as dangerous to others as to himself; it was not only that he did not mind accidents, he positively *liked* them; and when one unhappy gentleman was rash enough to venture into the Squire's gig, and, when having done so and had some slight experience of the resultant steeplechasing, he begged the Squire to consider their necks, the latter inquired: 'Were you ever much hurt then, by being upset in a gig?' 'No thank God,' was the reply, 'for I never was upset in one.' The next moment, all was confusion. For the Squire, much shocked by this omission on the part of Providence, ejaculated: 'What, never upset in a gig? What a damned slow fellow you must have been all your life,' and running the near wheel up the bank, he rectified the omission. Fortunately, according to Nimrod, neither gentleman was injured seriously.

Indeed, carriage accidents were Squire Mytton's strongest point. Having bought some carriage horses from a horse-dealer named Clarke, he put one of them into a gig, tandem, to see if it would make a good leader. 'Do you think he is a good timber-jumper?' he inquired of the alarmed Mr Clarke, who sat beside him. Not waiting for that unhappy gentleman's reply, the Squire exclaimed: 'We'll try him.' And a closed turnpike being before him, he gave the horse his head. The horse did himself credit, leaving Squire Mytton, the other horse, Mr Clarke, and the gig at the other side of the gate in grand style and almost inextricable confusion. But once again, nobody was hurt. The Squire had, too, a horse that would rear up in his gig at the word of command, 'until the hinder part of it absolutely touched the ground'. But in spite of this talented animal's frequently repeated achievement, the Squire remained alive.

Master and horses were so friendly with the country people that they would help themselves to anything that took their fancy on their way home from hunting, and Squire Mytton, if his coat was wet, would think nothing of taking a country woman's red flannel petticoat from a hedge, slipping it over his head, and leaving his coat drying in its place. It was, too, not in the least unusual for Squire Mytton, if he felt cold when out hunting, to go into the house of a cottager, accompanied by his favourite horse Baronet, and ask her to light a good fire to warm Baronet and himself, for he did not believe in a heaven from which animals were excluded. Baronet and he would then lounge by the fire, side by side, until they were warm again, and then they would start for home. But alas, there was one moment when disaster came from the master's habit of sharing all good things with the subject beast, for a horse named Sportsman dropped dead because John Mytton, out of kindness of heart, had given him a bottle of mulled port. There was a day, too, when disaster came because Squire Mytton deserted the horse as a steed and rode into the dining-room on a large brown bear. Dinner was waiting, and all went well until the Squire, who was dressed in full hunting costume, applied his spurs to the bear, whereupon that injured pet bit him through the calf of his leg, inflicting a severe wound. Nimrod produces, in his life of Mytton, a striking picture of the bear, who was of the gentler sex, with flames spouting from her nose and mouth, and Squire Mytton straddled across her back, in very much the attitude of Arion astride the Dolphin.

There was a heronry at Halston, containing from fifty to eighty nests, and Squire Mytton wished to have some herons taken, so that it might be proved if heron pie is more delicious than rook pie. The nests were on the tops of such high trees that neither keepers nor grooms dared to climb them. 'Here goes then,' said the Squire, and swarmed to the highest of the trees. Often he would be seen, with the temperature at zero, walking to his stables before breakfast, dressed only in a shirt, dressing-gown, and slippers.

Throughout his career, money fell like rain, dripped and melted like rain. In the last fifteen years of his life, indeed, more than half a million pounds drifted through his fingers.

Some of this, it is true, went on the upkeep of his foxhounds or his racing establishment, in which he had, as a rule, at least fifteen or twenty horses in training at the same time. Some of the money, again, was spent on those thin shoes which were worn out after two of his mad, storklike races over the stony countryside, through or over anything which came in his way, for this man's daily walks were a kind of symbol of his life and his half-crazy, driven mind.

He had a hundred and fifty-two pairs of trousers and breeches, and the same amount of coats and waistcoats, while, in his cellars, 'hogsheads of ale stood like soldiers in close formation'. So careless was he of money, that several thousand pounds were one night blown, by that high wind in which always he seems to have lived, out of his carriage, as he was returning from Doncaster Races – blown along the road and far away. For he had been counting the notes on the seat of the carriage, in which he was alone, and he had fallen asleep, and up sprang that cold night wind of fortune, and swept the notes away. Often, again, when going on a journey, he would take handfuls of bank-notes; and, without counting them, would roll them into a lump and throw them to his servant, as if they had been waste paper. On one occasion, Nimrod picked up one of these lumps, containing £37, in the plantation at Halston, where, to judge from its wet appearance, it must have lain for many days.

The strangest exploit, perhaps, in which Mytton was concerned, was the episode of the Nightshirt and the Hiccup. It is better to relate this story in the stately terms of his biographer Nimrod. 'You have read that somebody set fire to Troy, Alexander to Persepolis, Nero to Rome, a baker to London, a rascally caliph to the treasures of Alexandria, and the brave Mucius Scaevola to his own hand and arm to frighten the proud Lars Porsena into a peace; but did you ever hear of a man setting fire to his own nightshirt to frighten away the hiccup? Such, however, is the climax I have alluded to, and this was the manner in which it was performed. "Damn this hiccup," said Mytton, as he stood undressed on the floor, apparently in the act of getting into his bed; "but I'll frighten it away"; so, seizing a lighted candle he applied it to the tab of his shirt and, it being a cotton one, he was instantly enveloped in flames.'

In the subsequent mêlée, during which two intrepid gentlemen knocked down and rolled upon the Squire in their attempt to put out the flames, and the flames did their worst against both nightshirt and hiccup, the two gentlemen won, for they tore his shirt from his body piecemeal. As for the hiccup, it was frightened away. 'The hiccup is gone, by G—,' said the Squire, as, appallingly burnt, he reeled into bed.

The next morning, he greeted his friends with a loud 'view-halloo' to show them how he could bear pain.

This took place in Calais, whither he had fled in order to avoid his creditors; but as soon as he had recovered from his terrible burns, he returned to Halston in, I suppose, some mad fit of bravado, for he knew that every bailiff in England was on his track, and that his return must mean that he would be seized and put in a debtor's prison. It is better not to think of his sufferings in that chilled, deserted, and wretched place in which he had spent his childhood; but he was not to remain there for long. He was imprisoned in the King's Bench Prison, then in other prisons both in England and France, until, after the utmost misery of mind and body that such a man could know – his wife, whom he loved, had been forced to leave him – he died, at the age of thirty-eight, worn out by too much foolishness, too much wretchedness, and too much brandy.

Nimrod, who was his friend, says of him : 'As to his dying in peace with all mankind, how could he do otherwise who never attempted to revenge himself on any human being, but who, though his communication was not "yea, yea, or nay, nay", so far from demanding the eye for the eye, and the tooth for the tooth, would have actually given his cloak to him who stole his coat; whose heart was as warm as those of most of the world are cold; and whose warmth of heart had brought him into the prison in which he died.'

I hope that this pitiful creature has found a warm, country heaven of horses and hounds, an old and kindly heaven of country habits and country sweetness, with heavenly mansions where he and Baronet can sit by the fire together once more, horse and man, and where the master can forget the dirt and wretchedness of the debtor's prison, and the eight bottles of port a day, and all the ancient foolishness.

5

Some Amateurs of Fashion

OF those who, like Peter Schlemihl, sold their exaggerated
shadows, cast in fashionable places, to the Devil, or to the
dust, these Amateurs of Fashion, the Macaronis, the Jessamies, remain to us. Beau Feilding, that splendid figure of the
time of King Charles II, and Beau Nash, do not come into
our category; but their places are taken by the Abbé Delille,
who, besides being a priest, was perhaps the ugliest man of
his day, and who lost so little of his personal vanity that,
even in old age, he 'invariably had his hair dressed with powder *couleur de rose*'; and Prince Raunitz, who wore satin
stays and passed a portion of every morning in walking up
and down a room in which four valets puffed a cloud of
scented powder, but each of a different colour, in order that
it might fall and amalgamate with the exact shade that
suited their master's taste. '*Ils étaient*', observed a French
writer, '*des dévots à l'élégance, et en cela ils méritent nos
respects. Mais étaient-ils élégants? Voilà la question.*'

Amongst other celebrated Macaronis, or Jessamies, of the
late eighteenth and the early nineteenth centuries, were Lord
Effingham and Lord Scarbrough. The *Morning Post*, of
4th July, 1798, said: 'There is not a man of the nation, no,
not even Lord Effingham, who bestows so much time and
attempts in rendering the external appearance of his head,
elegant in the extreme, than the Earl of Scarbrough. It is
said that his Lordship keeps six French friseurs, who have
nothing else to do than dress his hair. Lord Effingham keeps
only five.'

And here come these beaux, and the feather-witted,

feather-crowned ladies who are their complements, driving round and round the Park, as if they were leaves, or feathers, blown by a cold wind. 'Our emaciated beaux in these quilted lapels and stuffed sleeves', said *The Times*, 'are like a dry walnut in a great shell'; whilst as to the ladies, the same commentator observes: 'The maroon fever had been succeeded by a very odd kind of light-headedness which the physicians call the pterio-mania, or feather folly.... The Ladies now wear feathers exactly of their own length, so that a woman is twice as long upon her feet as in her bed.... A young lady, *only ten feet high*, was overset in one of the late gales of wind, in Portland Place, and the upper mast of her feathers blown upon Hampstead Hill.' The feathers were those of the Argus pheasant, the Indian macaw, the Argilla, the flat and porcupine ostrich, and the Seringapotum; the rest of the attire was lighter than the feathers, and 'owing to the fashion of wearing muslin', we are told by another paper, 'eighteen ladies caught fire, and another eighteen thousand caught cold'.

Here comes an elegantly dressed, block-headed figure of whose coat Lord Byron once remarked, 'You might almost say the body thought.' It is Beau Brummell, the magnificent and admired friend of the Prince Regent, the grandson of a Treasury porter, and, as some say, the son of a pastry-cook. An equally magnificent personage stops his carriage for a talk with this shadow that forecasts fashion, saying: 'Brummell, where did you dine yesterday?' 'Dine, why with a person of the name of R—. I believe he wishes me to notice him, hence the dinner; but, to give him his due, he desired that I would make up the party myself, so I asked Alvanley, Mills, Pierrepoint, and a few others, and I assure you the affair turned out quite unique; there was every delicacy in and out of season; the Sillery was perfect, and not a wish remained ungratified; but my dear fellow, conceive my astonishment when I tell you that Mr R— had the assurance to sit down and dine with us.' At this point in the story, a great merchant, approaching, asked the honour of the Beau's company at dinner, whereupon he replied, with a laugh, 'with pleasure, if you promise not to tell'.

The huge evening sun cast the Beau's long shadow on the dust, for he had left his carriage for a moment's talk with these acquaintances. The shadow moved slowly, stiffly, grotesquely, as if it were very old, as if it were paralysed, and in rags. But Beau Brummell saw in it no foreshadowing of the time when, in disgrace with the Regent and living on an income of £80 a year at Caen, insufficient even for his washing-bill, a wretched semi-paralysed old man would creep with tottering and feeble steps along the side of the street, supporting himself by the wall, whilst the very children mocked and jeered at him, so forlorn was his appearance. Jeered at and mocked, he crept to a confectioner's at two o'clock every day, to obtain two of his favourite biscuits and a cup of coffee, his only luxuries, on credit; and when the old lady who kept the café would ask for the settlement of the bill the old Beau would reply with a bow: '*A la pleine lune, Madame, à la pleine lune.*' Sometimes he was reduced to begging for these poor comforts. His misery was increased by the following heartless verse, which appeared in the papers:

> Keen grows the wind, and piercing is the cold;
> My pins are weak and I am growing old;
> Around my shoulders this worn cloak I spread,
> With an umbrella to protect my head,
> Which once had wit enough to astound the world,
> But now possesses nought but wig well curl'd.
> Alas, alas, while wind and rain do beat,
> That great Beau Brummell thus should walk the street.

The winter, however, was kind to him; for, as his biographer remarks, 'His old cloak covered all his rags, and then his appearance was not so wretched.'

On this July day, thirty years before that time, who would have seen, in this magnificent figure, the unutterably wretched skeleton?

Beau Brummell has passed on, and here comes a magnificent curricle, 'shaped like a scallop shell', with the outside painted 'a beautiful rich lake colour', and bearing the owner's heraldic device, a cock, life-size, with outspread wings, and over it the motto, 'While I live, I'll crow.' The step or footboard of this imposing carriage is formed, also, in the shape of a cock. The wheels of the carriage are exceedingly high, and are picked out in all the most brilliant water-shining colours of the rainbow, and the curricle is drawn by two white horses 'of faultless figure and action'. Nothing could exceed the richness of the upholstery and the lining of the curricle, and on the cushions of this, dangling in a creole languor, half sits, half lies, a romantic and melancholy figure. Those austere features, that dark hair and those dark whiskers, enhancing the somewhat sallow tinge of the skin ... surely we have seen these before? ... This figure, wrapped in the richest and most priceless of furs, in spite of the hot and languid weather, seems surrounded by a halo of rainbow-gathering colours like those of the Antiguan moonlight, for diamonds, and the light of diamonds, are part of his being. Beneath the furs he wears a 'blue surtout coat, handsomely ornamented with frogged braid, and a high shirt collar, around which is tied a richly coloured bandana handkerchief. His legs are encased in well-wrinkled Hessian boots, whose tops are ornamented with large tassels.' Can this be that rich and celebrated Amateur of the Drama, Mr Robert Coates, known variously as Romeo Coates, Diamond Coates, and Curricle Coates? It is he!

But now Mr Coates awakens from his romantic languor, for here comes a sombre carriage, dignified and austere, containing a tall, upright, and noble-looking figure. It is Mr Coates' admired and reverenced friend, Lord Petersham, afterwards Earl of Harrington, the husband of the actress Maria Foote, of Covent Garden Theatre.

Lord Petersham's equipage makes a strong contrast to that owned by Mr Curricle Coates, acting, indeed, as a kind of dark and beneficent cloud to his friend's sun; for his lordship's carriage and his horses are brown, the harness is of an outworn design, whilst the servants are shrouded in long brown coats which muffle both necks and heels, and glazed hats whose large cockades have all the sobriety of the feathers worn by funeral mutes in other and more demonstrative days. Lord Petersham, in his youth, had been in the habit of cutting out his own clothes, and making the blacking for his shoes, but in later times he had become a great patron of the tailors, and these were so much in awe of him that they had called a certain pattern of greatcoat by his name. He was a connoisseur of snuff, and one room at Harrington House was filled with shelves bearing Chinese jars of great beauty which held the various kinds of snuff; he had, too, a collection of snuff-boxes; indeed, it was said that he used a different box on every day of the year. Captain Gronow reports that once, when Lord Petersham was using a fine Sèvres snuff-box, and this was admired, he replied that it was 'a nice summer box, but it would not do for winter wear'. Lord Petersham was a great connoisseur of tea, and Mr Timbs tells us that in the same room that contained the jars of snuff, were arranged tea-canisters containing Cougou, Pekoe, Souchong, Gunpowder, Russian and others. Indeed, his father's house, Harrington House, was long famous for its tea-drinking. Lord and Lady Harrington and their family would receive their visitors upon these occasions in the long gallery, and here the family of George III enjoyed many a cup of tea. Such, indeed, was the enthusiasm for tea, that when General Lincoln Stanhope returned home from India, after an absence of many years, he was welcomed by his father with the words, 'Hullo, Linky, my dear boy, delighted to see you. Have a cup of tea!'

Lord Petersham had not been talking to Mr Coates for many minutes, when, almost blinded by the splendour of an approaching equipage, he signalled to the coachman to drive on.

The magpie carriage, adorned by servants in superb uniforms, which had roused this consternation in the breast of Lord Petersham, had been designed to enhance the magnificence of the figure within, for it displayed to advantage Baron Ferdinand de Geramb's singularly tight-laced, gold-braided and bedizened uniform, and those huge pointed mustachios and superb whiskers which were the envy of the Prince Regent. The uniform, indeed, was the splendid original from which our more modest, less resplendent Hussars' uniform was taken. But the gold on the Baron's costume was the purest gold, and it was applied in every possible place. His spurs, when he attended balls and routs – and none of these were complete without him – were four inches long and of pure gold.

'This magnificent Personage', according to one admirer, 'was of French birth or extraction, and served in various foreign armies.' His service in the Austrian army was the most notorious, and, in the end, this amazing Chevalier de Fortune rose to such eminence that he became Chamberlain to the Emperor of Austria. He then married the widow of an enormously rich Hungarian noble, and certain malevolent persons, jealous, probably, of both whiskers and uniform, both braid and spurs, insinuated that he took unto himself not only the widow, but the title, of the deceased.

The bravery of the Baron was as striking as his appearance, and the uniform, however tight, however heavy with gold, does not seem to have hampered the expressions of his courage in the least, as we shall see from this notice in the Austrian *Court Gazette*.

'Presburg, 26th August, 1806.

'On the twenty-first of this month, at seven o'clock in the evening, a workman belonging to this place inadvertently fell into the Danube. On seeing him fall and hearing his screams, an immense crowd of persons soon assembled, but no one amongst them attempted to rescue him, and no boat was handy to send to his assistance. Every other means threatened inevitable death to those who had bravery enough to undertake the man's rescue, as the Danube (in consequence of the very heavy rains) overflowed, which, particularly in this part, added to the rapidity of the current. At this critical juncture, the Baron Ferdinand de Geramb, actual Chamberlain of Service to His Majesty the Emperor of Austria, who is so renowned for his many and exalted actions, and who in the last war raised the regiment of Her Majesty the Empress, which he conducted before the enemy, now appeared at the sight of the unhappy sufferer to fly to his relief by plunging into the waves, without even undressing. This was but the work of a moment, and after a short interval the Baron was plainly perceived, with the unfortunate he had saved, evidently struggling against the strength of the torrent, till at length, aided by an indomitable courage and dexterity, he brought the man safe on shore. In addition to this exemplary action, not content with having saved the man's life, he likewise made him a handsome present. He further ingratiated himself with his fellow-officers and comrades in the Austrian army, by erecting a monument to the memory of the Austrian Generals, Palsay Piazeck and Holtz, on the battlefield upon which they so

gloriously fell. The Baron had, whilst in Palermo during the
year 1807, *une affaire d'honneur* with a military officer of
high rank based on a rather curious agreement, to the following effect. The meeting was to take place on the summit
of the volcano, Mount Etna, and that if either of the combatants fell, the crater was to become their tomb.' The
Baron's opponent escaped this novel burial by being put *hors
de combat* at the second discharge of pistols, with a battered
arm, whilst his ball passed through the Baron's hat.

Renowned and admired, the Baron de Geramb decided
to conquer England. He made, therefore, 'overtures through
our Minister abroad, to be permitted to engage 24,000
Croatians for service in the English army. To discuss this
question more fully, Mr Bathurst, General Oakes, and Mr
H. Wellesley granted him passports to prosecute his journey
to this country for the purpose of seeing the authorities at
the War Office.' London was soon brightened, therefore, by
flashes from the Baron's gold braid, and from the macawlike
colouring of his uniform and those of his regiments of servants. London was taken by storm, the Prince Regent was
so overcome by the splendour of the whiskers and of the uniform that the Baron became, according to one enthusiastic
admirer, 'one of the most favoured guests as Carlton House,
where his opinion was eagerly sought by the occupant on
matters of dress, both for private and military purposes'. As
a result, the Baron, courted by the whole fashionable world,
forgot his military mission. The twenty-four thousand Croatians melted from his memory; and his splendour enlivened
London for twenty-two months. During these twenty-two
months he had forged bonds of the deepest friendship with
Mr Romeo Coates, for a brave man can recognize gallantry
when he sees it, and Mr Coates was in the habit of risking
life and limb in his stage performances, since the audience
could not, would not, and did not, endure his interpretations

of the classics. A riot was the inevitable result, death or serious injury the probable outcome, of these attempts.

But here was the intrepid Mr Coates, who was to brave these terrors on that very evening, stopping his curricle in order to have a talk with the Baron, who, on the occasions when his friend appeared on the stage, was in the habit of sitting in the stage box, and acting as a kind of second in Mr Coates' very unequal duel with the audience. The creole grandee and the Baron had met on the north side of the Park, but no little cold air drumming among the leaves warned them of the future battle of Bayswater, which was to take place at the end of March, 1812, when the inhabitants of that neighbourhood were drawn together by the sight of an immense poster floating from the top of the Baron's house. This poster, which floated as if it were a flag, bore the device: 'My house is my castle. I am under the protection of the British law.' Unhappily, the British Law, far from protecting the Baron, wished to reject him, for a warrant from the office of the Secretary of State had been issued under the Alien Act for his arrest, and the Baron, on his side, had refused to surrender, and had barricaded himself in, though not before flying the flag of liberty.

Those persons who had been deputed to arrest the Baron, discomfited, retired to the office for orders, returning to the house of the Baron with two gentlemen named Harrison and Craig. These authorities, stern and intrepid, called upon the Baron to surrender; whereupon that gentleman not only refused, but stated in unequivocal terms that he had two hundred pounds of gunpowder in the cellar, and that 'if they persevered in their efforts to dislodge him, he would blow them and himself up'.

In the face of this threat the authorities, armed with hatchets, hacked down the Baron's garden gate and braved the gunpowder; whereupon it transpired that the Baron had taken them for bailiffs, and therefore, moved by dim but poignant recollections of his pre-baronial days, had refused them admittance. On hearing who they were, the Chamberlain of the Emperor of Austria surrendered immediately, and having spent a night in Bridewell Prison, at Tothill Fields, was sent in a post-chaise to Dover the next day, and when there was put on a ship bound for Hamburg.

The fact was that the English government had become more than a little tired of the Baron's activities. In the first place they had traced to him a very strange correspondence with some dangerous persons in Sicily; secondly, his demands on the Government, his bills for expenses brought about by imagining those twenty-four thousand Croatians, were not only extortionate – they were fantastic. They were, as well, accompanied by threats; and the demands becoming more and more frequent, the threats more and more violent, it was judged best to send the Baron to shine at Hamburg. One bill, which he sent to the War Office, in account of services rendered, ran thus:

'Journey from Cadiz to London, £250; Establishment in London twenty-two months at £200 a month, £4400; Return to Hungary, £700. Total: £5350.'

This magnificent and bedizened ruin having landed at Hamburg, he, as I think, carelessly, indulged in a little poetry, celebrating in verse the fêtes at Carlton House, and the presence there of certain members of the former French dynasty, to whom he wished, in rickety couplets, a speedy restoration. This poem was destined to a wider public than the Baron could have hoped for, since the Emperor Napoleon was brought face to face with it, and promptly ordered the Baron's arrest, although he was on neutral ground. The Baron as a result found himself in the Château de Vincennes, and in daily fear of execution.

Having time for reflection, we are told, this superb

Italian-comedy adventurer, swaggerer and duellist, with his begonia-coloured metallic outward splendours vowed that should he ever regain his liberty he would lay down the sword and enter a monastery. This vow was fulfilled, for this strange man of honour, when he was set free from prison, entered the monastery of the Trappists near Reimingen, in Alsace, and in that silence became Abbot and Procurator General, writing several works on doctrine and the religious life, and, venerable and revered, dying in March, 1848, at the age of seventy-six.

The personage to whom the Baron was talking on this summer morning, many years before his splendours faded into the grey shades of the monastery, was a being as exotic, if less remarkable, than himself. That is to say, that Mr Coates, the Amateur of Fashion, was not so remarkable in his personality as in his appearance, and in the singular manner in which Misfortune dogged his footsteps. Sadly enough, Misfortune refused to wear her tragic mask when in Mr Coates' company, but insisted instead on appearing in the most antic of moods, tripping up her companion, and setting innumerable booby-traps for him, so that, as a result, his life was a kind of Greek drama, and the end of each adventure was inevitable and sure.

Born in Antigua in the year 1772, Mr Coates was famed in his native isle as much for his dramatic raptures as for the fountains of light shed by his profuse display of diamonds. If it had not been, indeed, for the intensely dramatic quality of his gestures, I doubt if the melancholy Mr Coates would have been perceptible amidst the lights which flashed from his person. But the gestures were admired, they were recognized, in the West Indies, where dramas on the stage were few and far between, no matter how many there may have been in real life. 'In the West Indies of that time,' we are told, 'there were no parks or walks, no concerts or ballrooms. In 1788, the first Antiguan theatre was formed by some amateurs, who generally engaged the band of the regiment then in garrison to act as Orchestra, with the consent of the Colonel. The performers were frequently supplemented by a company of players making the tour of the West Indies.' Encouraged by the elephant-like trumpeting of the military band, soothed by the plaudits of the Colonel, and by the gentle sound of the sea, Mr Coates flashed his diamonds, and his sword, in imitation of the Antiguan moonlight, raised his left arm to the heavens, in protestation of his honour, died, and rose again. How different was this happy life in the Garden of Eden to that life of danger into which his art must plunge him, once he had come to England. How high were his hopes – and how swift was their fall! But not more swift than was the fall of the curtain every time that Mr Coates trod the boards! And every time that he appeared, this intrepid man took his life into his hands – and not only his life, but the lives of his fellow-actors and actresses, as we shall see.

The first record of Mr Coates' appearance on the stage in England appears in Mr Pryse Gordon's memoirs. He tells us that: 'In the year 1809 I was at Bath and stayed at the York House, where I found this gentleman an inmate, and we generally met in the coffee-room at breakfast. He shortly attracted my notice by rehearsing passages from Shakespeare during his morning meal, with a tone and gesture extremely striking both to the eye and the ear; and, though we were strangers to each other, I could not help complimenting him on the beauty of his recitations, although he did *not always stick to his author's text*. On one occasion I took the liberty of correcting a passage from *Romeo and Juliet*. "Ay," said he, "that is the reading, I know, for I have the play by heart, but I think I have improved upon it." I bowed with submission, acknowledging I was not a profound critic. This

led to a dissertation on the merits of this fine tragedy. When
he informed me that he had frequently performed the part of
"Romeo" at Antigua, of which island he was a native, adding that he always travelled with the dress of that character amongst his other garments, I lamented that, with the
extraordinary talents he seemed to possess, he had not gratified the English public with a specimen of his powers. . . .
"I am ready and willing", replied our Roscius, "to play
Romeo to a Bath audience, if the manager will get up the
play and give me a good Juliet – my costume is superb and
adorned with diamonds, but I have not the advantage of
knowing the manager Dimonds." After laughing at his
excellent pun, in which he heartily joined, I observed that I
was acquainted with this gentleman, and would either make
the necessary arrangements, or give him a line of introduction, as he preferred.' In the end, the performance was
arranged, and took place on February the ninth, 1810, without any loss of life, since nothing heavier than orange peel
was thrown on this occasion. Nor did the curtain fall until
Act V, when Romeo seized a crow-bar in order to break into
Juliet's tomb. Then the attitude of the audience became so
menacing that as nothing but the crow-bar stood between
Mr Coates and imminent dissolution, it was thought wiser
to lower the curtain and declare the play at an end. His
biographers, Messrs John and Hunter Robinson, inquire,
not without justice: 'What cared they [the audience] if Mr
Coates appeared as Romeo (probably following the taste for
bright and striking colours which all inhabitants in tropical
climes possess in a more or less marked degree) in a spangled
cloak of sky-blue silk, crimson pantaloons and a white hat
trimmed with feathers, or that the ornament upon the hat
glistened with diamonds, which likewise appeared on his
knee and shoe-buckles – or for any new giving of the text?'

But Mr Coates was not to be daunted. He repeated the

performance at Brighton, where, according to one paper, it 'astonished the aquatics and submarines of the Sussex coast', and then with the utmost intrepidity he appeared in the part of Romeo at Cheltenham. Here he met with no very serious disaster, for the only untoward event was that just as he had repeated the line: 'Oh, let me hence, I stand on sudden haste', instead of acting according to that urgency, Romeo went down on all fours and in that position crawled round and round the stage. In vain did the prompter call, 'Come off, come off.' It was some time before Mr Coates heard him and, when he did, he responded that he would come off as soon as he had found his diamond knee-buckle! This pleased the audience, and they allowed the play to reach its proper conclusion, in the hope that something of the same kind might happen again.

Encouraged by this immunity, Mr Coates appeared at the Theatre Royal, Richmond, on the fourth of September, 1811, and again no attempt was made upon his life. Indeed, the only lives that were in danger were those of certain unfeeling young gentlemen, who, in the scene where the hero poisons himself, were seized with such immoderate paroxysms of laughter that a doctor who was present became alarmed at their condition, and ordered them to be carried into the open air, where they received medical attention.

This incident annoyed Mr Coates who, when the play was ended, strode towards the footlights and, pointing at the boxes from which the interruption had come, gave the famous recitation, 'Bucks, have at ye all.'

This severe indictment of the taste of the audience contained these lines:

> Ye Bucks of the boxes there, who roar and reel,
> Too drunk to listen and too proud to feel.
> Whose flinty hearts are proof against despair,
> Whose vast estates are neither here nor there.

Mr Coates was much applauded by a certain part of the audience, who admired him for his courage. But alas, matters were not always so easy for him. On the ninth of December, 1811, he appeared at the Haymarket Theatre in the part of the gay Lothario in Rowe's tragedy, *The Fair Penitent*, and in his hands tragedy lost all her gloom. The occasion was that of a benefit performance in aid of the widow Fairbur, and how huge were the crowds that besieged the doors of the theatre, eager to see the gifted amateur, the owner of the curricle, the owner of the diamonds! At least one thousand persons were turned away from the box entrance alone, whilst many people with money to spend besieged the stage-door and offered as much as five pounds for a single admission to go behind the scenes. Not an empty seat could be found. We read that 'Amongst the persons of rank and fashion present this evening to witness Mr Coates' rendering of the character of Lothario were the Duke of Brunswick, the Duke of Devonshire, the Portuguese Ambassador, the Earl of Kinnoull and family, Viscount Castlereagh, Baron de Geramb, Sir Godfrey Webster, Sir Charles Coote and family, etc.' We may imagine the feelings of Mr Coates as he approached that crowded entrance to the theatre. How great was the British love of Dramatic Art, how great the friendliness of the Nobility! How lustrous were the leaves of that laurel crown which awaited him, how deafening the plaudits of the audience! Alas! This was but another booby-trap laid by Fortune – or rather by Mr Coates' faithful and indefatigable companion, Misfortune! – for no sooner had the Baron de Geramb appeared in a box, than a large portion of the audience took a dislike to him, and showed this by hissing him and by loud and discordant screams, though other members of the audience thought that this was bad-mannered conduct towards an illustrious foreigner and a friend of the Prince Regent, and applauded him so vigorously that in the end their opponents relented and joined in the applause.

When, at last, the Gifted Amateur appeared, and made a special bow to the box containing the Umpire – the Baron de Geramb – the noise was cataclysmic. There were catcalls, there was much whistling, and shrieks of cock-a-doodle-doo – this latter expression of condemnation referred to the famous curricle and Mr Coates' crest. Calm and intrepid, that gentleman faced his traducers, in a dress of the utmost richness, wrought of 'a species of silk so woven as to give it the appearance of chased silver; from his shoulders hung a mantle of pink silk, edged with bullion fringe; around his neck was a kind of gorget, richly set with jewels, and at his side was a handsome gold-hilted sword. Coates' head-dress was composed of a Spanish hat surmounted by tall white plumes, while his feet were encased in shoes of the same material as his dress, and these were fastened with large diamond buckles.'

Unperturbed by the splendour of Mr Coates' costume, the audience would not allow him to reach that final scene which was, as a rule, the joy of all beholders. An eyewitness, describing this pregnant ending of the play, exclaims : 'Who shall describe the grotesque agonies of the dark seducer, his plastered hair escaping from the comb that held it, and the dark crineous cordage that flapped upon his shoulders in the convulsions of his dying moments, and the cries of the people for medical aid to accomplish his eternal exit? Thus, when in his last throes his coronet fell, it was miraculous to see the defunct arise, and after he had spread a nice handkerchief on the stage, and there deposited his head-dress, free from all impurity, philosophically resume his dead condition; but it was not yet over, for the exigent audience, not content that when the men were dead, why there's an end, insisted on a repetition of the awful scene, which the highly flattered corpse executed three separate times, to the gratification of the cruel and torment-loving audience.'

On this occasion the spectators, by their eagerness to annoy, cheated themselves of this magnificent death-scene, for, having yelled themselves hoarse, they found that Mr Coates was unable to compete with them, and the curtain fell, to rise no more. The audience faded away. The Duke of Brunswick, the Duke of Devonshire, the Portuguese Ambassador, the Earl of Kinnoull and family, Viscount Castlereagh, Sir Godfrey Webster, Sir Charles Coote and family went with the rest. One by one, the lights were turned out. I do not know if Lothario, returning to his solitary but magnificent lodging, ate a solitary and magnificent supper, or if his friend the Baron Ferdinand de Geramb shared this; but I do know that the attitude of the critics outshone that of the rest of the audience, and that Mr Coates felt constrained to write a letter to the *Morning Herald*, which contained these lines :

'In regard to the innumerable attacks that have been made upon my lineaments and person in the public prints, I have only to observe, that as I was fashioned by the Creator, independent of my will, I cannot be responsible for that result which I could not control. If the gentlemen who amused themselves in this *noble* way can derive either pleasure or profit from the indulgence of such desires, I regard the liberty of the Press as the keystone of that arch upon which our glorious constitution reposes in security; and I will not lightly question the extent of that liberty because envy, folly, or even a viler passion may stimulate a blockhead to violate the purity of such a privilege.'

On a subsequent occasion, Mr Coates reached the last scene of *The Fair Penitent* in perfect safety, rendered immune by the presence of His Royal Highness the Duke of Clarence and his suite, and by that of Lavendor, the police officer, whose services had been engaged by the not unnaturally nervous management.

At about this time, both Mr Coates and the Baron de Geramb became officially enamoured of Miss Tylney Long, an heiress of renowned beauty, but this rivalry did not in the least impair their friendship. Alas, even this infidelity towards the Thespian Muse proved to be only another booby-trap laid by Misfortune, for not only did Miss Tylney Long marry the Hon. Wellesley Pole, but Miss Euphemia Boswell, the daughter of Dr Johnson's biographer and victim, wishing to revenge herself on Mr Coates, because he would not succumb to her begging letters, wrote this sinister and veiled threat :

'I shall thank you to send me the copy of lines I wrote for you to send to Miss Tylney Long. I am urged to publish them.'

The masterpiece in question ran as follows :

> Titian, could he but view thy heavenly face,
> In vivid colours he'd each beauty trace.
> Lucretia's charms were great, but thine surpass
> Nature's first model – o'er that Grecian lass,
> Enchanting fair one, save, oh, quickly save,
> Your dying lover from an early grave.
> Lady, ah, too bewitching lady, now beware
> Of artful men that fain would thee ensnare,
> Not for thy merit, but thy fortune's sake,
> Give me your hand – your cash let venials take.

In celebration of this love, and that of the Duke of Clarence for the same lady, a paper called the *Scourge* published a coloured plate as a frontispiece to the December number for 1811; this is taken from an etching by George Cruikshank, and is entitled 'Princely Piety, or the Worshipper at Wanstead'. In the centre is Miss Tylney Long, seated upon a dais draped in crimson and gold, which is reached by

five steps, carpeted with the same colours; the first step bears
this device: 'Infancy, ten'; the second 'Puberty, fifteen'; the
third 'Womanhood, twenty'; the fourth 'Discretion, twenty-
five'; and the fifth, 'Old Maidism, thirty'. His Royal Highness the Duke of Clarence is on Miss Tylney Long's right
hand, and by him is the outraged Miss Jordan, who empties
over him a vial of her wrath, from which fall several persons
in naval and military uniforms; 'False, Faithless Clarence,
behold thy children. Ahem, Shakespeare.' The Duke, meanwhile, with the utmost determination, is trying to thrust the
Baron de Geramb into the background. The Baron is kneeling by the steps of the dais surrounded by bags, full of gold –
the result of his various adventures in the secret services and
the armies of the world. In the background, on the left, a
fool with a cap and bells, is playing a violin, and two dum-
mies are dancing to the music of this, whilst, in front of
these, two personages are kneeling on the steps of the throne.
One is an old beau, much resembling Sir Lumley Skeffington; his quizzing-glass is raised, and he holds a petition in
his hand; whilst the other figure bears the romantic appearance of Mr Romeo Coates. The head of this figure bears a
cock crowing, 'Cock-a-doodle-doo'. Romeo's hat and feathers
lie by his side, one hand is pressed to his heart, whilst the
other is outstretched. It is obvious that this hand has scattered the papers, marked 'Odes', which lie on the steps of
the throne.

As a result of his celebrated though thwarted worship of
Miss Tylney Long, his equally famous friendship with
Baron Ferdinand de Geramb, his riches, his diamonds, his
curricle, and his dramatic performances, Mr Coates was now
in a fair way of becoming a lion. No drama given in aid of
Charity was complete without him, even though his presence alone meant that the drama must come to an untimely
end, or, in any case, that disaster must ensue. There were,

however, one or two performances which drew to their close without any actual bloodshed, however threatening the attitude of the audience might be. Amongst these performances we may single out that given at the Haymarket Theatre on January the eleventh, where the riot was mainly vocal, and which was made memorable by the fact that, at the end, Mr Coates, in reply to repeated requests, came on the stage dressed in a scarlet military coat, a hat with a regulation feather, knee-breeches, silk stockings, and shoes sparkling with diamonds, and recited a set of verses named 'The Hobbies'.

And now Mr Coates was approaching the summit of his ambition, the dream which his loyal, and innocently snobbish soul had cherished for so long. For, after many subterranean burrowings, which were only equalled by his perfectly frank trumpetings for attention, Mr Coates, on the eleventh of February, 1813, was presented by General Baker to the Prince Regent at the Royal levee. How gracious was the Royal Personage, and how interested in the personality, the character, the history, the dramatic aspirations, and the diamonds, of Mr Coates. How full of wonders was the life of Mr Coates. How easily might ignorance and envy be forgiven. How quickly might the Gifted Amateur rise to an equality with his friend the Baron Ferdinand de Geramb, as a familiar of Carlton House.

Mr Coates was not in the slightest surprised, therefore, when he received, on the fourth of February, 1813, 'a portentous missive sealed with the Royal Arms, and left, so the attendants stated, by a gentleman in a scarlet coat'. Mr Coates with a trembling hand broke open the seal, and read the contents of the letter, which ran thus:

'The Lord Chamberlain is commanded by His Royal Highness the Prince Regent to invite Mr Robert Coates to a ball and supper at Carlton House on Friday evening. The company to appear in the costume of the manufacture of the country. Hour of attendance, ten o'clock.'

Mr Coates, overcome with joy and with pride, recognized that this invitation was but a natural sequel to the gracious interest shown by the Prince Regent on the occasion of the levee; so he ordered that his diamonds should be polished, that a suit of unparalleled magnificence should be made 'in order to do honour to so illustrious a host, the prince of connoisseurs as well as of the Realm'.

On the evening of the ball, Mr Coates could hardly contain himself till the moment of his departure. We are told that he left his lodgings in Craven Street 'a blaze of splendour; diamonds of the first water flashed upon his bosom, whilst those on the hilt of his sword, and upon his fingers, radiated with equal brilliancy. Having taken his seat in the chair prepared for his conveyance, he proceeded to his destination accompanied by two footmen in the most superb and costly liveries.'

When he arrived at Carlton House, and presented his card, Colonel Congreve, who was in attendance, told him, with the utmost politeness, that it was a forgery. So Mr Diamond, or Curricle, Coates, passed out of Carlton House into the brilliantly lighted street, where his splendours and his forlorn condition attracted the attention of the huge crowd that was waiting to stare at the guests; and having found, at last, a hackney carriage (his own magnificent chair had gone, long ago), this poor harmless kindly creature found his way back to his lodging. There he knew the utmost miseries of humiliation, remembering the horrors of his stage appearances, the cruel and perfectly unnecessary mockery, the pain that the crowds had inflicted upon him. But the humiliation on this occasion was not to be perpetual, for the Prince Regent, when told of the circumstances, was made so angry by the heedless and needless cruelty of the hoax, that he sent his secretary, the next day, to apologize to Mr Coates for the disappointment, which, had His Royal Highness known of the occurrence, would not have been inflicted; and Mr Coates was invited to come and view the decorations of the fête, which were still intact.

Fortune relented on this occasion, it is true, but on others her attitude became more and more harsh. And as the fame of Mr Coates increased, so did the terror of those who appeared on the same stage as the Gifted Amateur. The audiences knew this, and revelled in it, relying on mass hypnotism in order to terrify Mr Coates' fellow-actors into making the strangest admissions. One gentleman, for instance, driven half out of his mind with fear by the menacing attitude of the audience, substituted for the words 'I would I were a beggar, and lived on scraps' the phrase 'I wish I were a baker, and lived on sprats', an admission which was greeted with rapturous applause and the fall of the curtain. And there was another, and a more serious, incident of the same kind. The house was, as usual, crowded; the Baron Ferdinand de Geramb could be seen in his full splendour in the stage box. The occasion was, of course, a benefit performance in aid of somebody or other, the play was *The Fair Penitent*, the interruptions, the roars and the missiles were the usual interruptions and roars and missiles. Then, suddenly, the unfortunate gentleman who acted the part of Horatio, driven by terror at the almost unceasing clamour, substituted, in the lines, 'When you are met among your set of fools, talk of your dress, of dice, or horses, and yourselves; it's safer, and becomes your understanding better', the word 'curricles' for the word 'horses'. Some people say, indeed, that the actor inserted the lines:

> Why drive you in state about the town
> With curricle and pair – your crest a cock?

Mr Coates' honour was outraged. The Baron de Geramb's whiskers and moustaches could be seen to be bristling with rage. A duel was imminent. The fatal word set free all the feelings of the house, and raised such a clamour that for nearly a quarter of an hour not a word could be heard from the stage. As for Mr Coates, when he heard this purely involuntary personal allusion, he started back, overcome with indignation, and then advanced a pace or two, in apparent agitation, to the front of the stage. He then advanced upon Horatio as if to ask the meaning of this insult.

The petrified Horatio now came to life again, and tried to speak, but the clamour was such that his voice could not be heard. At last, when the audience had shouted itself hoarse, Mr Coates made the following speech, in a voice choked with indignation:

'Ladies and gentlemen, I was solicited to play for a lady who I was informed was an object worthy of attention. [Applause.] I further beg leave to state that there are several performers in this place who belong to our great theatres, and let me add that one of them has taken a most unwarrantable liberty with me. Many of you may have doubtless read the play of *The Fair Penitent*, and, if not, you may do so tomorrow, but there you will find something about horses and merriment. But a performer has no right to endeavour to hurt my feelings by inserting allusions to me not in his part. Let my equipage be laughed at by those that choose; my father, who left me a large fortune, wherewith I indulge my whims, likewise taught me good manners. I am little given to boasting, but if I may be allowed to say a few words on my own conduct, I can say I consider myself a most useful character; for if my dress be extravagant, it is this which supports the working classes. Does it not assist the tailors, mercers, and coach-makers? In these respects I set, what I think, a laudable example.'

Amidst the applause, shrieks and crowings of the audience, Horatio now stepped forward, and in a very manly and sincere manner disclaimed, on his honour, any intention of giving offence to Mr Coates.

The tension of the Baron's figure was seen to relax; honour was satisfied, the incident was over, and Mr Coates, after consulting the Baron and some friends in a stage box, shook hands with Horatio. The play then proceeded and came to an end where the author wished.

But there was a fresh scene, and this time of unexampled pathos, when Mr Coates appeared at the Haymarket Theatre in *Romeo and Juliet* on the occasion of a benefit performance in aid of Miss FitzHenry, the daughter of an old lady named Lady Perrott, who had invoked Mr Coates' aid on a previous occasion. Miss FitzHenry, as Juliet, became so terrified by the menacing attitude of the audience, that, shrieking, she clung to the scenery and pillars in great agitation; and could not be dislodged. Another time, in the duel scene where Romeo kills Tybalt, all was ruined, and the house was convulsed with laughter at the appearance of a bantam cock, which strutted at the very feet of Romeo, at whom it had been thrown. Mr Coates was in despair, but luckily, at the last and darkest moment, old Capulet seized the cause of the trouble and bore him, crowing loudly, and flapping his wings, off the stage.

His biographers inquire, not without indignation, 'what should we think now if an amateur of good private fortune made his appearance, drawing houses that even Garrick might have envied, and one who combined with dramatic taste that for unique and brillant equipages – what would the present generation think of such a person being received with cries derisive of his armorial bearing, real or assumed, together with remarks upon his carriage and servants?' What, indeed?

The play continued, though, when Romeo left the stage after killing Tybalt, he stood in the wings and shook his sword at the box from which the cock had been thrown on to the stage, with the result that the occupants of the box yelled that he must apologize for shaking his sword. Mr Coates, very naturally, refused to do so, and the interruptions continued until the occupants of the pit turned on the interrupters and pelted them with orange peel. The play continued, then, without any further interruption until the moment came when Romeo kills Paris. Then the latter, lying dead upon the ground, was raised to life by 'a terrific blow on the nose from an orange'. The corpse rose to his feet and, pointing in a dignified way to the cause of his revival, made his way off the stage. Mr Coates, we are told, was 'considerably annoyed' during the Tomb Scene, by shouts of 'Why don't you die?'

Amidst such scenes of unparalleled ferocity did Mr Coates woo the Thespian Muse, but not for much longer, for his love remained unrequited, and he was growing tired. Besides, the situation grew more and more dangerous, until at last he decided no longer to risk life and limb in this hopeless courtship, but to place his purse, instead of his person, at the disposal of his needy fellow-actors. We are told that he was seen but rarely 'on the tragic boards during the year 1815 – a period occupied in celebrating the overthrow of Napoleon'.

Mr Coates was looking a little older, a little more sallow, a little sadder. The splendours of the curricle, and of the diamonds, these, too, were dimmed, for the value of Mr Coates' estates in Antigua had fallen owing to the revolt of the slaves in Barbados, and Mr Coates felt that something was missing from his life. Perhaps it was that he missed his friend the Baron de Geramb, although he had many other friends – Lord Petersham, with whom we have seen him conversing in the Park, and Sir Lumley Skeffington, of whom the *Monthly Mirror*, in an ecstasy of admiration, wrote this eulogy : 'Those who best know him declare that in point of temper he may be equalled, but not surpassed; as to his manners, the suffrages of the most polished and polite circles in the kingdom have pronounced him one of the best-bred men of the present time, blending at once the *Vieille Cour* with the careless gracefulness of the present school. He seems to do everything by chance, but it is such a chance as study could not improve. In short, whenever he trifles, it is with elegance, and whenever occasion calls for energy, he is warm, spirited, and animated.'

But even the spirit and animation of Sir Lumley Skeffington could not make up to Mr Coates for his fading splendours, his unfading and unrealizable ambitions. He found, I hope, some consolation in his marriage with Miss Emma Anne Robinson, the daughter of Lieutenant William McDowell Robinson, of His Majesty's Navy, which took place at St George's, Hanover Square, on the sixth of September, 1823. Mrs Coates' portrait shows a pretty face with dark eyes rather overcharged with meaning, though it is impossible to guess what that meaning may be – a delicate nose, a silly rabbit-mouth, and a well-ordered stage crowd of dark curls and ribbons.

In the course of the 1830s, as a result of the trouble in the West Indies, Mr Coates' income sank, so that he was obliged, according to his biographers, 'to retire to Boulogne'. They add, with their customary delicacy, that 'no doubt this necessity might have been obviated had he wisely entered an appearance, or come to some arrangement about several actions pending against him. As prudence or foresight had not dictated this cause, he was forced to make an exile of himself for a time as the price of his neglect.'

In the end matters were arranged, and Mr Coates might

once more have been seen bobbing up and down in the sea of fashionable life, with some persistence.

But Fate had not yet exhausted her jokes at his expense. On February the fifteenth, 1848, a rather cheap-looking curricle, drawn by a dirty grey horse, was dashing along Russell Street, just as an old gentleman, elaborately dressed and of dark complexion, began to run from a theatre, with a curious poultry-like flutter, across the road. There was a shout from the crowd, a dreadful muffling silence, and then a high agonized unnatural sound like the crowing of a ranting, dramatically flapping cock.

Mr Romeo, Diamond, or Curricle Coates had been run over by a cheap imitation of his own famous carriage, and he died on the following Sunday, aged seventy-five years. Mrs Coates was not more faithful to his memory than had been his Muse; for she married on the twenty-third of December following, an old friend and associate of her husband, Mark Boyd, Esq., and with this marriage vanishes from our story.

So died an exaggerated shadow, cast in fashionable places.

Eight years before that time, in a small back room of a lodging-house in Caen, the whist table was set out, the candles were lit, and the lodging-house servant, opening the door, would announce the names of those who had been dead these thirty-five years or more, and of those who had deserted Beau Brummell in the days of his poverty. Then the old and paralysed man in the chair by the thin fire would try to reach the door to welcome his guests. 'His Royal Highness the Prince Regent,' announced the servant, and a little cold air entered from the dark passage. 'The Duchess of Devonshire', 'The Duke of Beaufort', 'Lady Jersey', 'Madame de Mangrattan'. 'Ah, my dear Duchess,' said the wheezing voice, coming with such difficulty through the paralysed jaws, 'how rejoiced I am to see you, ... so very amiable of you at this short notice. Pray bury yourself in the armchair; do you know it was a gift to me from the Duchess of York, who was a very kind friend of mine; but poor thing, you know, she is dead now.' And his vacant eyes would fill with tears. There he would sit, talking with these ghosts in his eerie voice until, at 10 o'clock, the servant announced the carriages, and the old man was alone again.

His state grew increasingly terrible, more and more distressing. At last his intestines became paralysed, and his bodily functions were no longer under control. It was impossible to keep him clean, and his wretchedness was made greater by the fact that warmth was now his only comfort, and that his monthly pension did not allow him enough fuel.

At length it was decided, without his knowledge, that the good and charitable nuns of the Bon Sauveur should take care of him, where every comfort awaited him, and a blazing fire with an armchair in front of it. But when his friend Mr Armstrong, the servant, and the landlord, went to his room, to lead him to the carriage, nothing would induce him to go. He continued lathering his wig, and exclaiming '*Laissez-moi tranquille.*' In the narrow staircase of the house, at last, came the three men carrying a collapsed and paralytic skeleton, whilst the house echoed with terrible screams from a voice which was now nothing but a memory, enclosed in the grave of those useless jaws. 'You are taking me to prison. Loose me, scoundrels, I owe nothing. I owe nothing.' The door opened and shut again, and one last cracked shriek pierced the door – 'I owe nothing.'

6

An Observer of Human Nature

In the study of the Hermitage at Bath, an estate which was made cheerful by the fact that one of his daughters by his first wife lay buried in the grounds, my old friend (and my ancestors' cousin), Captain Philip Thicknesse, sat writing the third volume of his memoirs.

His position as a soldier, and a Man of Wrath and of Honour, vied with his avowed position as an Ornamental Hermit, for he had lately declared that 'The duplicity of Mankind, and satiety of enjoyments, all tend to show that even the splendid scenes, which surround the palaces of wealth and greatness, are never thought complete, unless marked by some shady cave and the abode of an imaginary Anchorite. . . . I have obtained that which every man aims at, but few acquire: solitude and retirement.' And Captain Thicknesse, his manly face softened by emotion, adjusted his wig and wrote the following 'Hermit's Prayer':

'God of my Life, who numberest my days, teach me to meet with gratitude, or patience, the good or ill which the tide of time shall float down upon me; but never, O God, I humbly beseech Thee, withdraw from me those native spirits which have been the cheering companions of my existence, and have spread a gilding even upon my misfortunes.

'Continue to me, O God of Life, those powers, that I may view with rapture the inexhaustible Volume of Nature, which Thou hast spread before mine eyes; in every page of which I read the impression of Thy Omnipotent Hand.'

Captain Thicknesse paused, sighed, then added, slowly:

NOTE

'It is with inexpressible concern that I now find myself under the Necessity of Adding to the above Description, to my Paradisal Abode, the following advertisement, but I have lived to perceive that two Events are not very far remote, and if either of them happen in my Life, it will render my Residence here, uncomfortable with my scanty income.

ADVERTISEMENT

'On the 15th of June, 1789, will be Sold by Auction, St Catherine's Hermitage, near Bath. For further Particulars, Enquire of Mr Fores, Bookseller, Piccadilly; or of Mr Plura, Auctioneer, at Bath.'

This change of front was the result of 'Esquire Hooper telling me he would let the land all round my house to a parcel of Beggars on purpose to perplex me.'

For this reason, therefore, was the Captain obliged to give up his position as Ornamental Hermit, and to leave his place of retreat, which, according to himself, 'hangs on the side of Lansdown Hill', and from which he could watch 'the barks on the Avon, which I considered as messengers whom I have sent forth to fetch me Tea from Asia, Sugar from America, Wine from France, and Fruit from Portugal'.

Captain Thicknesse, after meditating for a few moments on the unfairness of fate, resumed the writing of his Memoirs, and told the interested, if slightly hostile, world, that 'I can at any time muster ten or a dozen knaves and fools, who will put a hundred pounds in my pocket, merely for holding them up to public scorn. Let me see? I will muster up my forces, and begin, as all scholards [sic] do, with my A.B.C. One rum Wiltshire fumigating Duke, ten Lords, a long white-headed travelling Parson, three Doctors of Physic, a broken, deaf and lame Sea-Duck, ten thousand

five hundred Male Midwives, and about the same number of
their silly female customers, a Bulgarian Bath Painter, two
hundred Black Legs, and a Dancing Master of the Ceremonies.'

Faced with this assorted army of enemies, Captain Thicknesse showed no fear. His character was liable to be misunderstood, for he was one of those unfortunate people who
cannot move one step in life without being injured by one
person, insulted by another, so that he was forced to engage
in perpetual warfare in order to preserve his dignity. So
much, indeed, was he misunderstood, that a schoolboy who
made his acquaintance told his father that he had expected
to find Captain Thicknesse 'a thin, peevish, fretful-looking
being, instead of which he found him fat, and as much disposed to laugh as any man'. Captain Thicknesse added:
'His father was pleased to inform his son that he believed
the latter to be my natural disposition, but that a great
variety of unfortunate events, having fell one after another
upon me, had in some measure rendered me liable to the
imputation of the former.'

Now this virtuous and warlike old gentleman, described
by himself on the title page of the Memoirs as 'Late Lieutenant Governor of Landguard Fort, and unfortunately father
to George Touchet, Baron Audley', was staging a highly
satisfactory quarrel with another old gentleman, James
Makittrick Adair, to whom he had dedicated his Memoirs
in a highly insulting preface. Mr Makittrick Adair had, it
seems, aimed 'a deeper blow to a susceptible mind, and to
an innocent man, than either lead or iron can impress'. He
had, in short, accused Captain Thicknesse, an officer and a
gentleman, not only of being 'a fugitive, to avoid personal
danger, by flying from his colours', but of boasting of his
own personal prowess, at the very instant when Captain
Thicknesse's victorious Sergeant, from whose side he had

fled, 'returned, surrounded by prisoners, and wearing upon his brow those laurels he [the Captain] had so shamefully blasted'.

The labyrinthine and tortuous windings of this quarrel are as difficult to follow as any of the other warlike expeditions which were Captain Thicknesse's delight, but so great was the interest which it aroused that the names of the subscribers to the Memoirs filled eight pages, that those pages are black with the names of bloodthirsty clergymen, and that, whilst the Honourable Horace Walpole was content with one copy only, the Duke of Northumberland was so voracious that he ordered ten. Amongst other subscribers, I find the name of Francis Sitwell Esq., of Renishaw Hall, Derbyshire, although as a rule that gentleman was a man of peace, and preferred playing Gluck on the flute to quarrelling.

Captain Thicknesse gave the errant Mr Adair a very thorough trouncing in the dedication and, amidst other charges, stated that 'this man obtained his boasted independance, by black and white practice, among the Negroes of the Island of Antigua, where he was known by no other name than James Makittrick; but as that was but an awkward name *to go to bed with*, among *white people*, he made a trip to Spa, where he found a very respectable practitioner of physic, of the name of Adair, and confined himself with his *family name*; in his medical *"morceau"*, he has taken care to let us know that he has seen the bed-chamber of the Queen of France, but as if that arid Island, upon the surface of which he obtained "his independance" had been sunk by an earthquake, he has omitted to let us know that the language, and manners of the Negroes, was the only living language he could utter a word of, for of the French he knows no more than the late learned pig.'

Captain Thicknesse ('unfortunately father to George

Touchet, Baron Audley') was deeply shocked at Mr Makittrick Adair's behaviour in holding up his own daughter to
shame. Indeed, he was so shocked that he thought it only
right to repeat the story in these words: 'I therefore call upon
you, James Makittrick, alias Adair, to tell the publick what
punishment you would think due to a man, were he to write,
to print, and privately dispense, five hundred pamphlets, as
you have done, stating that your daughter, who, for ought I
know, is of unsullied fame, and as chaste as she may be fair,
had been debauched at Antigua by a negroe-slave; that she
had been delivered of a mulatto child.' But at this point,
Captain Thicknesse's punctuation becomes so congested, as
a result of indignation, that it is impossible to follow the
story any further. For the Captain was a chivalrous gentleman, as we shall understand from the circumstances of his
first marriage, the later episode of the Widow Concanen, and
his own story about the Young Ladies and the Dog.

At last, driven to frenzy by the Captain's hints and but-
tings and shufflings, warlike excursions and feints and am-
bushes, Mr Adair wrote this reply, in a pamphlet: 'The
dunce has been a hackney scribbler for half a century, yet
his letter to A. exhibits, in every page, such gross ignorance
of grammer as would disgrace a footman or a cook-maid.'
He announced further, that if Captain Thicknesse did not
tell the whole truth, and nothing but the truth, one of his
Grub Street brethren would certainly be employed to publish
a cheap edition of his life, embellished with genuine anecdotes and explanatory annotations.

To this appalling threat, Captain Thicknesse returned the
following singularly mild answer: 'The Author is in his
Seventeenth Year, and never pretended to be an accurate
Writer.'

When Captain Thicknesse was angry (and this was his
usual state), or when he found a circumstance difficult to

explain to his advantage, he was in the habit of exuding clouds of ink, like an octopus, in which he could disguise the facts at will, and capture his audience. However, as far as I can make out from the stories told about him by other, and less fervent, admirers, the facts of his first marriage and of that episode with the Widow Concanen which led to his second marriage, were these. The story of the Young Ladies and the Dog will come later.

The first Mrs Philip Thicknesse was a rich young lady whose maiden name was Lanove; and Captain Thicknesse met her when he was twenty-two years old, whilst he was commanding Landguard Fort. The Captain, being wise in his generation, and realizing that her family would never allow him to marry her (and obtain possession of her money) unless he first involved her in a scandal, entered into a feigned marriage with her, so that her parents were only too glad to hurry on a real marriage, at whatever cost. This lady bore him three daughters, and then died, with two of her daughters, of a disease called Pelham sore throat, an appalling epidemic of the time, whose ravages were as terrible and as sudden, though less general, than those of the Spanish influenza of 1918. That queer irascible old rascal, Captain Thicknesse, who, in spite of his violent temper (which may have been due in part to the fact that he suffered from gallstones and was in the habit of drinking large quantities of laudanum in order to soothe the pain), had a real, if strangely constituted heart, and his descriptions of his sufferings when his wife and daughters died, is moving – all the more so, perhaps, because it is an artless production, for Captain Thicknesse was no writer. His description of the death and burial of a third daughter (in the grounds of the Hermitage) has also a touching quality. 'The long painful and hopeless illness of my daughter,' he tells us, 'which had worn her down to death, and her parents to such a deep sorrow, that the idea of the procession of removing her remains down the hill seemed to us but one remove less painful than that fatal remove between Life and Death; and therefore as she was virtuous, dutiful, and not void of some genius, we have deposited her body here with, the only monumental stone raised in Britain to the Greatest Genius that Britain, or perhaps any other nation under the sun, has produced.'

The genius in question was Thomas Chatterton, and although his poetic gifts have, I think, been grossly, if pardonably exaggerated, the poignant tragedy of his death has not. So I have a feeling of affection for my distant kinsman, because he erected this monument in his garden, inscribed with these halting lines:

> Sacred to the memory of
> Thomas Chatterton
> Unfortunate Boy.
> Short and Evil were thy days
> But the vigour of thy genius shall immortalize thee.

> Unfortunate Boy,
> Poorly wast thou accommodated
> During thy Short Sojourning among us,
> Thou liv'dst unnoticed,
> But thy Fame shall never die.

In spite, however, of the warmth of heart which is shown in these passages, Captain Thicknesse was no respecter of persons, and he did not allow any strange inward stirrings of the conscience to interfere with business.

Soon after the death of his first wife, the Captain met at Bath a rich widow named Concanen, whose husband, Matthew Concanen, had been impertinent to Pope, in a paper called the *Speculatist*, and had met with his reward, for he was imortalized in the lines:

Cook shall be Prior, and Concanen Swift,

True to the bottom see Concanen creep
A cold, long-minded native of the deep.

Mrs Concanen was as dark in complexion as her diamonds
were brilliant, and we understand, from a sinister passage
in the Captain's Memoirs, that she had a creole *manner*,
whilst, by the way in which the passage is written, we are
left with the impression that the Captain might have been
more explicit, and have said things of a deeper dye, if he
were not too much of a gentleman to do so.

Mrs Concanen was very rich, but Captain Thicknesse
could, at the moment, think of no plan by which he might
induce her to share her fortune with him. At last, however,
one of His Majesty's Judges, anxious to help the cause of
virtue, suggested to him that, should he insinuate himself
into the widow's house, which was in South Parade, at
night-time, and then, putting on his night-cap, look out of
the widow's bedroom window, when the walks were full of
company, the widow would, without a doubt, accept his pro-
posal of marriage with alacrity.

According to the Captain, he did not actually follow the
Judge's recipe, but I am unable to believe this, as he could
bring himself to repeat the story. According to his detractors,
Captain Thicknesse lost no time in following the Judge's
suggestion, which would, no doubt, have met with the desired results, had not Captain Thicknesse, immediately
afterwards, decided to marry instead the Lady Elizabeth
Touchet, sister of the Earl of Castlehaven and Baron Audley,
and heiress to the latter title. But he thought the story of the
widow too good a joke to be lost, and took every opportunity
of telling it : 'So I left the widow to finish her second mourn-
ing', he explained with his usual delicacy, 'and was soon
after married to Lady Elizabeth Touchet.'

No wonder that the virtuous Captain Thicknesse, shocked by the cynicism of the world in which he lived, wrote (in *The New Prose Guide*) ... 'The very action which youth and innocence naturally lead the honest, unsuspicious, often the best-hearted women into, are construed into vices of the deepest dye. The most wicked insinuations are thrown out, under the specious appearance of friendship, and when the subject is prepared to receive the variolous matter, it is poured forth with such torrents, that the contagion spreads far and wide, the domestic happiness of whole families is disturbed, to give place, and fortune, to these hellish gamblers, who by one infernal *coup de main* break through the bonds of all faith, honour and honesty.'

Lady Elizabeth Touchet provided her husband with three sons (George and Philip became, as soon as they were of an age capable of quarrelling, or of being quarrelled with, a source of constant interest to their father), and three daughters, two of whom were sent to nunneries in France.

Captain Thicknesse, as soon as his son Philip had attained his seventeenth year, arranged and staged a highly satisfactory quarrel between the two brothers, and in the interests of virtue, took the younger son before magistrates to swear that his elder brother had set him upon a runaway horse with the intention of killing him and inheriting his fortune – a wicked story which had, quite undoubtedly, originated in the mind of Captain Thicknesse, and which was afterwards proved to be a lie. Then after a while, to the Captain's great discomfiture, the brothers became friends, and from that time their indignant father could think of nothing bad enough to say about either of them. He was, in addition, grieved that he could not possess himself of their fortunes. For years a guerilla warfare was carried on. Eventually, Captain Thicknesse brought off a master *coup* of strategy. He was, by now, living at The Hermitage. His younger son, hearing that his father intended to live abroad, offered to buy the property for £100, but, being only eighteen years old, he was not, as yet, in possession of his fortune, and so gave his father an acceptance for this sum. A short while after, having obtained the money in question, he paid Captain Thicknesse the £100, but presented him with an extra £100. He must therefore have been a little surprised when, some years after, having spent large sums of money upon the house, and having offered to allow his father to rebuy the house on the repayment of the £100, that virtuous old gentleman produced the original acceptance with a flourish, and denied that he had ever been paid.

But interesting as were these slightly embellished stories to the readers of Captain Thicknesse's Memoirs, still more interesting were the histories of his encounters with the Great, his summing up and belittling of these.

Captain Thicknesse in the course of a long and rambling career (it was indeed nearly as rambling as his stories), had met John Wesley in Georgia, immediately after being brought face to face with the spectacle of twenty alligators basking on a muddy shore. But after this allegorical warning, the Captain, very naturally, did not enter much into the company of the preacher. It transpires in the Memoirs that Captain Thicknesse had showed his wisdom in refusing any intimacy, for Mr Charles Wesley, the brother of the rejected apostle, had written a number of letters to a young lady in which the care of the soul, and body too, seemed to claim much of his regard, and Miss Thicknesse, the Captain's sister, who happened to be the confidante of the young lady, and who 'had perhaps more knowledge of the world, and mankind, than Miss Hutton (for tho' of good understanding, she was very deaf), did not approve of that spiritual correspondence between Mr Charles Wesley and her female friend'.

This unfortunate effect upon the fair sex seems, moreover, to have been produced by both brothers, for when Mr John Wesley, the shunned acquaintance of Captain Thicknesse, went at the invitation of a 'frail lady, whom he had censured', to call upon her, the instant he entered her apartment, a most appalling scene ensued. For the lady, whose physical strength seems to have equalled her moral frailty, 'laid violent hands upon him', and, according to Captain Thicknesse, 'threw him upon the bed, and threatened him with the immediate loss of life, or what some men might deem as dear as life, nor did she dismiss him till she had deprived him of all the Adonis flowing locks, which at that time adorned one side of his neck and goodly countenance; yet such was his humility, that he appeared the Sunday following, at church, in his partial and ear-crop'd head of hair'.

I do not know if this appalling scandal ever reached the ears of Lady Huntingdon. However, Captain Thicknesse ends the painful story with this pregnant sentence: 'Let it be remembered that a desire of such spiritual correspondence with the sex, which appeared in both these brothers, might arise from the utmost purity, and virtuous intention; *however their letters might be construed to carry suspicion of sinister designs.*' (The italics are mine.)

But this was not the only occasion when the Captain saw the Great under curious, and rather intimate circumstances.

'About the year 1749,' he tells us, 'Mr Quin [the great actor] came into the lobby of the rooms at Bath, it was after dinner. Quin was what in another man we would call sack-mellow; at this time I was in conversation with an Esquire, to whom Quin walked as steadily up as he could, and putting his heels upon the Esquire's feet, made them *crash again*, and then without a word, walked off. Whether pain, surprise, or timidity, overcame the Esquire's *upper-works*, I cannot say, but as soon as he could speak he asked me whether I had observed Quin's conduct, and whether I thought it was some accident, or done with design, to affront him. . . . Quin answered: "The fellow invited me to his house in Wiltshire, laid me in damp sheets, and seduced my servant; fed me with red veal and white bacon, raw mutton, and bull beef"; adding, "and as to his liquor, by my soul it was every drop sour except his vinegar, and yet the scrub had the impudence to serve it upon dirty plates." '

The irate Captain, with that sudden volte-face which was his habit, his intricate method of terrorism, adds, 'I believe Quin's twinge on the toes of that gentleman is to this day visible in his face, if a face it can be called, yet I should not, at this distance of time, have shown in what manner Mr W. fed his friends, in the year 1749, had he not, in the year 1778, made his six-feet-high young wife write a very extraordinary letter to a certain copper-faced Captain.'

Captain Thicknesse's adventures among *avowedly* savage tribes, it appears, gave him more pleasure than his adventures among the savages of the drawing-room. The Red Indians, for instance, with whom he dwelt for some time, seem to have been the only people, if we except one or two forgers and a few bankrupts, with whom he did not succeed in quarrelling. He was on friendly terms with Tomo Chachi, the Creek Indian King, and thought him not only a very humane man, but also a very well-bred one.

Having built himself a wooden house among the Red Indians' encampment, Captain Thicknesse lived on squirrels and boiled rice, and such was his delight in this sylvan existence that he had almost determined to marry one of Queen Cenauke's maids of honour, presenting her by way of courtship with a pair of Indian boots, some paint, a looking-glass, a comb, and a pair of scissors; but this matrimonial scheme came to nothing because, whilst Captain Thicknesse was playing the flute, his 'affectionate and warm disposition' conjured up before his eyes the vision of his mother. The very natural result was that Captain Thicknesse returned straight to England, though not before he had been involved in a dangerous dispute with a very determined pair of rattlesnakes, and that Queen Cenauke's maid of honour was left disconsolate.

Captain Thicknesse did not remain in England for long, however, for he was soon sent with his regiment to Jamaica, and quartered on the north side of the island.

This strange, irascible, unjust, but humane man tells us that during his stay on the island 'I was frequently sent out with four- or five-and-twenty men, in search of wild negroes, as the assembly of that Island allowed seventy pounds for *every pair of wild-negroes' ears which were brought in*. Just in the same manner, as the *tame negroes* are allowed a bottle of rum for every dozen of *rat tails they bring in*; I thank God however, *in that business*, I was fortunate, for I never *gathered a single pair*. I thank God, too, that I very early in life had perception enough to learn that however honourable it may be deemed, to invade, disturb, or murder people of distant climes, it did not tally with my ideas of justice. I would fight and either perish, or conquer, men who came from afar, to disturb me from the enjoyment of that land, which my birth gave me a natural footing in; but I feel no disposition to murther those who, like Tomo Chachi are content with their own.'

At this point, Captain Thicknesse's narrative becomes clouded once more by indignation, for the moment had come to relate that warlike expedition on which Mr Makittrick had thrown doubts. 'I will not', the Captain exclaimed with commendable restraint, 'call this double-named doctor a beast, a reptile, an assassin, a murder-monger; but the reader will, I am sure, excuse me in saying he is a base libeller, a liar, and a wicked defamer, and has no pretensions to be a gentleman.'

Captain Thicknesse gives a very complicated account of the exploits against the formidable companies of wild Negroes, in the woods. These had no connection with each other, the west gang being under the command of a Captain Cuodje; the east under Captain Quoha. Indeed the old gentleman's garrulity is such, that all that emerges from the narrative is the fact that after climbing up and down mountains, and being pursued and preceded by wild Negroes, and 'standing a long time up to our hips in water, with a vertical sun upon our heads', Captain Thicknesse, to quote himself, 'lay down upon my back, by the side of my brother-officer, with my tongue out, and praying to God to let that dew fall, which is considered fatal to those who expose themselves to it. The next morning, providentially, we found an enormous cotton tree, the leaves of which grew so fantastically that they had formed a reservoir of rain water. It was as black as coffee, but it was more acceptable than a treasure of gold. On the evening of that day we got to the seaside, and among some inhabitants where hospitality and humanity were not wanting notwithstanding the present hue and cry about slavery, cruelty,' etc.

Eventually Captain Thicknesse arrived at some sort of terms with the wild Negroes, and took up his abode at Captain Quoha's residence, but when there he had the 'mortification of seeing the poor Laird of Laharets' underjaw, fixed as an ornament, to one of their horsemen's horns, and we found that the upper teeth of our men, slain in Spanish River, were drilled thro' and worn as ankle and wrist bracelets by their Obea women, and some of the ladies of the past fashion in town'.

After this protracted guerilla warfare, Captain Thicknesse

set sail for England; but whilst on board ship 'I bore my share in two of the greatest calamities to which mariners are subject – Fire, and Water – for in the windward passage, during very fine weather, and smooth water, the cooper dropped a lighted candle into a half-puncheon'. In the subsequent conflagration, Captain Thicknesse, naturally, performed miracles of valour. But no sooner was the fire subdued, than, in the latitude of the Bermudas, a furious gale began. Captain Thicknesse struggled out of his hammock, which the inconsiderate gale had flung into the gun-room and, clad in his shirt alone, gained the deck. 'But good God,' he exclaimed, 'what a sight did it exhibit! There lay poor old Commodore Brown; ladies, both black and white, naked among the fragments of furniture, bedding, sheets, blankets; all helter-skelter, without any covering but their wet shirts and shifts, and poor Captain Wyndham, a cripple with the gout, holding himself from being blown overboard, by the main-sheet.'

As usual Captain Thicknesse came to the rescue; but not without having a pot of ginger that had cost him seven pounds sterling broken in this encounter with the elements.

A short time after the Captain's return to Europe, when he was making his way to the Continent from England, presumably because he was, as usual, as unwanted by his friends as he was wanted by the bailiffs, he was defied by two young ladies of tender years and a dog, the former being as a result incarcerated in a convent, where the younger remained for the rest of her natural life.

These two young ladies, or rather children, had for parent a gentleman of Captain Thicknesse's own kidney, and he, having quarrelled with his wife, asked the Captain if he would allow these two young maidens to spend the summer with Mrs Thicknesse at Calais.

The Captain agreed and the cortège set out, with Jacko the monkey riding jockey-like on the horse that drew the chaise, and gesticulating from time to time at the scenery. Another member of the party was Mrs Thicknesse's parakeet, whose devotion to his mistress was such that he had before now travelled from Marseilles to Calais in an open chaise, quite at liberty and sitting, most of the time, upon Mrs Thicknesse's shoulder or bosom; when not in these places of rest, he hung by his bill from her tippet, 'gilding his eyes', as her husband tells us, 'with such delight that it would almost induce one to believe in the transmigration of souls'.

The young ladies, the elder of whom was fourteen, the younger between eleven and twelve, were thoroughly naughty, restless little girls; and, in addition to their fidgeting, the Captain and Mrs Thicknesse had to put up with the restlessness of a fussy, perpetuum-mobile-scratching little dog who had been imported by the younger girl. When the Captain's cortège halted at Canterbury, this burdensome addition to the family 'gnawed the carved clawed feet of the mahogany chairs, and did much injury'. But at Calais, two days after, he did more injury still, for having been put, I cannot conceive why, into the same closet which was used as the roosting-place of Mrs Thicknesse's pet, he made a hasty meal of the latter.

Mrs Thicknesse burst into floods of tears – and no wonder. The Captain was not unnaturally irate. But 'the little spoiled girl, with a single feather sticking in her hair, began to hum Lady Coventry's Minuet'. Captain Thicknesse's passion was aroused to such boiling pitch by this heartlessness, (and for once I find myself sharing his passion) that he threatened to cut the dog's throat – a threat that was not carried out. And next day both the young misses were taken to a convent and placed in charge of the Mother Superior. From that moment, as their father was only too pleased to be rid of them, they led, much against the grain, the religious life for three years, and one little girl died amidst these fastnesses. The Captain thought all this a grand joke, and wrote on the subject of the oblivious parent that it was 'a conduct I could not disapprove, yet a punishment, as it originated with me, I could not but lament'.

Meanwhile Captain Thicknesse kept up a guerilla warfare with both his sons, and announced that his brother, who was High Master of St Paul's School and who had had these errant youths under his charge, years before, disapproved of the eldest so strongly that he had determined to change his name unless his nephew did so. This gentleman was extremely sensible and an admirable instructor of youth; for according to the Captain: 'My brother always endeavoured to check the disposition of all ingenious men who were under him, when they betrayed a tendency to poetry. I recollect I have heard him say that he declined Dr Johnson's acquaintance, as he deemed him then only a poet.' To this strong criticism Captain Thicknesse, who was as just as he was severe, added the footnote: 'He since, however, became a great moralist.'

But Captain Thicknesse was growing older, and his sons would take little or no notice of his attempts to quarrel with them, and Mrs Catherine Macaulay, whom he had attacked in another work, had left Bath, and a crowd had attacked the Captain's house because he had caused his manservant to be taken by a press-gang as a punishment for seducing a maid. His creditors besieged the house, too. The Captain was growing older, and he was growing tired – even of quarrelling. The frills on his shirt-front still bristled like the fins of a fish, his wig and profile looked as martial as ever, but some joy had gone out of life. So the Captain announced that he intended to 'set out for Paris; a journey far preferable, I think, to see the wrangling there than to stay to wrangle here with an old superannuated hero and a mad Doctor'.

So, accompanied by the long-suffering Mrs Thicknesse and by the aged Jacko, who still rode the chaise horse postillion-wise, mopping and mowing, making queer gestures of anger and defiance at the gathering dust, the Captain set out for France, where he spent the remainder of his life. In 1792, just as he was about to start on a journey to Italy, this remarkable old gentleman died, leaving a will which began thus:

'I leave my right hand, to be cut off after my death, to my son Lord Audley; I desire it may be sent to him, in hopes that such a sight may remind him of his duty to God, after having so long abandoned the duty he owed to a father, who once so affectionately loved him.'

7

Portrait of a Learned Lady

ON a foggy evening in the month of October, 1846, had we peered through a window into the dining-room of a certain house in Chelsea, which was filled always with a shaggy Highland-cattle-like odour of homespun materials and by a Scotch mist of tobacco smoke, we might have seen a successful dinner-party in full blast. The host was Thomas Carlyle, the guest of honour an American lady of thirty-six, Miss Margaret Fuller, the author of *Woman in the Nineteenth Century* and the first editor of the *Dial*.

This chaste, passionate, and high-principled woman, at once splendid and ridiculous, was the direct outcome of the movement towards the Emancipation of Women, a movement in which learned, trousered and vivacious ladies like George Sand made presents of themselves with the same frequency, cheapness and indiscrimination as that with which other ladies present Christmas cards. This caused them to be collected with great eagerness by sex-snobs, who, unlike all other snobs, or collectors, prefer the ubiquitous to the rare.

Miss Fuller's principles, but not her behaviour, were derived from ladies such as these, and her friend Mr Emerson tells us that Margaret 'was always a most earnest, devoted champion of the Emancipation of Women, from their past and present condition of inferiority, to an independence on men. She demanded for them the fullest recognition of Social and Political Equality with the rougher sex; the freest access to all stations, professions, employments, which are open to men. To this demand I heartily acceded. It seemed to me however that her clear perceptions of abstract right were often overborne in practice by the influence of education and habit; that while she demanded absolute equality for women, she exacted a deference and courtesy from men to women, as women, which was entirely inconsistent with that requirement.

'So long as a lady shall deem herself in need of some gentleman's arm to conduct her properly out of a dining-room or ballroom, so long as she shall consider it dangerous or unbecoming to walk half a mile alone by night, I cannot see how the Woman's Rights theory is ever to be more than a logically defensible abstraction. . . . Whenever she (Margaret) said or did anything implying the usual demands of woman on the courtesy and protection of manhood, I was apt, before complying, to look her in the face and exclaim with marked emphasis – quoting from her *Woman in the Nineteenth Century* – *"Let them be Sea-Captains if they will."* '

However, according to Mr Emerson's letter introducing her to Mr Carlyle, she was 'a wise, sincere and accomplished, and one of the most entertaining of women, one of the noblest of women', although her appearance, according to the same gentleman's memoirs of her published after her death, 'had nothing prepossessing. Her extreme plainness,' he continued, 'a trick of incessantly opening and shutting her eyelids, the nasal tone of her voice, all repelled. It is to be said that Margaret made a disagreeable first impression on most persons, including those who afterwards became her best friends, to such an extent that they did not wish to remain in the same room with her. This was partly the effect of her manners, which expressed an overweening sense of power and slight esteem of others.'

Mr Emerson, however, admired Miss Fuller's 'severity of truth', for 'I have known her', he wrote, 'mow down the crop of evil, like the angel of retribution itself, and could not sufficiently admire her courage. My friends told me of a verdict, pronounced upon Mr — at Paris, which they said was perfectly tremendous. They themselves sat breathless; Mr — was struck dumb; his eyes fixed on her with wonder and amazement, yet gazing too with an attention which seemed like fascination. When she had done, he still looked to see if she was to say more, and when he found she had really finished, he arose, took his hat, said faintly "I thank you," and left the room.' Miss Fuller was in no doubt as to her own mental attainments, and Mr Emerson tells us that 'she would let slip, with all the innocence imaginable, some phrase betraying the presence of a rather mountainous ME, in a way to surprise those who knew her great sense'.

Mr Emerson was, however, grateful to her for he, owing to his years of arduous mental toil, had almost lost the 'capacity to laugh', and Mrs Emerson, deciding that he must make a new and thorough study of this useful accomplishment under the careful tutorship of Margaret Fuller, had invited that lady for a fortnight's visit, and had insisted that the two sages should take a daily walk together, with the result that the lessons were, after a while, crowned with comparative success. I can imagine the happy chatter, the gay *badinage* about metempsychosis and Goethe, Locke, English metaphysics, Racine, Körner, Truth, Liberty for Woman, Carlyle and Liberty for Man, the Christian religion, Plato, Socrates, Bigelow's Elements, Jacob's Letters to Fichte, which constituted those Lessons in Laughter. I can imagine too the spell of ordinariness which came over the Emerson household during these brief respites from Wisdom.

At first Mr Emerson did not find the lessons easy, for he tells us that he 'was, at that time, an eager scholar of ethics, and had tasted the sweets of solitude and stoicism, and I found something profane in the hours of amusing gossip into which she drew me'. Hollow sounds, as from an owl in a metaphysical holly-bush, an owl imprisoned in the mausoleum of Goethe, were heard floating over the woodlands. Then the sounds grew lighter, took on a more shrill and batlike note. In the end, however, though slowly and painfully, the accomplishment to which I have referred was restored to Mr Emerson through the tutelage of Margaret, and now he had passed his teacher on to his friend Carlyle, in the hope perhaps that he also might derive some benefit of the same kind.

Mr Carlyle however would not allow himself to receive any instruction of any kind, and Miss Fuller tells us that 'it is the usual misfortune of such marked men, happily not one invariable or inevitable, that they cannot allow other minds room to breathe, and show themselves in their atmosphere, and thus miss the refreshment and instruction which the greatest never cease to need from the experience of the humblest. Carlyle allows no one a chance, but bears down all opposition, not only by his wit, and onset of words, resistless as so many bayonets, but by actual physical superiority, raising his voice, and rushing on his opponent with a torrent of sound. This is not in the least from unwillingness to allow freedom to others. On the contrary, no man would more enjoy a manly resistance to his thought.' Still, Mr Carlyle would not allow Miss Fuller to speak, and Miss Fuller was used to talking uninterrupted and to interrupting others. 'The worst of hearing Carlyle', she assured her correspondent, 'is that you cannot interrupt him. I understand the habit of haranguing has increased very much upon him, so that you are a perfect prisoner when he has once got hold of you. To interrupt him is a physical impossibility. If you get a chance to remonstrate for a moment, he raises his voice and bears you down. True, he does you no injustice, and, with his admirable penetration sees the disclaimer in your mind, so that you are not morally delinquent;

but it is not pleasant to be unable to utter it.'

Another guest at this dinner-party was 'a witty French, flippant sort of man, author of a *History of Philosophy*, and now writing a *Life of Goethe*, a task for which he must be as unfit as irreligion and sparkling shallowness can make him. But he told stories admirably, and was allowed sometimes to interrupt Carlyle for a little.' This irreligious sparkling shallowness caused the witty flippant sort of man, whose name was George Henry Lewes, to enter into a *ménage* with that monument of lightness George Eliot.

The inability to interrupt seems to have been a great problem in literary circles, in the year 1846. For Miss Martineau, immediately before Miss Fuller's meeting with Wordsworth, which took place a month or so before her inability to interrupt Carlyle, warned her that 'He does all the talking, and never knows the name of the person he is addressing. He talks mostly about his poems and he is pretty sure to take the visitor to see the terrace where he has composed so many.' But then Miss Martineau did not entirely approve of her neighbours. She could, and did, give Margaret other and equally important information about the author of the *Ode on the Intimations of Immortality*. In the winter he wore a long cloak, a Scotch bonnet and great goggles. Usually a score of children ran along after him, coaxing him to cut switches out of the hedge for them. A curious combination of economy and generosity he was. If you dropped in to tea you were likely not to have enough cream to put into it, and yet Wordsworth gave away all the milk the household did not want to cottagers perfectly well able to buy their own. If you dropped in for any other meal, you were greeted with 'You are very well welcome to have a cup of tea with us, but if you want any meat you must pay for it.'

Others of Miss Martineau's neighbours were hardly respectable, but like a comfortable Christian woman Miss

Martineau said no more about them than would destroy their reputation for respectability and enhance her own. Take the Coleridges, for example. The poet's son, Hartley, had died of drink. De Quincey was not only on the verge of starvation, but, according to his virtuous neighbour, was in such a state that 'when he lived at Keswick he drank five or six wineglasses of laudanum a night. Coleridge was to blame for that of course, for De Quincey ran across him shortly after he came down from Oxford, and Coleridge was then drinking his tumblerful a day.'

After these revelations, we cannot for a moment doubt that Miss Martineau, with her striking virtues, was a more valuable inhabitant of the world than the authors of the 'Ode on the Intimations of Immortality', the 'Ancient Mariner' and 'Kubla Khan', and the *Confessions of an Opium Eater*.

Margaret Fuller however was not as critical of these benighted beings as was Miss Martineau, and she was glad to be in Europe, because her life in Boston must remind her of the imaginary being, clothed in actual flesh, whom she had lost.

Two years before Margaret Fuller's journey to Europe she had fallen passionately in love with a young gentleman named James Nathan, who came from Hamburg. Mr Nathan was younger than Miss Fuller, was pale, had long dark hair, played the guitar, spent his days in the City, and talked about the Soul. He was consistently and profitably misunderstood, as we shall see. 'His was no plebeian mind,' Miss Bell informs us in her book on Margaret Fuller. 'Not for him the utilitarian life, where leisure was considered a waste of time, and graceful indolence the pastime of fools and women. He felt a little out of place in the world of lower Broadway.'

The work-shy and superior Mr Nathan spent a good deal of time in being melancholy with the aid of Margaret, and between them developed one of those innocently incestuous brother-and-sister relationships which are always so grateful and convenient to the gentleman, so shattering to the nerves and dignity of the lady.

At first the nature of Mr Nathan's behaviour had not allowed Margaret to guess that she wàs his sister. Do gentlemen, she wondered, when the nature of the relationship had been made abundantly clear, pour blackberry blossoms into the laps of their sisters? She fancied not. Blackberry blossoms, though they are frail, seem to hold in them some promise of fruition, however cold, belated and hard. However, Mr Nathan proved to her that she was wrong; for after some time he discovered that she had no money, and this fact made their relationship clearer than ever. They had, he said, a *spiritual* affinity. He proposed that it should be recognized, that their relationship came from *within*, although I imagine that this high spiritual life was interspersed, even then, by interludes of a distressing tenderness.

At last, owing partly to overwork, partly to the wrack and worry and general wear and tear of this inhibited incest, Miss Fuller's face began to show increased signs of her age, and these signs were noted by Mr Nathan with distress and a profound distaste for the misunderstanding which had caused them. He meanwhile had been giving a good deal of time to the contemplation of himself, his prospects, his outlook, etc. . . . and the result was that, in Miss Fuller's eyes, his face was 'sicklied o'er with the pale cast of thought', though a prejudiced observer might have said that he was suffering from an enlarged liver. His curls, too, were less luxuriant than formerly. But these signs of mental pain only made the woman who loved him move more closely to him, with a deeper, more foolish, phoenix-like love.

The disillusioned Mr Nathan began to pick quarrels with Miss Fuller, but she replied only : 'You shall upbraid me to the stars, and I feel sure that you will not find me incompetent.' This irritated Mr Nathan so much that he found more and more faults in her.

At last, he wrote and told her that he was about to leave America and return to Europe, and this drove Margaret to despair, for she did not know what this might mean, or if he would ever return. Then, as she read his long and extremely noble letter, at last, at the very end of that letter, she found the heart which had inspired it. Mr Nathan needed money because he wished to explore the East, and be the first to navigate the Dead Sea. Also, he wanted to go to Jerusalem. Margaret, he felt, might ask her rich and influential friends for some money which would make these aspirations possible. He would be glad, too, if she would take charge of his Newfoundland pup Josey, and the irresistible guitar.

The money was, of course, forthcoming; Margaret saw to that; and for some time Mr Nathan was too busy packing and making arrangements for the explorations to pay her a visit. But at last, just a week before he sailed, he found time to come and see her, bringing Josey and the guitar, and explaining that he would carry her letters with him wherever he went.

When he had gone, Margaret, in her loneliness and sadness, wrote: 'I have lost my dear companion, the first I ever had who could feel every better side of life and beauty as exquisitely as myself.'

Other sides of life and beauty, however, were occupying the thoughts of Mr Nathan, and, although Margaret wrote often, two months passed before a letter reached her in return. But then how noble was the letter, and how long! 'Let me lie down and die,' exclaimed Mr Nathan, 'rather than my presence abet falsehood.' It was not till the end of that long letter, that the unpractical and unworldly Mr Nathan inquired if his correspondent would secure for him a letter of introduction from Mr George Bancroft, the Minister of Marine, and place Mr Nathan's articles on travel under the editorship of Mr Greeley.

The months passed and Mr Nathan's letters grew fewer and fewer: her heart knew that the tone of those rare letters had changed. Perhaps, she might have broken the bond that held her, but although Mr Nathan felt himself as free as air, it would have injured his high ideals to see any signs of such a frailty on the part of Woman, whose legendary fidelity is her birthright, bestowed upon her by heaven. What an inspiration is this fidelity to Man, supporting as it does his belief in human nature on those many occasions when he is weighed down by the disillusionment brought about by the contemplation of his own lack of fidelity. Besides, any shadow cast on Mr Nathan's belief in Woman would have been particularly tragic at this moment, since – although Margaret did not know this – he was about to marry another and a younger woman. Margaret wrote to him, 'You will love me as much, as long, and as carefully as you can, will you not?'

The months dragged on, and it was only a fortnight before Margaret sailed for Europe that she received his reply to this letter. He had arrived in Hamburg, where he was the centre of attention, the guest of honour at dinner-parties and receptions . . . but his funds were exhausted. Where could he get a book published? Would Margaret see to it that Mr Greeley published this? . . . Then comes this sublime and characteristic touch, showing all Mr Nathan's childlike and beautiful gift for casting other people's bread upon the waters: 'As for Josey [his Newfoundland pup], if he is too much trouble and if Mr March cannot keep him for me and you know of no other person that will, just have him sold at auction, *or run loose away, or what he may do, a kind Providence will have a care of him.*'

When Margaret was in Edinburgh, she received another letter from this childlike believer. She too might run loose away, or do what she might do, and a kind Providence would have a care of her, for Mr Nathan was soon to be married to the younger lady.

But Mr Nathan would not entrust the letters, that the celebrated older lady had written him, to the care of Providence. They might, he thought, prove valuable yet. In answer to her request that he would return these pledges of her affection, he wrote, 'My loving regard is and was too sincere and earnest and holy as to change with any new ties or external events. . . . And to permit me to part with things so dear, so suddenly. Let me entreat you to let the spiritual offspring of our friendship remain in the home they were born to and intended for, until on our return to New York we will talk the matter over more fully and fairly. In the meantime, let me assure you, they enjoy the sacredness and privacy of this uninterrupted and uninterfered with from any foreign alliance or relationship, and that at our meeting there I shall do nothing but what is right, manly and honourable.' Anxious to add one further incitement to madness, he proclaimed that he felt 'a deep admiration for your great, superior well-stored mind, an equally true regard for the integrity, profundity, and holiness of your character and for the many womanly virtues and sentiments of your capacious heart and true love for the purity of your soul, from which noble source I have drawn many deep inspirations'.

It may be that the thought of these letters written to the unworldly Mr Nathan, gnawed into Miss Fuller's mind as she sat, listening to the thunder of Carlyle's talk, and being allowed, once an hour or so, to speak, 'enough to free my lungs and change my position, so that I did not get tired'. Or perhaps she thought of the difference between her repressed childhood and youth, and the freedom that had come to her by way of her friendship with such people as the Emersons, and Horace Greeley and his wife. She was in many ways a remarkable woman, and we find ourselves agreeing with Emerson's verdict that, although 'Margaret often loses herself in sentimentalism, here was a head so creative of new colours, of wonderful gleams, so iridescent that it piqued curiosity and stimulated thought and communicated mental activity to all who approached her; though her perceptions were not to be compared to her fancy, and she made numerous mistakes. Her integrity was perfect, and she was led and followed by love, and was really bent on truth, but was too indulgent to the meteors of her fancy.'

She lived, indeed, a life full of noble ideals, Backfisch nonsense and moonshine, silly cloying over-emotionalized friendships and repressed loves (friendship being often disguised as love, and love as friendship), extreme mental and moral courage, and magnificent loyalty to her ideals, friends, and loves.

Miss Fuller's life was one mass of symbolism; even the magnificent and tragic shipwreck with which her life, together with those of her young Italian husband and her baby boy ended, was symbolic. It is impossible not to feel an embarrassed sympathy, and a kind of affection for her, since the whole record of her life leaves us with the impression of a certain nobility and uprightness, blurred over by an overheated nervous sensibility masquerading as imagination. She had a certain non-productive intellect, and considerable rectitude, but these qualities were balanced, to some degree, by her almost incomparable silliness. As in the case of nearly all remarkable women, opinions were strongly divided about her, and one hostile biographer exclaimed that her writing was 'a striking illustration of the propensity of all strong-minded ladies to Monster Nothings'. Miss Fuller took an untiring interest in everything and everybody, including herself, and wrote that 'mine is a large, rich, but unclarified nature. My history presents much superficial temporary tragedy. The woman in me kneels and weeps in tender rapture, the man in me rushes forth, but only to be baffled.'

Alas, this was only too true, and when Miss Fuller inquired of herself and of others: 'Who may understand me?' the answer was 'None.'

This unconscious candidate for the attentions of the yet unborn Professor Sigmund Freud was, according to her biographer Miss Margaret Bell, 'hungry for soul demonstrations of love ... so hungry that she pressed the flowers passionately to her lips, and to her breast, and tried to imagine that they gave her all she needed'.

Her childhood and early girlhood were not devoid of incident or excitement, for, among other remarkable phenomena, she had been brought face to face with 'an old man in a cocked hat carrying a circular canopy over his head. This was Dr Popkin, introducing the first umbrella to Cambridge. It was not long till the tax-collector had one, then Professor Hedge was seen carrying one back and forth from lectures.' In spite, however, of these excitements, Miss Fuller longed for experiences of a more romantic spiritual order, in which all symbols were to be mixed together into a rather heavy pudding. For instance, she told her admirers that 'when I first met with the name of Leila, I knew it to be mine. I knew that it means night – night which brings out truths.' She found, too, that there was much to be said for the symbolism of precious stones, and she became a firm believer in talismans and omens. It appears that she herself was a stone of the masculine gender, a living carbuncle – for carbuncles were divided into two sexes. The female casts out light, the male has light within itself. Mine is the male. Accordingly, when Miss Fuller wrote a letter to a much valued friend, she wore a male carbuncle upon her finger, but when she wrote to a slighter acquaintance, the stone worn would be an onyx or an amethyst, according to the degrees of friendship which prevailed.

This bunkum may, or may not, have been the result of a schoolgirl friendship with a nauseatingly silly English woman. 'I was reading *Guy Mannering*,' Miss Fuller tells us, 'and my eyes were wet and dim with tears drawn forth by the loss of little Harry Bertram, when an English lady of supreme beauty, who was on a brief visit to that part of America, observing me, approached and accosted me. She did not question me, but fixed on me looks of beautiful love. She did not speak many words; her mere presence was to me a gate of Paradise. I laid my head against her shoulder and wept, dimly feeling that I must lose her and all who spake to me of the same things – that the cold waves would rush over me. She waited till my tears were spent, then, rising, took from a box a bunch of golden amaranths. They were very fragrant. "They came to me", she said, "from Madeira." The departure of the lady threw me into a deep melancholy, from which I was with difficulty aroused. I kept the amaranths during seventeen years. Madeira, for long, long afterwards, was pictured in my imagination as an Island of the Blest. And when ships sailed past the coast, their white wings gleaming in the sunlight, I fancied they might be bound for happy, fortunate Madeira.'

The young men were, at first, less attracted to Miss Fuller's friendship than were women. It is true that one young man, Mr Henry Hedge, would and did talk about philosophy with her, whilst others listened with a strained expression to her monologues on the subject of Greek mythology, precious stones, Maria Edgeworth, Goethe, and

Madame de Staël. But it was a young lady named Anna Barker who was the recipient of confidences such as this: 'I sometimes see myself in a large hall, it is the age of feudalism; a charming company is assembled, and a minstrel is playing on a harp. Torches flicker and now and then one hears the clank of armour, as the sentries at the doorways change their places. . . . The night wears on; servants bring refreshments, there is a flash of golden goblets and the sound of gold falling at the feet of the minstrel.'

From the preceding passages, and from Miss Fuller's unfortunate love-passages with Mr Nathan and a previous friend, Mr Samuel Ward, we can see that European culture, the romance of the Middle Ages, and the Rights of Women, as inculcated by such teachers as Mary Wollstonecraft and the trousered and volatile Mme George Sand, had worked equal havoc with her life. It was, I imagine, as a result of the teaching of these ladies, that she contracted the unfortunate daily habit of sending bouquets of flowers to Mr. Samuel Ward. As a not unnatural result of this habit, Miss Fuller was rewarded by the sound of scampering feet, disappearing into the far distance.

When Miss Fuller had waited for several months for some sign from Mr Ward, she wrote to him the following letter: 'You do not wish to be with me. Why try to hide it from me, from yourself? You are not interested in any of my interests; my friends, my pursuits are not yours . . . the sympathetic contemplation of the beautiful in nature, in art, is over for us – that for which I loved you first and which made that love a shrine at which I could rest upon my weary pilgrimage. You come home to go away again, and make a call upon me in the parlour. . . . You write me to say you could not write before. My heart deceives me widely if this be love.'

Mr Ward replied, as I imagine, with a letter which agreed

with these sentiments, for Margaret, in reply, wrote this letter, inspired by her innate nobility of soul and of heart, which, when that soul and that heart were profoundly moved, could not be smeared over or spoiled by the sentimentality which was the only cause of any foolishness in her :

'My dearest Samuel,

'Although I do not feel able at present to return a full answer to your letter, I will not do myself the injustice of preserving entire silence. Its sincerity of tone is all I asked. As I told you, I should never make any claim upon the heart of any person on the score of past intercourse . . . but, on the minds of those who have known me, I have always a claim. My own entire sincerity in every passage of life gives me a claim to expect that I shall never be led by unmeaning phrases or attentions.

'For the rest, believe me, I understand all perfectly, and though I might grieve that you should shut me from you in your highest hour and find yourself unable to meet me on the very ground where you had taught me to expect it, I would not complain that the past had bound either of us at the present.

'I had thought that in ceasing to be intimates, we might cease to be friends. I think so no longer. My attachment was never so deep as now; it is quite unstained by pride or passion; it is sufficiently disinterested for me to be sure of it. Time, distance, different pursuits, may hide you from me, yet will I never forget to be your friend, or to visit your life with a daily benediction.

'Do not bid yourself remember me, but should an hour come by and by when you have any need of me, you will find me in my place and find me faithful to you.'

But now, unshadowed by Dr Popkin's and the tax-collector's umbrellas, unshadowed, perhaps, by memories of the strange behaviour of Mr Ward and Mr Nathan, this large-souled, noble, but over-dramatic lady sat listening to the torrents of Mr Carlyle's conversation.

At their first meeting, Mr Carlyle let his American guest down gently, and she, writing of the encounter to Mr Emerson, had said: 'I admired his Scotch, his way of singing his great full sentences, so that each one was the stanza of a narrative ballad. That evening, he talked of the present state of things in England, giving light, witty sketches of the men of the day, fanatics and others, and some sweet homely stories he told of things he had known of the Scotch peasantry. Of you he spoke with hearty kindness; and he told, with beautiful feeling, a story of some poor farmer, or artisan, in the country, who on Sundays lays aside the cant and care of the dirty English world, and sits reading the Essays, and looking upon the sea.'

How typical of the Victorian age was their conversation. Indeed, it seems to smell of the time, and in feeling, the story of 'the poor farmer, or artisan,' resembles closely Mr Ruskin's rhapsody over a picture by Mr Landseer – a shepherd, a rhapsody that was disinterred for us by Miss Margaret Barton and Sir Osbert Sitwell, and enshrined in their joint *Victorians*. 'Take', said Mr Ruskin, 'one of the most perfect poems or pictures' (I use the words as synonymous) 'which modern times have seen, "The Old Shepherd's Chief Mourner". Here the exquisite execution of the glossy and crisp hair of the dog, the bright, sharp touching of the green bough beside it, the clear painting of the wood of the coffin, and the folds of the blanket, are language – language clear and expressive in the highest degree. But the close pressure of the dog's breast against the wood, the convulsive clinging of the paws, which have dragged the blanket off the trestle, the total powerlessness of the head laid, close and motionless, upon its folds, the fixed and tearful fall of the eye in its utter hopelessness, the rigidity of repose which marks that there has been no motion nor change in the trance of agony since the last blow was struck on the coffin-lid, the quietness and gloom of the chamber, the spectacles marking the place where the Bible was last closed, indicating how lonely has been the life – how unwatched the departure of him who is now laid solitary in his sleep – these are all thoughts – thoughts by which the picture is separated at once from the hundreds of equal merit, as far as mere painting goes, by which it ranks as a work of high art, and stamps its author, not as the neat imitator of the texture of the skin, but as the Man of Mind.'

A Landseer-like smell of homespun, Highland cattle, shaggy lonely shepherds, the liberty of man, and mountain peaks, must have pervaded the conversation, and we may be sure that Margaret enjoyed it. But there was sparkle and fun too, of the order that was countenanced in that age, and Margaret could not forbear giving her former pupil in the difficult accomplishment of laughter a slight rebuke in that connection : 'Carlyle is worth a thousand of you, for that he is not ashamed to laugh when he is amused, but goes on in a cordial human fashion.'

In the few years that remained to Margaret Fuller, years that were to bring her the friendship of Mazzini, a young Italian husband, Count Ossoli, a baby son, and that strange, dramatic and tremendous shipwreck in which she, her husband, and her baby, lost their lives, Margaret remembered, often, her conversations with Carlyle, how the great man, inveighing against poetry, 'came back to some refrain, as in the French Revolution, of the Sea-Green'. In this instance, it was Petrarch and Laura, the last word pronounced with his ineffable drawl of sarcasm. Although he said this 'over fifty times, I could not help laughing when *Laura* would come, Carlyle running his chin out, when he spoke it, and his eyes glowing till they looked like the eyes and beak of a bird of prey. . . .'

On another occasion, Mr Carlyle spent some hours in rebuking Mazzini and Miss Fuller for their 'rose-water imbecilities'.

Scholars have, it seems, always despised this quality; but they are notoriously difficult to please; stupidity and flippancy in women, learning in women, all these offences may, at different times, prove equally unpalatable to them, though the last offence is usually the most unforgivable – largely, I imagine, because it is sometimes a little too readily assumed that heaven deems the charms of the mind to be sufficient of an endowment, and therefore bestows no other. In any case I suspect that the feeling cherished by both Mr Emerson and Mr Carlyle towards the learned Miss Fuller was very much the same as that natural male feeling expressed by Mr Fatigay, in my friend Mr John Collier's *His Monkey Wife*, when he learns that his pet monkey has taught herself to spell: 'Come, come, Emily, if you are as clever as all that, you must be sold to perform on the Halls.'

8

Some Men of Learning

AFTER reading the previous chapter we may, perhaps, find ourselves inclined to agree with those persons who insist that the Graces and the Muses are but rarely on visiting terms. Professor Porson, who was a generation older than Miss Fuller, Dr Parr, who contradicted Dr Johnson, and Dr George Fordyce, are other startling examples of this breach between sisters. Mr Timbs, the chronicler of both these gentlemen, becomes particularly morose when dealing with Professor Porson; and tells us that 'it is sufficiently notorious that Porson was not remarkably attentive to the decoration of his person'. But the decorations that adhered to him seem to me, on the contrary, of a very remarkable character; and a writer in the *Monthly Magazine* was much struck by his appearance, 'with a large patch of coarse brown paper on his nose, the rusty black coat hung with cobwebs'; whilst another friend, who met him in 1807, was dumbfounded 'by his fiery and volcanic face, and by his nose, on which he had a perpetual efflorescence, and which was covered with black patches; his clothes were shabby, his linen dirty'.

Yet, in earlier life, who more gallant than the Professor, who more assiduous in their attentions to the Fair? It is rumoured, indeed, that he once carried a young lady round the room in his teeth. But that was before dinner, and after dinner, the Professor, though equally manly, was less urbane. Indeed Mr Timbs tells us that, whilst as Cambridge, 'his passion for smoking, which was then going out among the younger generation, his large and indiscriminate potations, and his occasional use of the poker with a very refractory controversialist, had caused his company to be shunned by all except the few to whom his wit and scholarship were irresistible'. Apparently, the gifts in question did not always prove irresistible to the Fellows of Trinity, who, when the use of the poker seemed imminent, would slink out of the Common Room, and leave the Professor sitting at the table, emitting no sign of life excepting a perpetual eruption of smoke. In the morning, the servants were accustomed to seeing him sitting where he had been left, with no appearance of having moved, even once, during his night-long vigil.

These vigils became a source of anxiety in the houses which the Professor frequented, and it became necessary, at last, for the sake of preserving the health and sanity of the hosts, that the Professor should be told that he must never stay to a later hour than eleven. He showed no resentment at this mandate, but kept the agreement, honourably, and to the letter. But, 'though he never attempted to exceed the hour limited, he would never stir before', and woe betide the host who suggested such a breach of faith. But this state of affairs did not extend to every house, or to every host, and there were houses in which the Professor behaved like a lion rampant. The unfortunate Mr Horne Tooke, for instance, was one of Professor Porson's unhappier hosts, for he was foolish enough to invite the Professor to dine with him on a night that he knew had been preceded by three nights in which the Professor had refused all entreaties on the part of his hosts that he should go home to bed. Mr Tooke thought, therefore, that Professor Porson would relent on this occasion. But the night wore on, and Mr Tooke was worn out, for the Professor became more and more animated, passing from one learned theme to another. The poker was out of sight and out of mind, but insensibility, at any costs, might have been preferred. Dawn broke, the birds sang, the milkmen shouted, the Professor continued his monologue.

At last, in mid morning, the exhausted Mr Tooke proclaimed that he had an engagement to meet a friend for breakfast in a coffee-house at Leicester Square. The Professor was delighted, and announced that he would come too. But in the end, Providence came to the rescue of Mr Tooke and, soon after the Professor and he were seated in the coffee-house, the Professor's attention was distracted for an instant, and Mr Tooke, seizing the opportunity, fled as fast as his legs would carry him, nor did he pause for breath until he had reached Richmond Buildings. Having reached this haven of refuge, he barricaded himself in, and ordered his servant not to admit the Professor even if he should attempt to batter down the door. For 'a man', Mr Tooke observed, 'who could sit up four nights successively, could sit up forty'.

Mr Tooke won a victory over the Professor on another occasion, when the latter had threatened to 'kick and cuff Mr Tooke', and to bring in the poker as umpire. Mr Tooke said that the duel must be fought not with pokers but with brandy, and quarts of brandy at that. When the second quart was half-finished, the Professor sank into unconsciousness beneath the table, and the triumphant Mr Tooke, in what appears to me to be a spirit of bravado, drank the health of the vanquished in another glass of brandy and, after instructing the servants to 'take great care of the Professor', joined the ladies, weaving his way, without ostensible difficulty, into the drawing-room, where tea was being served.

In spite of this victory, however, and of his successful flight, Mr Tooke feared Professor Porson in controversial matters, because, after remaining silent for some aeons, he would then 'pounce upon him with his terrible memory'. Indeed, the position of host to the famous Greek scholar was no sinecure, and his rival Dr Parr informed Dr Burney, who had wished to invoke the Professor's aid on some question of the classics, that 'Porson shall do it, and he will do it. I know his terms when he bargains with me: two bottles instead of one, six pipes instead of two, Burgundy instead of claret, liberty to sit till five in the morning, instead of sneaking into bed at one – these are his terms.'

It was impossible, too, for the hostess to guess what food the Professor would indulge in; for at breakfast he called frequently for bread and cheese, and would then, as Mr Timbs remarks, take his porter as copiously as Johnson took his tea. With the aid of these methods, he once confined the wife of Dr Goodall, of Eton, to the breakfast table, throughout the whole of a Sunday morning, and the Doctor, returning from church, was just in time to see the sixth pot of porter being carried into the house. It is true that the Professor preferred port to porter, but he could, and would, drink anything, even water. Nor would he exclude a bottle of spirits of wine, or an embrocation. There were moments, however, when he would eschew these habits, and once, when he paid a visit to his sisters, in 1804, he confined himself to drinking two glasses of wine a day for eleven weeks.

But when in less chaste company, he would become melancholy, if not warlike, and, whilst he was at Cambridge, after sitting for two hours over a couple of bottles of sherry, 'he began to clip the King's English, to cry like a child at the close of his periods, and in other respects to show marks of extreme debility'. It is gratifying to know that in the end the Professor recovered sufficiently to find his way downstairs, without however recognizing the presence of the company, and to the outskirts of Cambridge. After some time, an anxious admirer tracked him down, and found him reclining upon the arm of a bargeman, 'and amusing him by the most humorous and laughable anecdotes'. But it must be said that he preferred learned company to that of bargemen, and

that, in praise of one of his academic visits to Germany, he
wrote the following poem:

> I went to Frankfort, and got drunk
> With that most learn'd Professor Brunck;
> I went to Würtz, and got more drunken
> With that more learn'd Professor Runcken.

In spite of the physical danger run by those who entered
into conversation, or at least argument, with Professor Porson, he could be, and was, an entertaining companion, as his
wits were as sharp as his learning was great. He had a
happy enough gift of phrase, as when, for instance, he
described a certain prospect as resembling a fellowship, since
it consisted of a long dreary walk with a church at the end
of it. It was unsafe, for a man of less sharp wits than the
Professor, to attempt impertinence in his presence, though
strangely enough the poker was never brought into play
on these occasions, for the Professor relied on verbal effects
alone. When at dinner some person who had tried, un-
advisedly, to argue with the great scholar, ended by saying:
'Dr Porson, my opinion of you is most contemptible,' 'Sir,'
replied Professor Porson, 'I never knew an opinion of yours
that was not contemptible.' Dr Parr and Mr Dodd were
other victims of this quickness – the former bringing disaster
upon himself by asking the Professor, in the presence of a
large and interested multitude, 'what he thought about the
introduction of moral and physical evil into the world'.
'Why, Doctor,' was the reply, 'I think we should have done
very well without them.' As for Mr Dodd, the Professor
refused to argue with him, no matter how drunk he might
be, saying, 'Jemmy Dodd, I always despised you when sober,
and I'll be damned if I'll argue with you now that I am
drunk.'

In such a manner did the Professor dispose of the harmless

Dr Dodd, and of the great Dr Parr, who stamped at Dr Johnson, in the course of an argument. Dr Johnson, much impressed by the manly firmness of the divine, made this statement: 'I do not know when I have had an occasion of such free controversy. It is remarkable how much of a man's life may pass without meeting with any instances of this kind of open discussion.' Dr Parr, on his side, recorded the incident thus: 'I remember the interview well. I gave him no quarter. The subject of our dispute was the liberty of the Press. Dr Johnson was very great; whilst he was arguing, I observed that he stamped, upon this I stamped. Dr Johnson said "Why do you stamp, Dr Parr?" I replied, "Sir, because you stamped; and I was resolved not to give you the advantage of a stamp in the argument."' There were, indeed, 'giants in those days'!

Conversation in the presence of Professor Porson, when it turned upon matters of learning, was an especial danger, as we may understand from the fate of Dr Parr and of Mr Dodd, and from the unhappy adventure of the young gentleman, fresh from Oxford, who, whilst in a hackney coach, dared to make a quotation from the Greek, in the hope of impressing the ladies. The Professor, a stranger to him, had appeared to be asleep, but was roused immediately by this daring on the part of the young gentleman, and, leaning forward, he said: 'I think, young gentleman, you favoured us just now with a quotation from Sophocles; I do not happen to recollect it there.' 'Oh, sir,' replied the unwary young gentleman, 'the quotation is word for word as I have repeated it, and in Sophocles too; but I suspect, sir, it is some time since you were at college.' The Professor, after fumbling for some time in his greatcoat, produced a small pocket edition of Sophocles, and commanded the young gentleman to produce the quotation. After some moments' unhappy turning of the pages, he was obliged to confess that he could not find it, recollecting upon second thoughts, that 'the passage is in Euripides'. The Professor, with a frown gathering upon his brow, produced the works of that author for the young gentleman's inspection, saying: 'Then perhaps, sir, you will be so good as to find it for me, in that little book.' The young gentleman was, by now, thoroughly terrified, but, unwilling to give way before the ladies, he ejaculated: 'Bless me, sir, how dull I am; I recollect now, yes, yes, I remember that the passage is in Aeschylus.' The Professor produced a book from his pocket. But the young gentleman, who had had enough of learning, cried, 'Stop the coach. Let me out. Let me out, I say. There's a fellow here has got the Bodleian Library in his pocket; let me out I say, let me out, he must either be the devil, or Porson himself.' In such a manner did the Professor 'pounce with his terrible memory'.

But there were moments when his memory failed him; and he would forget to eat dinner, though he never forgot a quotation. Once when Rogers invited him to dine, he answered, in an abstracted tone: 'Thank you, no, I dined yesterday.'

In early life, he was wretchedly poor, and in later years would say: 'I was then almost destitute with less than £40 a year for my support, and without a profession; for I could never bring myself to subscribe to the Articles of Faith. I used often to lie awake for a whole night, and wish for a large pearl.'

Dr George Fordyce, the great anatomist and chemical lecturer, resembled Professor Porson in the strength and length of his libations, nor was he less remarkable for his powers of absorbing food. A great admirer of the lion, his studies in comparative anatomy had brought him to conclude that this sagacious animal is the wisest eater; for he eats but once a day, and then as much as nature will permit.

So for twenty years Dr Fordyce followed the same régime as the object of his admiration, although, as we shall see, he did not confine himself to drinking water. Every day at four o'clock he would enter Dolly's Chop House, in Queen's Head Passage, Paternoster Row, and immediately on his arrival the cook would put a pound and a half of rump steak on the gridiron, whilst the waiter brought the Professor some *hors d'œuvre*, in the shape of half a broiled chicken or a large plate of fish, together with a silver tankard of strong ale, a bottle of port, and a quarter of a pint of brandy. All these vanished in the twinkling of an eye, for the Doctor, like the lion, did not toy with his food, or his drink – he ate and he drank as if he were performing a race for a bet. Having finished his meal, he then made his way to the Chapter Coffee House, in Paternoster Row, where he drank a glass of brandy and water; a second glass was provided at the London Coffee House, and a third at the Oxford, after which the Professor, considerably refreshed, returned to his house in Essex Street, and thundered out his lectures on chemistry. Nor did he eat again until, at four o'clock on the following day, he returned to Dolly's.

This habit, however, led to strange results at moments; and on one occasion, when Dr Fordyce attended a lady who had been stricken with illness of a sudden and mysterious nature, he found he was unable to count the beats of her pulse. This, indeed, seemed to have discovered the secret of perpetual motion, whirling madly round and round in one direction, whilst Dr Fordyce's brain persisted in whirling equally madly in the contrary sense. Irritated by this phenomenon, but tracing it to its source in Dolly's Chop House, the Professor ejaculated: 'Drunk, by the Lord!' Rather to Dr Fordyce's surprise, the lady wept silently, and Dr Fordyce, having prescribed some remedy, left the room with dignity and precision. Next day, he received a message begging for an immediate interview with him, and as soon as he arrived the lady, bursting into tears, confessed that he had diagnosed her illness only too correctly. The reproof administered by the Professor was severe in the extreme, and the lady promised that there should be no recurrence of the malady.

Mr Herbert Spencer was of a totally different character to the gentleman described above. Though almost equally surprising in his habits, he was urbane and paternal, and cultivated a peculiar sense of humour. Indeed, examining the form taken by these verbal quips, I cannot help feeling that he must have been the life and soul of the London boarding-house in whch he lived for twenty-six years.

Two of the ladies with whom, after the twenty-six years in question, he made his home, as some kind of paying guest, have given us a very adequate portrait of Mr Spencer's home life, in a book called *Home Life with Herbert Spencer*, by Two (Simpkin Marshall), as well as a charming portrait of themselves.

The house which Mr Spencer took, under this arrangement, No. 64 Avenue Road, Regent's Park, was, according to these ladies, 'essentially a *man's* house, with its bright rooms, lofty ceilings, and big windows', and throughout the book we are given the impression that there is something very odd and unusual, but at the same time delightful, in being a man. 'The house', they continue, 'contained no corners or nooks, with their endless possibilities of giving the rooms that home-like, comfortable touch which cosy corners and deep window-seats would have done.' There was, in short, no place in which to play 'hunt the spider', that entrancing game which is so inexplicable to the male mind, so wrapt in that mystery which, according to woman, is part of her charm. In the end, the ladies became reconciled to the house; and family life, into which the great philosopher entered heartily, was carried on to the mandolin-like accompaniment of the sound of tinkling teaspoons and happy girlish laughter, and the subterranean rumbling of Mr Spencer's jokes. The covering of Mr Spencer's chairs, however, was a source of worry to the ladies, for he had a particular fancy for a colour which he described as 'impure purple', and so much did he insist upon this colour being imported into the Home Life, that one of the staple jokes of the ladies was the insistence that this kindly old gentleman must, in his youth, have been in love with a lady with an impure-purple complexion. In the end, the chairs were covered with dark-green velvet with a binding of the beloved hue, in order to brighten the effect.

Another favourite joke with Mr Spencer was one relating to George Eliot, and it must be said that Mr Spencer had, earlier in life, devoted a long space of time to wondering whether it was his duty to marry this lady. In the end, however, he had decided that it was not; mainly, I believe, because her nose was too long, and somebody had told Mr Spencer that a long nose was incompatible with charm in a woman, a statement which, owing to lack of experience, he was obliged to take on trust. I cannot vouch for the truth of this story, but I do know that his respect for this stern-minded woman remained undiminished, and his joke about her was merely a little gay *badinage* between one great personage and another. He had often teased her, he explained to the listening, wondering ladies, about her 'diabolical descent', and he hastened to explain that as her name was Marian she was also a Polly Ann (Apollyon).

At times, however, this brightness, this gay wit and happy chatter, was overshadowed by the fact that Mr Spencer wished to take his pulse; sometimes, again, he would be averse to conversation, and on these occasions, he would put his ear-stoppers into his ears, and sit mum. The ear-stoppers, we are told, 'were formed of a band almost semi-circular in shape, with a little velvet-covered knob at either end, which was pressed by the spring in the band on the flaps over the hole of each ear'. He would accompany the production of this necessary instrument by the injunction: 'Mustn't talk now'; and the bubbling girlish chatter would cease.

The taking of Mr Spencer's pulse was one of the great ceremonies of the day, and often, when out driving in his victoria, a cry of 'Stop' would be heard by the coachman, and then, no matter where the equipage might find itself, in the middle of the busiest traffic, in Piccadilly or in Regent Street, the carriage would stop dead, disrupting the traffic in question; and silence would reign for some seconds, whilst Mr Spencer consulted the dictates of his pulse. If the oracle proved favourable, the drive was continued; if not, Mr Spencer was driven home.

Mr Spencer, like all great men, was an admirer of feminine prettiness, and, as we can see from the anecdote (probably apocryphal) about George Eliot's nose, disapproved of plainness in a woman. One unhappy lady, a Mrs O— 'of a most homely countenance', so upset him with her plainness, that on one occasion, hearing that she was to lunch with his young friends, 'he refused to come in, preferring a solitary meal in the drawing-room to sitting opposite anyone who was "so ugly".' 'There is no greater nonsense', he would say, 'than the absurd phrase, "beauty is but skin deep". It is a skin-deep saying, for beauty of features is generally accompanied by beauty of nature, so that it means a good deal more than appears on the surface.' A Miss E—, however, found favour in his eyes, and Mr Spencer proposed to call upon her, adding, 'Now had I met her forty years ago. . . .' But in the end this belated romance fizzled out, for Mr Spencer saw the lady in profile, and found it 'too nutcrackery'.

No wonder that, on one occasion, he was haunted, in spite of his love of Beethoven (well or badly played), by that lively and significant tune : 'A naughty little twinkle in her eye'. As a result of this elderly effervescence, a pretty young lady exclaimed : 'The darling, I should like to kiss him.'

Fatal words. The sound of teaspoons now, from time to time, was disturbed by the gay threats of the ladies in charge of Mr Spencer that they would warn their charge of these designs upon him. They seem to have done so, for one day, after a considerable amount of teasing, the great philosopher said, beaming : 'You know I *know* what she said. When you see her you can tell her she may if she likes.'

She did. The opportunity came when the song called 'Three Old Maids of Lee' was being performed in the drawing-room. The pretty young lady's back hair wore 'the hideous mask of an old woman, into which she turned by swinging round for the last verse of the song'. Mr Spencer enjoyed this ridiculous situation as much as anyone, and he was particularly delighted when the young beauty rushed up to him, 'giving him little pecks with her repulsive mask' and crying, 'You said I might if I liked.'

The enchanted spectators tell us that 'He tried to seize her, but she escaped; and although he was sunk in the depths of a very low chair, he quickly struggled up, was after her like a flash, and captured her as she reached the door, when he twisted her round, and gave her a resounding kiss on her own lips, and in the midst of a perfect deluge of laughter quickly disappeared from the room.'

'Naturally', the narrative continues, 'a bad night followed the philosopher's unwonted excitement; so we, to whom he had given the title of "keepers", informed him we must certainly in future put an embargo upon the kissing of girls. He declared, however, it was not the kiss that had upset him but the laughter and hilarity so late in the evening, when he should have had perfect quiet.'

Great as were these excitements, however, that of being cicerone of Mr Spencer on a railway-journey was greater. The preparations were like those of a Roman army on the march, complete with elephants. There was, for instance, a 'carrying-chair, a hammock, his rugs, air cushions, and end-less small paraphernalia', including a manuscript which was tied round his waist by a thick piece of string, with a trailing cord two or three yards long. This end, issuing like a tail from the back of his coat, was attached to the brown-paper parcel containing the manuscript, which, at the same time, he held in his hand.

These impressive preparations raised great expectations in the minds of the railway officials, who were rarely absent, *en masse*, for more than two minutes, but who were in the habit of approaching, in crocodile form, and inquiring 'Would Mr Herbert Spencer like this?' 'Would Mr Herbert Spencer have that?'

The last scene, however, was the most impressive of all. For Mr Spencer had been 'taught by experience that by travelling in a hammock when going a long journey he avoided the evil consequences which usually followed the shaking of the train'.

The slinging of the hammock in the saloon carriage re-served by Mr Spencer was no light matter; indeed it aroused the interest of all the denizens of the station; but when Mr Spencer became aware of this interest, he called out in sten-torian tones: 'Draw down those blinds.' The four officials who were temporarily under bondage to him did so imme-diately, so that all the fun was spoilt, as far as the crowd was concerned. Mr Spencer continued his survey of the hammock-slinging, and then, as the train was about to start, he bestowed warm words of praise upon his companion, bending from the hammock to do so: 'You have done very well. Good-bye.' 'I wish I could take you with me.'

'Lingering for a moment to see the last sign of the train,' we are told, 'she began to wonder whether all the attention he had received was due to respect felt for "the greatest mind of the age"....' As the thought crossed her mind, a porter stepped forward, and with a jerk of his head towards the departing train addressed her:

'Beg pardon, Miss, is he Earl Spencer?'

Here then is a frail bouquet, resembling, in some ways, the life work of a certain Mrs Dards, whose personality is, otherwise, shrouded in mystery.

'No one', said the ingenious Mrs Dards to Mr Rainy Day Smith, 'seeing this immense collection of artificial flowers, made entirely by myself with fishbones, the incessant labour of many years, can imagine the trouble I had in collecting the bones for that bunch of lilies-of-the-valley. Each cup consists of the bones which contain the brains of the turbot, and from the difficulty of matching the sizes, I should never have completed my task had it not been for the kindness of the proprietors of the London, Freemason's, and Crown and Anchor Taverns, who desired their waiters to save the bones for me.'

9
Some Travellers

'EVEN though the phrase, the romance of Commerce is now a *cliché*, the maps in a commercial atlas neatly cut up, coloured, analysed and diagrammed, are a rich feast for the fancy. To *see* where not only castor, camphor, colocynth and cocaine come from, but whence also the emerald, the chryso-prase, the topaz and the tourmaline; where impregnable forests brood, and the yellow fever skulks, and the Buddhist abounds; where those tempests called cyclone, hurricane, typhoon rise up and travel and pass away; what Penang lawyers, supple-jacks, bdellium and carambola may be; and what precise delicacies have their origin in Jipijapa, Rosario and Trebizond – all this can scarcely be acquitted of a romantic flavour.'

Thus wrote that great traveller of the mind and of the spirit, Walter de la Mare, in *Desert Islands*. The soul needs, not only a resting-place, but a distant land where it may find romance, and those truths that are not clothed in the accus-tomed, dusty garb of every day.

In the eighteenth and early nineteenth centuries, when the Grand Tour was the fashion, in the later nineteenth century, when the exploration of savage lands was the most chivalrous of all deeds, travelling, if not in the body, at least in the spirit, was not only a pleasure, it was a necessity.

In the library at Strawberry Hill, one fine day in July, 1774, busy, gossiping Mr Horace Walpole, sitting down to write a letter to his friend Sir Horace Mann, exclaims suddenly, '. . . All Europe will not furnish me with another paragraph; Africa is, indeed, coming into fashion. There is just returned a Mr Bruce [James Bruce the traveller, who lived from 1730 to 1794], who has lived three years in the court of Abyssinia, and breakfasted every morning with the maids-of-honour on live oxen. Otaheite and Mr Banks are quite forgotten; but Mr Blake (who betted on the man's living under water twelve hours) I suppose will order a live sheep for supper at Almack's, and ask whom he shall help to a piece of the shoulder. Oh yes; we shall have negro butchers, and French cooks will be laid aside. My Lady Townshend, after the Rebellion, said everybody was so bloodthirsty that she did not dare to dine abroad, for fear of meeting with a rebel-pie; now one shall be asked to come and eat a bit of raw mutton. In truth, I do not think we are ripe for any extravagance. I am not wise enough to wish the world reasonable – I only desire to have follies that are amusing, and am sorry that Cervantes laughed chivalry out of fashion.'

Mr Walpole was, as usual, right in his theory that Africa was coming into fashion, but it transpired that not only Africa, but Asia and Australasia were to become equally fashionable, and equally the speculation of travellers: whilst those who could not explore these distances in person, did so in mind, with, very often, considerable financial advantages. Amongst these latter travellers were the Princess Caraboo, and the far more remarkable M. Louis de Rougemont, whose narrative rivals that of Sir John Mandeville; whilst among the more actual travellers we have Lady Hester Stanhope, Edward Wortley Montagu, and the enchanting Squire Waterton, the account of whose virtues should fill a whole book, but which, on this occasion, must be compressed into one chapter.

Mr Edward Wortley Montagu seems to have caused a considerable amount of astonishment in his day; for William Robinson, in a letter to Mrs Elizabeth Montagu, dated 1762, writes: 'I have much regretted Lady Mary Wortley leaving Venice, as I was in great hopes of seeing that extraordinary phenomenon, but have had some consolation in meeting the son, who is not less curious in his way. He is preparing himself for his Eastern expedition by learning Arabic, and really studies very hard. He rises before daylight, and has let grow his whiskers, which, with the addition of a turban, which he wears in the house, makes him a very odd figure. Nor is his household less oddly formed than himself. He has a sister-in-law with him as he calls her, a Miss Cast – you will say a good name for one of his females. He has, too, a young girl of 12 years old whom he proposes to make a nun of; he has lodged her with a priest of St Peter's with the view of instructing her in the Roman Catholic religion. I forgot to tell you she is his daughter. Upon being told that he could not make her a nun upon the account of her religion, he said that would be no obstacle and they were all alike to him. He purposes being in the East eight or ten years which is a considerable time for a man turned fifty, and from which, indeed, he will probably never return. I saw him the other day when he was very busy in drawing up a letter to the Royal Society in regard to a discovery you must have heard of, of the similarity between the Chinese and Egyptian characters.'

Mr Walpole, with regard to Mr Wortley's election to the Royal Society, after explaining that this gentleman (whose father 'scarcely allows him anything') 'plays, dresses, diamonds himself, down to distinct shoe-buckles for a frock, and has far more snuff-boxes than would suffice a Chinese idol with a hundred noses' – exclaims 'the most curious part of his dress, which he has brought from Paris, is an iron wig; you literally would not know it from hair. I believe it is on this account that the Royal Society has chosen him of their body.'

In spite of Mr Wortley's incurable habit of travelling, or perhaps because of it, he was, as we shall see, equally addicted to matrimony, though he was as much a wanderer in this sphere of activity as in any other for he married, first a washerwoman, and then, bigamously, Caroline Dormer.

Nor did his thirst for domesticity content itself with these two ladies, for he deserted Miss Dormer for a Nubian girl, and, as well, eloped with Miss Ashe – Pollard Ashe, as Horace Walpole called her. The iron wig could have been seen, now in Egypt, now in Jerusalem, in Leghorn, in Smyrna, and in Rosetta, from whence he returned to Venice, where he very suitably adopted the costume of a Turk, and was, as we have seen, the source of a good deal of astonishment to English visitors to that City. His death took place at Padua in April 1776, and he no doubt left several inconsolable widows.

At about the same time, other and less adventurous travellers were enjoying equally surprising journeys, but to a less distant bourne.

The Reverend Henry Blaine, Minister of the Gospel at Tring in Hertfordshire, for instance, found his journey to Ramsgate was not only full of the most perilous incidents, but also that it served him as a model on which to build a Tract, in which he compared the dangers of the voyage to the perils of the Soul in her Earthly Journal, etc.

The Reverend Mr Blaine must have been an enchanting acquaintance, if we may judge by the Tract in question, though I imagine the enchantment would be realized only when it was past. When present, it may have been a little too continual.

The tract which I have culled from, Mr John Ashton's *Eighteenth-Century Waifs*, contains fifty-four pages, and begins thus:

'In hopes of recovering that invaluable blessing, health, on Friday, 10 August, 1787, I embarked on board the ship *Friends* bound for Ramsgate, in Kent. I had heard there was such a place; and many had raised my expectations by their reports of the efficacy of sea-bathing; and others encouraged my hopes by repeating their own experiences of benefit received. By these means I was induced to determine on this little voyage. It reminded me of the never-to-be-forgotten season, when, urged by some motives, and impelled by a power unseen, but not unfelt, I entered on board that stately vessel which the Lord's prophet saw in a storm. Isaiah liv, 11.'

This is a sample of the tract. He then goes on to say: 'While we waited for the time of sailing [for different purposes, I suppose], many came to board, and appeared, to me at least, as if they intended to embark with us; but they left not the harbour, but, urged by other occasions and inducements they took leave of their friends and departed; while we, who were bound for a distant place, kept steady to our purpose, turned our backs upon home and waited patiently for the gentle breeze and driving tide to convey us to the desired port.

'When our sails were displayed, and our cable unloosed, assisted by a gentle gale, we began by degrees to view the lofty towers, the aspiring churches, and all the grandeurs of London at a distance behind us; in hopes of finding something we could not find in town, we turned our attention from the pleasures, and riches, of London; we bade farewell for a time, to our dearest friends; we laid aside our daily and domestic cares, and cheerfully forsook the dear delights of home.'

At length they were fairly started on their voyage, which from the crowded state of the river, and the excessive timidity of the writer, must have been vastly perilous. 'Our vessel, though it set sail with a fair wind, and gently fell down the river towards her destined port, yet once or twice was nearly striking against other vessels in the river, to her own injury; but, by the care of the steersman and sailors, she was timely prevented.... There was no spectacle more affecting, in all the little voyage, than the bodies of those unhappy malefactors which were hung up, *in terrorem*, on the margin of the river Thames. Surely these was some of the execrable characters whom Justice pursued who, though they "escaped the sea, yet vengeance suffered not to live"? Acts xxviii, 4.... Having passed these spectacles of horror, a fair wind and flowing tide smoothly carried us towards the boundless ocean.

'When we drew towards the conflux of the river Thames, there were two objects that attracted our notice; the one, the King's guardship, placed there for the purpose of good economy; the other a large painted vessel, which floated on the surface of the water, and is called a buoy. While we were passing the King's ship, I heard the report of a cannon, and saw the flash of the charge at some distance; and, on inquiring the reason of such a circumstance, was informed it was customary for every ship which passed, by way of obedience, to lower her topsail; but the firing of the gun made them hasten to show their obedience, for fear of a more unfavourable salute; for, though a flash of powder might give us some alarm, the discharge of a ball might make us *feel* the effects of disobedience.... Hitherto the generality of our company appeared to carry jollity and mirth in their countenance; but now we began to see the blushing rose die in the sickly cheek, and several of our passengers began to feel the sickening effects of the rolling sea; they withdrew from their mirth, and in pleasure crept into a corner, and silently mourned their lost pleasures in solitude.... Thrice happy the souls who are by Divine grace made sick of unsatisfying objects, and seek and find permanent bliss in the friendship of Immanuel.

'There had been the appearance of affability and good humour kept up among the passengers of our vessel, and a reciprocal exchange of civilities had passed between them; our bad tempers were for awhile laid aside, and we seemed mutually agreed to make each other as innocently happy as our present condition allowed. If the same mode of conduct was observed through the whole of our department, how would the ills of life be softened, and the ties of society sweetened!

'The eyelid of the day was now nearly closed upon us, and the gloom of darkness began to surround us, which, together with the hollow bellowing of the wind, and dashing waves, had a tendency to create very solemn ideas in the mind; and I, being a stranger to such scenes, had my mind exercised upon things of greater importance. . .

'About ten o'clock on Friday night, we were brought safely into the harbour of Margate, and then cast anchor in order to set a great number of our passengers on shore, who were bound for that place of rendezvous. How great are the advantages of navigation. By the skill and care of three men and a boy, a number of persons were in safety conveyed from one part to another of the kingdom. . .

'When we had safely landed our passengers at Margate, we weighed anchor at eleven o'clock at night, in order to sail round the North Foreland for Ramsgate. The North Foreland is a point of land which stretches out some way into the sea, and is the extreme part of our country on the right hand, when we sail down the river Thames; and sailing round the point into the British Channel is esteemed by sailors rather dangerous. However, there was danger enough to awaken the apprehensions of a freshwater sailor. Yet here with some degree of confidence in Him who exercises His power over the sea and dry land, I laid me down and slept in quietness, while the rattling waves drove against the sides of our vessel, and the rustling winds shook our sails and made our yielding masts to speak. I was led to reflect that now there was but a feeble plank between me and the bottomless deep, yet, by a reliance on the divine goodness, my fears were hushed, and a divine calm prevailed within. "Thou will keep him in perfect peace, whose mind is stayed on thee. . . ." Isaiah xxvi, 3.

'On Saturday morning, I awoke and heard a peaceful sound from shore, which informed me it was two o'clock; and, inquiring where we were, I found we were safe anchored within the commodious harbour of Ramsgate. Being so early an hour, we again composed ourselves to sleep, and lay till five o'clock; then leaving our sleeping apartment, and mounting the peaceful deck – not like the frighted sailor, who leaves the horrid hulk to view a thousand deaths from winds, and waves, and rocks, without a friendly shore in view, but to see one of the finest retreats from all these dangers, which Providence has provided for the safety of those who are exposed to the violence and rage of angry elements. The commodious Pier of Ramsgate seems admirably calculated to shelter and protect vessels which are threatened with destruction from winds and waves. This beautiful piece of architecture is built in the form of a Crescent, or half-moon, the points of which join to the land. The whole of this building of utility appeared to bear a clear resemblance to the glorious Mediator in his offices, who is appointed for a refuge from the storm. . .

'By six in the morning we went on shore, and joyfully met our friends, who were brought down the day before; but in their passage were overtaken by a violent storm of thunder and lightning, whilst our voyage was smooth and prosperous; but, in the morning, we all met in peace and safety. Thus we sat down to a friendly breakfast, and cheerfully talked over the adventures of the little voyage. Something like this, I think, may take place in the state of blessedness. . . . While we were thus employed, we consulted how to dispose of ourselves while we continued at Ramsgate; we naturally agreed to form ourselves into a little family, and though we could not all lodge, yet we wished to board together in the same house. This is a pleasing instance of *bonne camaraderie* engendered, in a short time, among agreeable companions.

'In order to pursue the design of our coming, some of our company mixed among the bathers at the seaside. The convenience of bathing, the coolness of a fine summer's morning, the agreeable appearance of company so early, and the novelty of the scene, had a very pleasing effect. . . . We began to look around us; and though we were not presented with objects of taste and elegance, yet the town and environs afforded us some rural prospects, which yielded both instruction and pleasure. Upon our left hand, as we ascended from the seaside, stands the seat of observation, erected on a point of land and commanding an extensive prospect over that part of the sea called the Downs, where you behold a number of ships lying at anchor, or on their passage to different parts of the world. From thence you may likewise see the lofty cliffs of France, and reverberating the light of the sun; while, at the same time, you may, by way of amusement, watch the motions of every boat coming in and going out of the harbour; and, as the sea is always varying, its appearance altogether affords an agreeable amusement. Here the Company frequently stop to rest themselves after a morning's or an evening's walk, and are sweetly regaled by the cool refreshing breezes of the sea. . .

'It might be thought strange was I to say nothing of Margate, that being the chief resort for bathers, and of growing repute. The town of Margate is in a very increasing state, and its principal ornaments consist of its late additions. The chief concern of the publick seems to render it as much a place for pleasure as utility, as, under colour of utility, persons can pursue pleasure without censure. A mother, for instance, might be highly blamed by her acquaintance for leaving her family for a month, and going to spend her husband's money; but who can blame her when her health requires it? They are modelling it according to the taste of the times. They have, indeed, built one place of worship, but a playhouse nearly four times as large. Thus, when ill health does not interrupt the company's pursuit of amusement, they are likely soon to be accommodated to their minds. Such is the provision already made, that the consumptive cough of a delicate lady may be furnished with the relief of the fumes of a smoking-hot assembly-room, and the embarrassed citizen may drown his anxiety in the amusement of the Card-table...

'The libraries are decently furnished, and may serve as a kind of lounging Exchange, where persons over-burdened with money and time may ease themselves of these with great facility. The most healthful amusement and best suited to invalids, that is pursued at Margate, is that of the bowling-green, where upon the top of a hill, and in full prospect of the sea, in a free open air, gentlemen may exercise their bodies, and unbend their minds; this, if pursued for the benefit of health and innocent recreation, with a serious friend, appears to have no more criminality in it than Peter's going a-fishing...

'Having staid as long at Ramsgate as our affairs at home would, with prudence, admit, we went on board the same ship, and re-embarked for London. In order, I suppose, to take the better advantage, we sailed some leagues right out to sea; but, it being a dead calm, we hardly experienced any other motion than was occasioned by the tide and swell of the sea for that night. The cry of the sailors, Blow, Blow, reminded me of that pathetic exclamation of the ancient Church. The next day proved equally calm, so that we had little else to divert us but walk about the deck, and watch the rolling of the porpoises in the sea. We had an old sailor on board, whose patience being tried, declared he preferred being at sea in a storm to being becalmed on the ocean, which struck me with the propriety of the observation, when applied to Christian experience; for a storm, under Divine direction, is often made the means of hastening the Christian's progress, while a dead calm is useless and unsafe.'

It took them two days to get to Margate, and another day to reach Gravesend. On their way they passed a vessel cast on shore, which 'cut a dismal figure, such as they make, to an enlightened eye, who make shipwreck of faith, whom Christians see, as they pursue their course, run aground, and dash to pieces'.

All travellers, however, were not content with drawing symbols from journeys to Ramsgate – they must invent, and be the natives of far more distant and perilous lands.

Thirty or forty years after this time, England received the visit of certain foreign potentates, who must no doubt have viewed our habits with as much astonishment as that with which we regarded theirs. The first potentate to arrive was Caraboo, Princess of Jevasu, who was wafted to our shores by some mysterious agency; and who eventually, according to rumour, captured the affection of the Emperor Napoleon I, who would willingly have divorced Marie Louise for her sake. Eight years after her arrival and departure London was enlivened by the view of the King and Queen of the Sandwich Islands, and the visit was celebrated in the song 'The King of the Cannibal Islands'.

The Princess Caraboo was the exotic visitor who caused the greatest surprise, aroused the most interest, arriving as she did, no one knows how, from a kingdom whose situation wavered from continent to continent, between ocean and ocean. Asia, however, seemed to be its preferred continent; and its principal habitation, within that limit, was now China, now the Indies, with a particular predilection for Sumatra.

The Princess of this errant land[1] arrived on Thursday evening the third of April, 1817, at a cottage in the village of Almondsbury, and by the means of modest but significant signs showed that she wished to spend the night beneath its roof. The inhabitants, finding that she was unable to speak or understand English, 'referred to Mr Worrall, a Magistrate for the county, for his advice'. The young and interesting female seemed to understand, by some mysterious means, that she was to be brought face to face with Mr Worrall, and showed the strongest disinclination for this meeting. But after a good deal of semi-forcible persuasion, the meeting was brought about, and not with Mr Worrall, alone, but with Mrs Worrall also. This lady and gentleman were unable to understand the strange language in which she spoke to them, but in the end, by means of signs, they succeeded in conveying to her that they wished to see any papers which she might possess; whereupon she took from her pocket a few halfpence and a bad sixpence. The small bundle she carried contained a few necessary articles, including a small piece of soap pinned up neatly in a piece of linen. Her dress was modest, and gave no hint of her royal rank, for it consisted of a gown of black stuff with a muslin frill round the neck, a black cotton shawl on her head, and a red-and-black shawl round her shoulders – 'both loosely and tastefully put on in imitation of the Asiatic costumes'.

Mrs Worrall arranged that the romantic stranger should sleep at the village inn, and sent her maid and footman to see that her bed was comfortable and her meal sufficient.

'When shewn to the room in which she was to sleep', we

1. '*Errant*: To wander; to err; wandering, roving, rambling, especially roaming in search of adventure, as a knight-errant.' – *Dictionary*.

are told, in a pamphlet published in the year of the Princess' arrival, 'she appeared reluctant to go to bed, and pointed to the floor, but upon the landlady's little girl getting into the bed and making her understand the comfort of it, she undressed, and after kneeling and appearing to say her prayers, she consented to lie on the bed.'

Early the next day, the stranger received visits not only from Mrs Worrall, but from the excited clergyman of the parish, who brought with him various pictures of distant climes, and especially of places situated in the East, in the hope that she might show some signs of recognizing these.

We are told that 'upon looking them over, she gave the spectator to understand that she had some knowledge of the prints that were descriptive of China, but made signs that it was not a boat, but a ship, which had brought her to this country'. This inquiry seemed to lead nowhere in particular, so the indefatigable Mrs Worrall decided to lead this mysterious foreigner back to Knole,[2] and to keep her there until some sort of solution of the mystery was reached. The mysterious foreigner showed every sign of reluctance at the prospect of re-entering Knole; but there was nothing to be done, and she was ushered once more under that too hospitable roof. Once there, she was taken into the housekeeper's room, where the servants were at breakfast, and, 'observing some cross-buns on the table (it being Good Friday), she took one, and after looking earnestly at it she cut off the cross and placed it in her bosom'.

This action of simple piety served only to deepen the mystery, proving as it did that the Wanderer's native land, however savage, was addicted to Christianity.

It seems that Mrs Worrall, whilst in church, took counsel with herself, and on her return addressed the stranger in the

2. This house is not the seat of Lord Sackville, but is situated in Gloucestershire.

following soothing and compassionate language. 'My good young woman, I very much fear that you are imposing upon me, and that you understand and can answer me in my own language. If so, and distress has driven you to the expedient, make a friend of me; I am a female as yourself, and can feel for you, and will give you money and clothes, and will put you on your journey, without disclosing your conduct to anyone; but it must be on condition that you speak the truth. If you deceive me, I think it right to inform you that Mr Worrall is a magistrate, and has the power of sending you to prison, committing you to hard labour, and passing you as a vagrant to your own parish.'

The beautiful countenance of the stranger showed no signs of embarrassment or shame as Mrs Worrall reached the peroration of this address. On the contrary, she showed plainly enough that she had no comprehension of the language in which she was addressed, and made what seemed to Mrs Worrall to be a voluminous speech in her own tongue. Mrs Worrall, indefatigable as ever, then attempted to induce the romantic stranger to divulge her name, by writing her own name upon paper and handing it to her, giving her at the same time a pen, and uttering long and piercing cries of 'Worrall, Worrall', smiting herself, as she did so, upon the breast. The Princess rejected the pen, and in her turn cried persistently: 'Caraboo, Caraboo', pointing to herself. It must have been an impressive scene, and the Princess carried this system of annoyance by rejection still further at dinner, where she put from her all animal food, beer, cider, etc.

The Princess Caraboo remained under Mrs Worrall's roof until the following Monday, when she was taken to a home for the destitute at Bristol. As soon as her story, or rather, lack of a story, became known, this haven of refuge was besieged by the curious, bringing with them any foreigner on whom they had been lucky enough to lay hands, in the hopes that by this means her nationality might become known. Among these foreigners was a Portuguese from Malay, who, it transpired, understood the language spoken by this interesting wanderer. She was a princess of the blood royal, he informed the awestricken audience, had been decoyed by pirates in some mysterious manner from Jevasu, her island home in the East Indies, brought, for an equally mysterious reason, to England, and then deserted by her heartless abductors, who had, it seemed, made the trip from Jevasu to England for the sole purpose of depositing the enchanting Princess Caraboo upon our shores. Heedless of danger they had come; heedless of danger they had stolen away; nor did they leave so much as a footprint upon our land. The story was dramatic and romantic in the extreme. Even Mrs Worrall's doubts were set at rest, and the Princess found herself once again at Knole, where she kept the household in a perpetual state of tension, and gave as much trouble as possible.

'Upon giving her some calico,' we are told by the pamphlet which was devoted to her, and which is quoted in Miss Margaret Barton's and Sir Osbert Sitwell's *Sober Truth*, 'she made herself a dress in the style she had been accustomed to wear. It was very short in the petticoat, the sleeves uncommonly wide, and long enough to reach the ground, but only half-scored up, and confined at the wrists. She wore no stockings, but open sandals on the feet with wooden soles. She expressed much pleasure at the sight of a Chinese chain purse, which was shown to her, and which she put on, first in the Chinese and afterwards in the Jevasu fashion – in both instances veiling her face. She sometimes twisted her hair and rolled it up on top of her head, fastening it with a skewer. A vocabulary of words, and the meanings to which she applied them, were collected, and she was always consistent and correct in using them in the same sense, meaning, or object. Mrs Worrall's housekeeper, who slept with her, never heard at any interval any other language or tone of voice than that which she at first assumed.'

Her habits were martial and unaccustomed, and she must have terrified the Worrall household. 'During her stay,' continues the pamphlet, 'she used to exercise herself with a bow and arrows, and made a stick answer to a sword on her right side, the bows and arrows slung on her left shoulder. She sometimes carried a gong on her back, which she sounded in a very singular manner, and a tambourine in her hand, a sword by her side, and a bow and arrows slung as usual, her head dressed with flowers and feathers, and thus she made it appear she was prepared for war.'

Whether Mrs Worrall was also prepared for war I know not; but life must have been by no means easy, as none could foresee where the Princess' native habits would lead her next. On one occasion, for instance, the watchful Mrs Worrall took an evening off, for the purpose of being present at a wake in the parish, and on her return the Princess could not be found. The gardens were searched, irrepressible joy mingled with a decorous and dutiful despair. But both emotions were destined to be dashed to the ground, for after the household had become exhausted through looking for her, a faint rustling was heard from the top of a particularly high tree, and there was the Princess, perched on the summit, and complete with bow and arrows. She had climbed this tree, she explained, because all the females in the house had gone into the village, and she feared the effect that her unchaperoned state might have upon the men.

The household resumed their normal activities. But not for long. One day at the beginning of June, the interesting captive, unable to bear the watchful eyes of Mrs Worrall any longer, crept out of the house and made her way to Bath. It is one of the mysteries of nature that the Princess of that far and savage isle must, undoubtedly, have known, by the instinct that wild peoples possess in such acuity, that Bath was at that time the centre of fashion. For why, otherwise, should her steps have led her thither? Once there, she was lionized by the fashionable society, eager for a new sensation; and rumours of this lionization reached the faithful Worrall, with the result that this lady followed her charge within a week of her escape, determined, at all costs, to protect her, and if possible to reimprison her.

'She found the Princess at the very pinnacle of her glory and ambition in the drawing-room of a lady of *haut ton*. Cervantes himself could not have expected the realization of so fine a scene. What was the situation of Sancho Panza at the palace of the Duchess, in comparison with the Princess of Jevasu in the drawing-room of Mrs —? The drawing-room was crowded with fashionable visitants, all eager to be introduced to the interesting Princess. There was one fair female kneeling before her, another taking her by the hand, another begging a kiss. . . .'

Dr Wilkinson of Bath was another of the *cognoscenti* who was led likewise by the same love of the marvellous to try his skill at developing the character and nation of the unknown foreigner.

'Her mode of diet seems to be Hindustani,' wrote the Doctor to the *Bath Chronicle*, 'as she lives principally on vegetables, and is very partial to curry; whatever she eats, she prepares herself. She is extremely neat in her attire, is very cautious in her conduct with respect to gentlemen; never allows them to take hold of her hand, and, even if her clothes should casually come into contact with theirs, she retires from them; when she takes leave of a gentleman it is by the application of the right hand to the right side of the forehead, and, in like manner, on taking leave of a lady, it is with the left hand. She appears to be dumb; and on a certain day in the week is anxious to go to the top of the house and there to pay adoration to the sun from the rising to the setting. She carries about with her a cord, on which some knots are made, like the Chinese abacus, which afterwards gave rise to the sliding beads. She writes from left to right, as we are accustomed. She has made Mrs Worrall understand that in her country neither pens nor paper are used; but what is supposed to be a camel's-hair pencil and a species of papyrus. All the assistance to be derived from a Polyglot Bible, Fry's *Pantographia*, or Dr Hager's *Elementary Characters of the Chinese*, did not enable us to ascertain either the nature of her language, or the country to which she belongs; one or two characters bear some resemblance to the Chinese *sho*, a reed. There are more characters which have some similitude to the Greek ... different publications have been shown to her in Greek, Malay, Chinese, Sanscrit, Arabic, and Persic, but with all she appears entirely unacquainted. Her letter has been shown to every person in Bristol and Bath versed in Oriental literature, but without success. A copy was sent to the India House, and submitted by the Chairman of the Company to Mr Raffles, one of the best Oriental scholars, yet he could not decipher it. The original letter was sent to Oxford, and the members of that university denied it being the character of any language; it has been by some conjectured as being an imperfect Javanese, others have supposed it the style of the Malay and Sumatra. From my own observation, although entirely unacquainted with any single character of her writing, I have deemed her more resembling a Circassian; her countenance, her complexion and her manners, favour such a supposition; and probably her appearance here may be connected with the Corsairs who have been hovering about our coast. The Supreme Being she styles Alla Tallah. All who have seen her are highly interested about her.'

Reading this, I regret more than ever that Princess Caraboo

did not delay making an appearance till this age, when she might have been brought face to face with my friend Mr Arthur Waley. I should have enjoyed the meeting, although I am afraid that it would have led to the retirement of Princess Caraboo from public life. Mr Waley is unconquerable. I remember, for instance, the day when he was expected for the week-end at my brother Sacheverell's house in the country, and my sister-in-law and I, finding in the library a small and ancient book in an unknown tongue, placed it beside Mr Waley's bed in the hope that he would confess himself defeated. Next morning, Mr Waley looked a little pale; his manner was languid, but as he placed the book on the breakfast table he announced in a faint voice: 'Turkish. Eighteenth century.' The pages were few; and after an interval of respect we inquired: 'What is it about?' Mr Waley, with sudden animation: 'The Cat and the Bat. The Cat sat on the Mat. The Cat ate the Rat.' 'Oh, it is a child's book.' 'One would imagine so. One would *hope* so!'

How pleasing then would have been the meeting between Mr Waley and Princess Caraboo. Alas, it was not to be. Nor did the meeting with Dr Wilkinson have results which were fortunate either for the Princess or for that innocent old gentleman. For a certain lodging-house keeper read Dr Wilkinson's narrative, and thought that the appearance and exotic behaviour of Princess Caraboo were reminiscent of a certain Mary Baker, who had been her lodger for a short time some months before.

The stories told by Miss Baker had been so wildly fantastic that the lodging-house keeper had feared for her reason. So this interfering lady bustled to Bath, and no sooner was she confronted with Princess Caraboo, than the latter burst into tears and owned that she was an impostor. The history she gave of her previous life was, however, just as extraordinary and improbable as was her previous role –

and nobody knew what to believe. Only one real fact emerges about her; and that is that she was 'a servant-girl from Devonshire with a far from unblemished reputation'. Her incurable love of romance, and love of wandering, both actually and in imagination, caused her to lose every situation she took, so that in the end she roamed about from place to place, until she took it into her head to woo romance by pretending to be a princess.

I cannot see that her behaviour was as bad as it has been held to be; she harmed no one, and brought a great deal of interest and romance into the lives of Mrs Worrall and Dr Wilkinson. Perhaps, after the sharp feeling of disappointment at her exposure had worn off, even those who had shown the most interest in the mystery forgave her. At any rate, it is certain that Mrs Worrall, that kindly and well-meaning busybody, pitied her and helped her to emigrate to America; and here our story would come to an end, if it were not for this strange story of the meeting between Princess Caraboo and the Emperor Napoleon at St Helena.

The story was printed in Felix Farley's *Bristol Journal* on September 13th, 1817:

'A letter from Sir Hudson Lowe, lately received from St Helena, forms at present the leading topic of conversation in the higher circles. It states that on the day preceding the date of the latest despatches, a large ship was discovered in the offing. The wind was strong from the S.E. After several hours' tacking, with apparent intention to reach the island, the vessel was observed to bear away for the N.W., and in the course of an hour the boat was seen entering the harbour. It was rowed by a single person. Sir Hudson went alone to the beach, and to his astonishment saw a female of interesting appearance drop the oars and spring to land. She stated that she had sailed from Bristol, under the care of some missionary ladies, in a vessel called the *Robert and*

Anne under Captain Robinson, and destined for Phila-
delphia; that the vessel being driven out of its course by a
tempest, which continued for several successive days, the
crew at length perceived land, which the captain recognized
to be St Helena; that she immediately conceived an ardent
desire of seeing the man with whose future fortunes she was
persuaded her own were mysteriously connected; and her
breast swelled with the prospect of contemplating face to
face an impostor not equalled on earth since the days of
Mohammed; but a change of wind to the S.S.E. nearly overset her hopes. Finding the Captain resolved to proceed
according to his original destination, she watched her opportunity, and springing with a huge clasp-knife into a small
boat which was slung at the stern, she cut the ropes, dropt
safely into the ocean, and rowed away. The wind was too
strong from the land to allow of the vessel being brought
about to thwart her purpose. Sir Hudson introduced her to
Bonaparte under the name of Caraboo. She described herself as Princess of Jevasu, and related a tale of extraordinary
interest, which seemed in a high degree to delight the Captive Chief. He embraced her with every demonstration of
enthusiastic rapture, and besought Sir Hudson that she
might be allowed an apartment in his house, declaring that
she alone was an adequate solace in his captivity.'

Sir Hudson adjoins: 'The familiar acquaintance with the
Malay tongue possessed by this most extraordinary personage (and there are many on the island who understand that
language), together with the knowledge she displays of
Indian and Chinese politics, and the eagerness with which
she speaks of these subjects, appear to convince everyone
that she is no impostor. Her manner is noble and fascinating
to a wonderful degree.'

A private letter adds the following testimony to the above
statement: 'Since the arrival of this lady, her manners, and

I may say the countenance and figure of Bonaparte, appear to be wholly altered. From being reserved and dejected, he has become gay and communicative. No more complaints are heard about inconveniences at Longwood. He has intimated to Sir Hudson his determination to apply to the Pope for a dispensation to dissolve his marriage with Maria Louise, and to sanction his indissoluble union with the enchanting Caraboo.'

This is the last we hear of the lovely and unfortunate Princess Caraboo – excepting for a rumour that she returned to England and made a living by selling leeches, and eighty-one years passed by before another traveller at once so romantic, and with such a tragic history, visited our land. This traveller was M. Louis de Rougemont, and his adventures, narrated as they were in the *Wide World Magazine* for August 1898, caused a stir throughout the whole of our Empire. Once more I find myself obliged to turn to *Sober Truth*, the authors of which have with the utmost industry and sympathy dug up and reproduced for us M. de Rougemont's history.

The *Wide World Magazine*'s announcement of M. de Rougemont's narrative of his adventures begins thus:

'We now commence what may truly be described as the most amazing story a man ever tried to tell. In all the annals of geographical science there is practically but one case that can be compared for a moment with M. de Rougemont's, but in that instance the man returned to civilization a hopeless idiot, having lost his reason years before, amidst his appalling surroundings. Quite apart from the world-wide interest of M. de Rougemont's narrative of adventure, it will be obvious that after his thirty years' experience as a cannibal chief in the wilds of unexplored Australia, his contribution to science will be simply above all price. He has already appeared before such eminent geographical authorities as Dr

G. Scott Keltie, and Dr Hugh R. Mill, who have heard his story and checked it by means of their unrivalled collection of latest reports, charts, and works of travel. These well-known experts are quite satisfied that not only is M. de Rougemont's narrative perfectly accurate, but that it is of the very highest scientific value. We also have much pleasure in announcing that arrangements are being made for M. de Rougemont to read an important paper before that great scientific body, the British Association for the Advancement of Science, at their next Congress, which will be held in September at Bristol.

'The narrative is taken down verbatim from M. de Rougemont's life and, apart from all outside authorities and experts, we have absolutely satisfied ourselves as to M. de Rougemont's accuracy in every minute particular.'

Life among the cannibals had, it seemed, taught M. de Rougemont to 'size up' human nature fairly accurately; and none knew better than he the value of the 'Dog-the-Friend-of-Man' theme as a softening factor. No head so soft, no heart so soft, that these could not be mollified still further by a really good story about a virtuous and courageous dog. M. de Rougemont's history therefore ran thus. In the early 'sixties he was engaged in pearl-fishing off the South coast of New Guinea, and in the course of this industry, and in mid ocean, he found himself alone save for the Captain's Dog. A storm arose. Where was the Captain? Where was the ship's Company? Where was M. de Rougemont's partner? They had vanished, leaving M. de Rougemont in charge of the Dog. For a fortnight these two inseparable companions navigated the ship, drifting hither and thither, and sharing each other's joys and sorrows, and then – probably just as M. de Rougemont was telling the Dog some simple poignant story – the ship struck a reef and was seen to be sinking, Man and Dog sprang into the sea, and began to swim towards a small island; but the tide was too strong for M. de Rougemont, and he, like the ship, was seen to be sinking. Then it was that the Friend of Man, sagacious and faithful, held out his tail to the drowning M. de Rougemont, who with a last effort seized it between his teeth, and in this manner was towed ashore. The companions found themselves on a small island one hundred yards long, ten yards wide and eight feet above the sea-level. Here they made themselves as comfortable as they could, by means of the furniture from the wreck, and settled down to a life of work and of thought, and of such sports as turtle-riding, and deepsea diving on the backs of the turtles. 'I used', he tells us, 'to wade out to where the turtles were and, on catching a big six-hundred pounder, would calmly sit astride on his back.

'Away would swim the startled creature mostly a foot or so below the surface. When he dived deeper I simply sat back on the shell, and then he was forced to come up. I steered my queer steeds in a curious way. When I wanted my turtle to turn to the left, I simply thrust my foot into his right eye and vice versa for the contrary direction. My two big toes placed simultaneously over both his optics caused a halt so abrupt as almost to unseat me.'

Here they remained for two years, undisturbed, and then four naked savages, a man, a woman, and their two children, were blown up to the island by another gale. The savages were friendly, especially the woman; they seemed pleased to see M. de Rougemont, and he learned their language, and was informed by them that they were Australian aborigines. The woman, whose name was Yamba, was peculiarly intelligent, and taught him many things about the customs and language of the Australian Negroes, which proved invaluable to him when he came to reign over them.

It may be said that M. de Rougemont had, by this time, discarded all clothing, in preparation for his future state.

These inseparable friends at last decided that they would try to reach the mainland in a boat they had constructed, so, after full preparations, they set out on their journey. A few days passed, land appeared on the horizon, and Yamba and her husband and children proclaimed joyfully that it was their native country. They decided, however, that the joy of arriving there immediately after such an arduous journey would be too much for them, and they therefore landed on an island, in the mouth of a large bay, and here Yamba lit fires which were to serve as a signal to her friends on the mainland. The result was that when, after a few days' complete rest, they arrived in sight of Yamba's native country. M. de Rougemont was much impressed by the sight of a huge shouting crowd of Negroes, excited, singing, and gesticulating, pouring down to the shore to welcome them. The enthusiasm, the friendliness, the respect of this simple people knew no bounds. They insisted indeed that M. de Rougemont must make his home with them, and to this he agreed, because, as Miss Barton and Sir Osbert Sitwell inform us cynically, 'he had no alternative'. His new friends then insisted on finding a wife for him, but the faithful M. de Rougemont would look at nobody but Yamba, and so, after some amount of amicable bargaining with her former husband, he married her. The marriage was a happy one, for M. de Rougemont had high ideals of womanhood, and Yamba fulfilled these to a remarkable degree. Her husband tells us, 'Often has that heroic creature *tramped on foot a hundred miles* to get me a few sprigs of saline herbs; she had heard me say I wanted salt.' And later, as we shall see, she proved her devotion in a manner even more striking and even more grateful to the masculine belief in that wise predilection of Providence for the heavier battalions. 'The battle goes to the strong,' cries heaven. And heaven may not easily be put in the wrong.

Life amongst the subjects of M. de Rougemont was extremely simple. We are assured that 'Every morning I was astir by sunrise, and, hope springing eternal, I at once searched for the faintest indication of a passing sail. Next I would bathe in a lagoon protected from sharks, drying myself by a run on the beach. Meanwhile, Yamba would have gone out searching for roots for breakfast, and seldom returned without a supply of my favourite water-lily roots. . . . The natives themselves had but two meals a day – breakfast, between 8 and 9 o'clock, and then an enormous feast in the late afternoon, their ordinary food consisting of kangaroo, emu, snakes, rats, and fish, an especial dainty being a worm found in the black avia tree, or in any decaying trunk.

'These worms were generally grilled on hot stones, and eaten several at a time like small whitebait. I often ate them myself, and found them most palatable.'

At this point, the readers of the *Wide World Magazine* became so violently excited by the prospect of seeing the hero of these adventures face to face, that the Editor inserted this notice : he was receiving, we are informed, 'shoals of letters daily from all quarters asking whether M. de Rougemont is likely to afford the British Public an opportunity of seeing him in the flesh. To these correspondents we can only say that it is very probable M. de Rougemont may shortly be induced to lecture in the principal towns and cities in the United Kingdom. Moreover, he at present is sitting to that well-known artist Mr John Tussaud, who is preparing a portrait-model of this marvellous man, which will shortly be on view at the world-renowned Galleries in the Marylebone Road. It is impossible for us to reply to even a tithe of our de Rougemont correspondents, and M. de Rougemont himself is busy working up his scientific material for the learned societies tracing his relatives in Lausanne and Paris, etc.'

The duties of a prospective Cannibal Chief were as painful,

at moments, as they were arduous, and M. de Rougemont gave the appalled readers of the *Wide World Magazine* this description of the sequel to a battle. Having explained that the dead were placed on litters made out of spears and grass and carried into the camp, he tells us that 'the chiefs decked themselves with gorgeous cockatoo feathers, and painted their bodies in stripes with red and yellow ochre, and other glaring pigments'. The narrative continues:

'There were so many signs to presage what was coming, that I knew a cannibal feast was about to take place; but for obvious reasons I did not protest against it, nor did I take any notice whatever. The women (who do all the real work) fell on their knees, and with their fingers scraped three long trenches in the sand, each about 7 feet long and 3 feet deep. Into each of these ovens was placed one of the bodies of the fallen warriors, and then the trench was filled up – firstly with stones, and then with sand. On top of all a huge fire was built and maintained with great fierceness for about two hours. There was great rejoicing during the period of cooking, and apparently much pleasurable anticipation among the triumphant blacks. In due time the signal was given, and the ovens laid open once more. I looked in and saw that the bodies were very much burnt. The skin was cracked in places and liquid fat was issuing forth. . . . But perhaps the less said about this horrible spectacle the better. With a yell, several warriors leapt into each trench and struck spears into the big "joints". At the moment the roasted carcasses were taken out of the trenches the whole tribe literally fell upon them and tore them limb from limb. I saw mothers with a leg or an arm surrounded by plaintive children, who were crying for their portion of the toothsome dainty.'

'The women are not prepossessing, and not nearly so peaceful in their bearing and gait as the men. Poor creatures, they did all the hard work of the camp – building, food-hunting, waiting, and serving – occasionally however the men did condescend to go out fishing, and they would also organize battues when a big supply of food was wanted. These great hunting-parties were arranged on an immense scale, and fire figured largely in them. The usual routine was to set fire to the bush, and then as the terrified animals and reptiles rushed out in thousands into the open, each party of blacks speared every living thing that came its way within a certain sphere. The roar of the fast-spreading fire, the thousands of kangaroos, opossums, rats, snakes, iguanas and birds that dashed hither and thither, to the accompaniment of bewildering shouts from the men and shrill screeches from the women, who occasionally assisted, flitting hither and thither, like eerie witches amidst the dense pall of black smoke, all these made up a picture which is indelibly imprinted in my mind. As to the fishing-parties, these went out either early in the morning, soon after sunrise, or in the evening, when it was quite dark. On the latter occasions, the men carried big torches, as they waded out into the water with their spears poised in readiness to impale the first big fish they came across. Sometimes a hundred men would be in the shallow water at once, all carrying blazing torches, and the effect as the fishermen plunged and splashed this way and that, with shouts of triumph or disappointment, may be better imagined than described.'

At this point, M. de Rougemont narrates a discovery which must have roused a kind of furore of excitement amongst natural-history societies. For he tells us that 'One day I decided to go and explore one of the islands in search of wombats, whose skins I wanted to make into sandals for myself. I knew that wombats haunted the islands in countless thousands, because I had seen them rising in clouds every evening at sunset. As usual, Yamba was my only companion, and we soon reached a likely island.'

Miss Barton and Sir Osbert Sitwell, in a note, remark with justice and admiration, 'A wombat is an animal closely resembling a small bear. The existence of flying wombats, it may readily be imagined, caused a stir among naturalists.' Whilst engaged in the search for this volatile quadruped M. de Rougemont met with an adventure which would have ended badly for any man less intrepid than this great traveller. But, like all M. de Rougemont's other adventures, it only brought him more honour and a greater fame amongst his chosen people. Let us tell the story in his own words.

He explains that 'I had not gone many yards along this track (in the forest) when I was horrified to see, right in front of me, an enormous alligator. The great reptile was shuffling along down the path towards me, evidently making for the water, and not only blocked my advance, but also necessitated my immediate retreat. The moment the brute caught sight of me, he stopped, and began snapping his jaws viciously. I confess I was quite nonplussed for the moment as to how to commence the attack upon the unexpected visitor. It was impossible for me to get round him in any way, on account of the dense bush on either side of the narrow forest track. I decided, however, to make a bold dash for victory, having always in mind the prestige that was so necessary to my existence amongst the blacks. I therefore walked straight up to the evil-looking monster, and then, taking a short run, I leaped high into the air, shot over his head, and landed on his scaly back, at the same time giving a tremendous yell in order to attract Yamba, whom I had left in charge of the boat.

'The moment I landed on his back I struck the alligator with all my force with my tomahawk, on what I considered the most vulnerable part of his head. So powerful was my stroke, that I found to my dismay that I could not get the weapon out of his head again. While I was in this extraordinary situation – standing on the back of an enormous alligator, and tugging at my tomahawk embedded in its head – Yamba came rushing up the path, carrying one of the paddles, which, without a moment's hesitation, she thrust down the alligator's throat as he turned to snap at her. In this way the monster was prevented from moving his head either backward or forward, and then, drawing my stiletto I blinded him in both eyes, afterwards finishing him leisurely with my tomahawk, when at length I managed to release it. Yamba was enormously proud of me after this achievement, and when we returned to the mainland she gave her tribesmen a graphic account of my gallantry and bravery. After the encounter with the alligator, they looked upon me as a very great and powerful personage indeed.'

Great and powerful, however, as was M. de Rougemont, he decided that it was, by now, time that he should shine once more in the outer world, and as he had given up hope of being rescued by any passing ship, he decided to make a journey overland, acompanied by the faithful Yamba. With him he took, not only Yamba, but a 'native passport – a kind of masonic mystic stick, inscribed with certain cabalistic characters. Every chief carried one of these sticks, stuck through his nose. I, however, invariably carried the passport in my long luxuriant hair, which I wore "bun" fashion, held in a net of opossum hair. This passport stick proved invaluable as a means of putting us on good terms with the different tribes we encountered.'

Here the Editor of the *Wide World Magazine*, stirred to the foundation of his being by the events narrated by M. de Rougemont and by those which followed, explains that 'The publication of the preceding instalments have, we may say, caused some truly amazing developments of the story, people having turned up here long since believed to be dead. We cannot say much about these developments, but we earnestly advise our readers to follow the story with the closest interest. Arrangements are already being made for its translation into several European languages from Spain to Sweden. M. de Rougemont begs his hundreds of thousands of friends not to think him discourteous if he is at present obliged, through pressure of work, to decline all social engagements, lectures, arrangements, etc.'

And now, quietly and soberly, the idealistic M. de Rougemont gives us the most amazing instance of the devotion of Woman, 'before it was corrupted and turned selfish by civilization'. For M. de Rougemont, attacked by malarial fever in its most terrible form, and nursed night and day by Yamba, when he came round a little, fancied he noticed a great change in Yamba. 'I asked her if anything had occurred to her during my illness. I then learned something which will haunt me to my dying day. There is perhaps no more extraordinary instance of womanly devotion recorded in the annals of the human race. To my unspeakable horror, Yamba quietly told me that she had recently given birth to a child, *which she had killed and eaten*. It took me some time to realize a thing so ghastly and so horrible, and when I asked why she had done it, she pleaded: "I was afraid that you were going to die – going to leave me; and besides, you know that I could not have nursed both you and the baby, so I did what I considered best." She saw I was perfectly horror-struck, but she altogether failed to understand my point of view. For a long time after this incident, however, Yamba carried a little parcel in bark round her neck, and this she appeared to treasure very much.

'One day when I had recovered, she told me that the little packet contained some of the small bones of the infant, which she was preserving out of love for its memory.'

I do not think it is possible to deny that, from a man's point of view, Yamba was the Ideal Woman, combining as she did in one person the virtues of an overwhelming understanding of the importance of man, strong practical common sense, and mother love.

However, to continue our narrative, M. de Rougemont now underwent a most remarkable and efficacious cure for the chilly feeling by which he was beset as a result of his illness. Having killed a big bull, 'I determined to test the efficacy of a very popular native remedy for fever – for shivering fits still continued to come upon me at most abnormal times – usually late in the day. No matter how much grass poor Yamba brought me, I never could get warm, and so now I thought I would try some animal heat.

'Scarce had the life left the body before I ripped the buffalo open between the fore and hind legs, and then crawled into the interior, fairly burying myself in a deluge of warm blood and intestines. My head, however, was protruding from the animal's chest. Yamba understood perfectly well what I was doing, and when I told her I was going to indulge in a long sleep in my curious resting-place, she said she would keep watch, and see that I was not disturbed. I remained buried in the bull's interior for the rest of the day, and all during the night. Next morning, to my amazement, I found I was a prisoner, the carcass having got cold and frigid, so that I had literally to be dug out. As I emerged I presented a most ghastly and horrifying spectacle. My body was covered with congealed blood, and even my long hair was all matted and stiffened with it. But never can I forget the feeling of exhilaration and strength that took possession of me as I stood there looking at my faithful companion. *I was absolutely cured* – a new man, a giant of strength.'

Alas, this story, and others, equally remarkable, proved too much for certain members of the public, and these persons (as I think, very unkindly) set about exposing this poor harmless creature, who had injured nobody, and whose worst crime was that he had given a little innocent amusement to others, brought a little harmless romance into his own threadbare life. Letter after letter appeared in the *Daily Chronicle* challenging the Cannibal Chief to prove the truth of his statements, to appear in person. Naïvely and courageously, he agreed to appear at the offices of the *Daily Chronicle* in order that he might be asked questions, and his persecutors were surprised to see 'an elderly man, slightly built, with a tanned, wrinkled face, the upper part of which bore obvious signs of marked intellectual power. In a pleasant, cultured voice, he gave such ready replies to the questions that were put to him that his examiners were disconcerted.' This, too, was the fate of those persons who baited him at public lectures.

But the *Daily Chronicle* was determined on his ruin, and, after having made the most exhaustive inquiries, it published the true story of poor M. de Rougemont's uneventful threadbare life.

He had never been a cannibal chief, though he had, once, risen to the position of being butler to a Lady Robinson in Australia. His real name was not de Rougemont, but Grin; he was a native of Switzerland, and had once been footman and courier to Fanny Kemble. In the early seventies, he led a wandering life in Australia, and then, in 1898, enlivened our shores with his presence. The Library of the British Museum may, or may not, have inspired in him the desire to be known as a cannibal chief, for it is certain that he spent many weeks in that haunt of learning before appearing in the presence of the awestruck Editor of the *Wide World Magazine* in the character of M. Louis de Rougemont. I am glad to think that he enjoyed fame and prosperity, even for such a short time, but his subsequent fate is cruel and undeserved. Sis Osbert Sitwell, in his preface to the book from which I have culled this narrative, tells us that 'the writer remembers so well and for so many years seeing a tall bearded figure, lank and stooping, selling matches in Shaftesbury Avenue or Piccadilly. This ghost of the streets was dressed in an old ragged overcoat, over the top of which the thin hair fell, and showed above it a calm, philosophical, curiously intelligent face.' He was told repeatedly that this man was Louis de Rougemont. Whether this information was accurate or not, certainly with the reported death of the explorer or impostor, whichever he was, this sad thoughtful spectre withdrew itself from the haunting of a busy world.

I wonder if the persecutors of this harmless creature ever passed the man they had so wantonly ruined, and, if so, if they felt ashamed before that mild and uncomplaining gaze.

10

Charles Waterton: The South American Wanderer

ON sunny days in the year 1862, an octogenarian of acute and alarming agility might have been seen climbing 'like an adolescent gorilla', as Mr Norman Douglas very rightly remarks, into the topmost branches of an oak in the Park of Walton Hall, in order to observe the habits of some bird of retiring nature.

Below the tree, Mrs Bennet, the Rumpless Fowl, disported herself, cackling and squawking, Dr Hobson, Squire Waterton's friend, watched the branches of the tree with anxiety, and in the grotto beyond the lake all was joy, all was innocent mirth, and occasional sounds of song and dance and gay laughter floated on the breeze, for the inmates of the local lunatic asylum were holding a dinner-party and conversazione in the grotto by the invitation of the Squire.

But the care-worn Dr Hobson paid no attention to the sounds arising from these social amenities, but remained, with upturned eyes and clasped hands, waiting for his aged friend to fall from the branches. The great naturalist and South American Wanderer did nothing of the kind, but continued climbing higher and higher.

Mr Waterton saw nothing extraordinary in these gymnastics, for, as Father J. Wood tells us in the Biography which prefaces the *Wanderings in South America*, 'He had no idea that he was doing anything out of the general course of things if he asked a visitor to accompany him to the top of a lofty tree to look at a hawk's nest, or if he built his stables so that the horses might converse with each other, or his kennel so that his hounds should be able to see what was going on.'

Dr Hobson's experiences with the agility of Mr Waterton were, to say the least of them, alarming. 'His remarkable suppleness of limb', we are told, 'and elasticity of muscle, I have often seen marvellously and most amazingly displayed in his eighty-first year, by a variety of physical contortions. When Mr Waterton was seventy-seven years of age, I was witness to his scratching the back part of his head with the big toe of his right foot. He knew no fear.' And again: 'I have frequently, in painful suspense and much against my own inclinations seen the Squire, when beyond seventy years of age, hop on one leg along the brink of a rock forming the highest terrace in the grotto, whilst the other leg was dangling over the chasm below: and, when thus hopping at a rapid rate, he would return again by hopping on the contrary leg. On my cautioning him, he would reply: *"Non de ponte cadit qui cum sapientia vadit"* – "He falls not from the bridge who walks with prudence." '

Perhaps as a result of her mother watching the Squire performing these gymnastics, a duck was hatched on the estate with her head reversed, and her bill pointed out, 'and, indeed, immediately situated above' the elegant feathers of her tail; so that whenever food was placed upon the ground, she must turn a somersault before seizing it. This remarkable bird had no webs between her toes, but by dint of using her intelligence, swam as well as, or better than, the rest of the brood. She aroused the liveliest feelings of admiration in the heart of the Squire.

Reflecting on Mr Waterton's habits and tastes, it is a little difficult to know why he refused the request of M. Blondin to be allowed to exercise his gifts on a tight-rope over the lake at Walton Hall.

For the pranks of Mr Waterton were as unexpected as

they were endless. Dr Hobson tells us that 'To show the playful levity of my octogenarian friend, I may mention a circumstance which occurred without a moment's warning [*sic*] of a very unexpected nature. In the north-east corner of the first entrance hall of the mansion stood a table, on which to place the hats and greatcoats, gloves, etc., of arriving visitors, which was covered by a large cloth, hanging down to the floor. On seeing me drive up to the bridge in front of the house, the Squire has more than once secretly crept on all fours like a dog under the table, waiting in order that I might place my greatcoat upon this table; and whilst I was thus unsuspiciously engaged, he has, in his private retreat, commenced to growl like a savage dog behind the cloth, and has seized my legs in such a practically canine manner that I really had no idea at the time but that some fierce dog was attacking my lower extremities.'

At last, after his legs had experienced the sharpness of the aged Squire Waterton's teeth on several occasions, Dr Hobson thought it better to 'drop a hint of the fortuitous hazard incurred, stating that many instances were recorded, on undoubted authority, where even permanent aberration of the mind had been the result of such a sudden and unexpected shock to the nervous system'. Overcome with remorse at this revelation of the risk that had been run, Mr Waterton promised not to bite his friend's legs again, and Dr Hobson's reason remained unimpaired. In future, the Squire welcomed Dr Hobson by 'dancing down the whole length of the broad flagged walk, and from time to time (even when the snow lay deep upon the ground) throwing one of his loose slippers from his foot high up in the air above his head and expertly catching it in his hand in its descent. . . . The wetness of the flags underfoot,' we are told, 'or a shower overhead, never constituted any impediment to an exploit of this character.'

Nor was this the only exploit of the South American Wanderer, now that old age had confined him to his native land. For his anxious and much-harassed friend tells us that 'Mr Waterton had considerable inventive genius, especially in the actual formation of supposed extinct animals, generally of a most horrid form and appearance, by a skilful union of separate portions of reptiles.' By the way, his inventive powers had nearly brought this experimental ingenuity to a fatal issue, for it seems that Mr Waterton had, for some time, conceived the idea that 'the art of flying was within his grasp, and that he would, in a short time, become a second Pegasus'. Under 'this surprisingly delusive impression', as Doctor Hobson tells us, not without a certain gloom, the Squire had constructed 'duplicates of a peculiar character of mechanism, as substitutes for natural wings', which he proposed to fix to each arm, although, as Dr Hobson adds, 'How the Squire proposed to dispose of his lower extremities he did not explain to me, but I remember he stated that a man's legs, however symmetrically formed, were inconveniently long and heavy for an atmospheric trip, unless they could have something more sustaining than air on which to rest.' In fact, the only time when the Squire had ever found his legs unwieldy, and unmanageable – so he informed his friend – was when he was about to fly.

At last, the wings were brought to perfection, and this spirited old gentleman, having fixed them to his shoulders, climbed to the roof of an outhouse, and was about to soar into the air when Dr Hobson arrived at the scene of action and, by dint of many and most urgent entreaties, induced the second Pegasus to return to earth in a less sudden manner.

Mr Waterton's exploits were performed, indeed, in every country he visited. For instance, on one occasion when in Rome, Mr Waterton climbed up the angel surmounting the Castle of Sant-Angelo and, having reached that remark-able eminence, persisted in standing on one foot upon its head, in 'a position', as Mr Norman Douglas points out, 'that would have made any self-respecting chamois seasick'. And he adds, 'All Rome rings with the exploit, even the Pope becomes interested in the mad son of Albion.'

His exploits were countless, and nobody understood the fun and oddity of these better than their performer. Amongst the most striking was the episode of the sprained ankle. Mr Waterton, whilst in the United States, was so unfortunate as to meet with this accident, and being extremely annoyed by the inquiries of other less-adventurous gentlemen, staying in the hotel, as to the progress of his 'gout', he remembered that in the past, when his ankle had been badly sprained, a doctor had ordered him to hold it under the pump two or three times a day. It struck him therefore that it might be a kind of super-cure if he held his ankle under the Niagara Falls.

'As I held my leg under the Fall,' he tells us, 'I tried to meditate on the immense difference there was betwixt a house pump and this tremendous cascade of nature, and what effect it might have upon the sprain; but the magni-tude of the subject was too overwhelming, and I was obliged to drop it.'

Nobody could foretell what form the next pranks would take. Fortuitous hazards, indeed, were run by all visitors to the Squire, for if their legs were not bitten their nerves might be broken at any moment, as I have hinted, by com-ing into contact, on a dark landing or in a dark corridor, with some appalling-looking reptile or huge beast of prim-eval appearance, which had been concocted by the Wanderer from a variety of creatures, and bore a label with the name of some famous Protestant or another. A huge bust for instance, formed from the head and skin of an enormous ape, but bearing the smooth unfurrowed brow of Man, stood on the staircase of Walton Hall. 'There was an union of a variety of knowledge,' says his biographer, 'which enabled Mr Waterton to produce a prodigy of apparent nature, and when I observed, "How could you dream of such an idea as to turn the monkey into man," he replied: "I fear you do not indulge in the scientific and progressive ideas of the day. Are you not aware that it is the present fashionable thing that monkeys are shortly to step into our shoes? I have merely foreshadowed future ages or signalized a coming event by giving to the tribe a human formation of face, and to this face an expression of intellectuality, since I daresay there are in the medley of humanity a few here and there who would consider that a fair exchange would be no robbery." '

Life at Walton Hall was full of surprises, and it need hardly be said that the Squire's daily round was planned on lines entirely different to that of anybody else. He never slept in a bed, for instance, but on the floor, wrapped in his cloak, and with a block of beech-wood for a pillow. He rose at 3.30, and after lighting his fire, spent half an hour in the chapel, and then began his day's work. He detested smart young gentlemen, whom he christened 'Miss Nancies' and 'Man milliners', but, beyond these, loved all human creatures.

He cherished a great friendship, for instance, with a young lady chimpanzee, who, in her caged condition, suffered from ill health. The Wanderer visited her daily and, on leaving, invariably imprinted a gallant kiss upon her cheek.

As for owls, the twenty-seventh lord of Walton Hall once journeyed from Italy to England with cages filled with these; and, having succeeded in passing his friends through the not unnaturally astonished Custom House of Genoa, he decided that as a bath was necessary to him it was necessary also to the owls. Alas, the bath was not a success, and many of the owls died.

This sweet and lovable nature was not easily disturbed or made angry; but on one occasion Dr Hobson found him in a state of excited anger and distress, because one of God's creatures had been despised. 'Yes,' he exclaimed, 'I am grieved to the backbone; Mr — whom you would just now meet in the carriage road and who proposes to be enchanted and in raptures with the works of God's creation, has just left the house; and – what do you think – he coolly turned up his nose at my Bahia toad, calling it an ugly brute.

'That a gentleman, avowing himself a lover of natural history, and pretending an anxiety to work in the same vineyard with me, should profanely designate one of God's creatures "an ugly brute", was enough to put me out for a week, so I left him in the staircase to his own cogitations.'

Indeed, the holy mind and heart of this man could see nothing ugly, nothing repulsive, in any of the works of God – excepting, of course, in the unfortunate Hanoverian Rat, a quadruped which I am shocked to say he persecuted unremittingly. The great naturalist would pick up, fondle, and admire that poor, harmless, and despised creature the toad, speaking to it gently, smoothing its head, with a sort of loving delight; he would 'expatiate in evident pleasure' on the beauty, the depth, the brilliance of its eyes, on its usefulness to man in destroying insects – in spite of man's ingratitude. He would speak gently of the harmlessness of one that has been so persecuted, and would dwell, with delight, on its form, its colour, as though that despised creature were an object of interest and admiration, although, as Dr Hobson tells us, 'he had no friend to support him'.

There was in fact no living creature – excepting, as I have said, the Hanoverian Rat – to which he did not extend love and pity. The Sloth, for instance, which to the casual observer might lack charm, called forth from Mr Waterton the following beautiful and moving passages in the history of his South American wanderings:

'His looks, his gestures, and his cries, all conspire to entreat you to take pity on him. These are the only weapons of defence which nature hath given him. While other animals assemble in herds, or range in pairs through these boundless wilds, the sloth is solitary, and almost stationary. He cannot escape from you. It is said that his piteous moans make the tiger relent and turn out of the way. Do not then level your gun at him, or pierce him with a poisoned arrow, he has never hurt one living creature. A few leaves, and those of the commonest and coarsest kind, are all that he asks for his support. On comparing him with other animals you would say that you could perceive deficiency, deformity, and superabundance in his composition. He has no cutting teeth and, though he has four stomachs, he still wants the long intestines of ruminating animals. He has only one inferior aperture, as in birds. He has no soles to his feet, nor has he the power of moving his toes separately. His hair is flat, and puts you in mind of grass withered by the wintry blast. His legs are too short; they appear deformed by the manner in which they are joined to the body; and when he is on the ground they seem as if only calculated to be of use in climbing trees. He has forty-six ribs, while the elephant has but forty, and his claws are disproportionately long. Were you to mark, upon a graduated scale, the different claims to superiority amongst the four-footed animals, this poor ill-formed creature's claim would be the last upon the lowest degree.'

Then comes this paragraph, more beautiful still in its love and understanding: 'He appears to us so forlorn and miserable, so ill put together is he, and so unfit to enjoy the blessings which have been so bountifully given to the rest of animated nature – for as it has formerly been remarked, he has no soles to his feet, and he is evidently ill at ease when he tries to move upon the ground. It is then that he looks up in your face with a countenance that says "Have pity on me, for I am in pain and sorrow." Indeed, his looks and his gestures betray his uncomfortable situation, and, as a sigh every now and then escapes him, we may be entitled to conclude that he is actually in pain.'

Mr Waterton once kept a Sloth in his room for months, and this forlorn and unhappy creature seems to have returned his affection. He would place himself in a position of the most comfort that was possible to him, and, after getting all his legs in a line on the back of a chair, would hang there for hours, and 'often, with a low and inward cry' would seem to invite his friend to take notice of him.

At moments, however, Mr Waterton's sympathy and admiration led him into dangerous paths, as when, for instance, whilst travelling in South America, he was much struck with the habits and appearance of the Vampire Bat, and defended that volatile being against the charge of living entirely on blood. 'When the moon shone bright', he tells us, 'and the fruit of the banana tree was ripe, I could see him approach and eat it. . . . There was something, also, in the blossom of the sawarri nut tree which was grateful to him.' Mr Waterton was, however, in spite of this sympathy, obliged to confess that 'The Vampire has a curious membrane which rises from the nose, and gives him a very curious appearance!'

Undeterred by this very curious appearance, Mr Waterton was seized by a strong wish to have his big toe sucked by the Vampire Bat, just once, so that he could say that this adventure had befallen him. Night after night, therefore, he slept with his foot out of the hammock, but all was in vain, for the Vampire, in spite of the fact that he shared a bedroom, or rather loft, with his admirer for some months, never came near him, but, presumably out of obstinacy, preferred the big toe of a neighbouring Indian. This, the Wanderer adds, with a sort of gentle pique, 'seemed to have all the attractions'.

In spite of this setback Mr Waterton did not cease to admire the Vampire Bat, nor did any slight disadvantages possessed by the Vulture and the Carrion Crow detract from his admiration of those bipeds. 'The head and neck of the King of the Vultures', he exclaims in a kind of ecstasy, 'are bare of feathers, but the beautiful appearance they exhibit fades in death. The throat and the back of the neck are of a fine lemon; both sides of the neck, from the ears downwards, of a rich scarlet; behind the corrugated part there is a white spot, the crown of the head is scarlet, betwixt the lower mandible and the eye, and close to the ear, there is a point which has a fine silvery-blue appearance. . . . The bag of the stomach, which is only seen when distended with food, is of a most delicate white, intersected with blue veins, which appear on it just like the blue veins on the arm of a fair-complexioned person. The tail and long feathers are black, the belly white, and the rest of the body a fine satin colour. Kind Providence has conferred a blessing on hot countries in giving them the Vulture.' As for the Carrion Crow: 'This warrior bird is always held up to public execration. The very word carrion, attached to his name, carries something disgusting with it, and no one ever shows him any kindness, though he certainly has his vices – still, he has his virtues too.' And Mr Waterton hastens to assure us that 'the Carrion Crow is a very early riser'.

The Orang-utang, too was a subject of constant interest and affection to Mr Waterton and, on one occasion at least, this cousin of Man seems to have returned these feelings. The occasion was in the year 1861, when Mr Waterton, watched

by a large crowd, and warned by the keepers of the Zoological Gardens, all of whom assured him that his host would
'make short work of him' since he had just been teased by
some impudent boys, entered the cage of an enormous
Orang-utang whose reputation for savagery was remarkable and unsurpassed. This visit was paid against the wish
of the curator of the Zoological Gardens, but, to the surprise
of everybody excepting Mr Waterton, the meeting gave host
and guest an equal pleasure. Indeed, Dr Hobson assures us,
'the meeting of those two celebrities was clearly a case of love
at first sight, as the strangers not only embraced each other
most affectionately, but positively hugged each other and,
in their apparently uncontrollable joy, kissed one another
many times'.

Mr Waterton had paid this visit in the hope of being allowed to inspect the palm of his host's hand in life, instead of
in death, and to examine the teeth of his newly found friend
at close quarters. Both of these investigations, we are told,
'were conceded to the Squire without a moment's murmur',
and Mr Waterton was allowed to cram his hand into the
Orang-utang's mouth. This ceremony being over, the Orang-
utang thought it would only be courtesy in he returned the
compliment, and he bent, with furrowed brow, over his
guest's head and felt Mr Waterton's teeth with great
thoroughness. Having done this, he 'went over' Mr Waterton's face, and ended up by sitting down and subjecting Mr
Waterton's hair to 'a careful and even examination, or
probably I ought to say, an elaborate search'.

But Mr Waterton's adventures, and the perpetual strange-
ness by which he was surrounded, even when, as a result of
his marriage and the birth of his son, he had returned from
his wanderings – these were endless, and the tribute paid by
Mr Norman Douglas, in *Experiments*, to Dr Hobson's *Life
of Charles Waterton*, is well deserved. As Mr Douglas very

justly remarks: 'The Table of Contents alone of this re-markable book is a joy for ever. It contains items like this: "An Ox-Eye Titmouse builds her nest in the Trunk of a Tree prepared for Owls, but declines occupying it in future years because a Squirrel had used it. On the Discriminating Courage of the Squire with an Orang-utang from Borneo, in the Zoological Gardens" – followed by: "The Ape Searching the Squire's head reminds him of a Cambridge anecdote". Or take these stimulating entries: "An Allusion to a stench from a dead herring near the Grotto induced the Squire to relate an incident regarding dead letters". "Mr Waterton faces a snowstorm without his Hat, and throws his Slippers over his head when approaching his eightieth year". "Mr Waterton distressed because his Bahia toad was called an 'Ugly Brute'".'

To these headings, chosen with so much wisdom by Mr Douglas, I would add: 'Perverted Judgement as regards the Destruction of Birds', 'Special Immunity in the Female Sex from Death by Lightning', 'The Author suspects that the Squire had a foreknowledge of the trees' suicidal termination when he trained them', 'Mr Waterton's opinion of the ac-cusation against the Carrion Crow of sucking the Eggs of other Birds, with Evidence somewhat mitigating the Charge', 'Capricious Freak of a Duck, by building her nest in an Oak Tree, twelve feet from the ground', 'The majestic Figure and singularly striking Peculiarities of the Heron', 'Monogamy of a Common Goose', and 'Mr Waterton not always discreet in the use of Animal Food, when The Pad-lock was removed from his Grinders by the Pope'.

These are only a few of the delights held out to us by Dr Hobson's reminiscences of his friend.

The great naturalist and traveller made four journeys to the New World in search of adventure, and in order to find the woorali poison, which was one of the chief interests of his existence. In 1812, the date of his first journey, he found that the region had undergone but little change since the time of Raleigh. Knowing that the towers of El Dorado were but castles in the air, he wished to know if Lake Panina were a myth.

It was during these wanderings that Mr Waterton took a ride upon a crocodile, and, in his anxiety to study the dental arrangements of the serpent, shared his bedroom for one night with a Coulacanara, 'fourteen feet long, not poisonous, but large enough to have crushed one of us to death. A Coulacanara of fourteeen feet in length is as thick as a common boa of twenty-four,' as Mr Waterton remarked drily.

The capture of Mr Waterton's room-mate was as dangerous as anything that could be imagined, for the serpent had to be dug out of his home; the accompanying Negroes were in a state of abject terror, and even Mr Waterton, brave as he was, acknowledged that his 'own heart, in spite of all I could do, beat quicker than usual; and I felt those sensations which one has on board a merchant vessel in wartime; when the Captain orders all hands on deck to prepare for action, while a strange vessel is coming down upon us under suspicious colours'.

The description of the capture is exciting in the extreme. 'On pinning him to the ground with the lance, he gave a tremendous loud hiss, and the little dog ran away howling as he went.' The fight was long and furious; in the end, Mr Waterton and a few Negroes, pale grey from fear, sat on the serpent's tail. Then Mr Waterton had a brilliant idea: 'I contrived to unloose my braces, and with them tied up the snake's mouth.' On the way back to the encampment, the serpent fought furiously and ceaselessly, but Mr Waterton and the Negroes won the battle, and the serpent spent the night imprisoned in a huge sack in Mr Waterton's bedroom. 'I cannot say he allowed me to have a quiet night,' the Wanderer tells us; 'My hammock was in a loft just above him, and the floor between us half gone to decay, so that in parts of it no boards intervened between his lodging-room and mine. He was very restless and fretful and, had Medusa been my wife, there could not have been more continued and disagreeable hissing in the bedchamber that night.'

I am grieved to say that at dawn Mr Waterton cut the serpent's throat, to the accompaniment of sympathetic sounds from the Negroes whose aid had been invoked. It was then found that the teeth were a disappointment, for 'they were all bent like tenterhooks, pointing down his throat, and not so large or strong as I expected to have found them'.

Mr Waterton's ride on a crocodile was an equally remarkable feat, and I expect that the irrationality of the idea must have given the Wanderer considerable pleasure, for he was never so happy as when performing the unexpected. The story of the exploit must be told in his own words: 'The people pulled the cayman (or crocodile) to the surface; he plunged furiously as soon as he arrived at these upper regions, and immediately went below again on their slackening the rope. I saw enough not to fall in love at first sight. I now told them we would run all risks and have him on land immediately. They pulled again, and out he came. *"Monstrum, horrendum, informe."* This was an interesting moment. I kept my position firmly with my eye fixed steadfast on him.

'By this time the cayman was within two yards of me. I saw he was in a state of fear and perturbation. I instantly dropped the mast, sprang up, and jumped on his back, turning half round as I vaulted, so that I gained my seat in a right position. I immediately seized his forelegs, and, by main force, twisted them on his back, where they served me for a bridle.

'He now seemed to have recovered from his surprise, and,

probably fancying himself in hostile company, he began to plunge furiously, and lashed the sand with his long and powerful tail. I was out of reach of the strokes of it, by being near his head. He continued to plunge and strike, and made my seat very uncomfortable. It must have been a fine sight for an unoccupied spectator.

'The people roared out in triumph and were so vociferous that it was some time before they heard me tell them to pull me and my beast of burden further inland. I was apprehensive the rope might break, and then there would have been every chance of going down to the regions under the water with the cayman. That would have been more perilous than Arion's morning ride:

' "*Delphini insidens vada caerula sulcat Arion*".

'The people now dragged us above forty yards on the sand; it was the first and last time I was ever on a cayman's back. Should it be asked, how I managed to keep my seat, I would answer, I hunted some years with Lord Darlington's foxhounds.'

Mr Waterton, I may say at this point, was more merciful to a little half-grown, ill-conditioned bug, met in the course of his wanderings, than he had been to either serpent or cayman, though it is doubtful whether the bug's eventual hosts were grateful for this exhibition of mercy.

This small and enterprising creature made its presence felt on Mr Waterton's neck whilst he was travelling down the St Lawrence River in a steamboat, and Mr Waterton felt it would be a shame to kill it, so, very considerately, he threw it amongst some luggage belonging to another passenger, and recommended it to get ashore at the first opportunity.

As for the woorali poison, that much-cherished, much-sought-for treasure, it is satisfactory to know that Mr Waterton did meet with it at last, and that he bore it home in triumph to England. He claimed that it would cure hydrophobia – I do not know for what reason – and his experiments with the treasured woorali were as fantastic as any of his other exploits. On one occasion, he and his friend Mr Higginbotham, the eminent surgeon of Nottingham, poisoned a donkey, not very charitably, as I think, with the beloved but feared woorali, producing apparent death. Then, with a lancet, they made an incision in the long-suffering quadruped's windpipe, producing artificial respiration. Life returned, the donkey rose, Mr Waterton rode round the room upon its back, and it was for many years afterwards a pensioner on the estate at Walton Hall.

Mr Waterton's letters are a great delight, and bear the strongest personal flavour of that charm, goodness, and fantastic gaiety which made him so remarkable.

For instance, writing from Scarborough in November, 1854, he gives us a glimpse of his attitude towards Commerce and the Gunpowder Plot:

'My dear Sir – We have received your last communication with great pleasure, and read it with contented smiles. Having now taken our last dip in Neptune's briny wash-tub, nothing remains but to square accounts between ourselves and good Mrs Peacock, of Cliff No. 1, which we always arrange satisfactorily on both sides.

'Tomorrow morning we shall leave Scarboro' with a sigh, and journey on to those gloomy regions, where volumes of Stygian smoke poison a once wholesome atmosphere; and where filthy drainage from hells upon earth is allowed by law, for the sacred rights of modern trade, to pollute the waters in every river far and near. Tomorrow being our great detonating festival, I shall have a leisure hour to ruminate on the dreadful consequence of old Guy's atrocity, had he succeeded in blowing to atoms a few dozens of miscreants who ought to have been hanged for their crimes against heaven and earth.'

Here, too, is another full-flavoured letter:

'My dear Sir – Last Saturday night I sang "Cease rude Boreas, blustering wild" and called most lustily upon that frigid god to relax his terrors and thus afford to our dear Doctor Hobson a safe highway from Leeds to Walton Hall. I have just been saying, that I was in possession of a bait to coax you down here. We have two fine cormorants, which daily swim on the lake within a stone's throw of the drawing-room windows, and I know that you would rather gaze on a cormorant in such a position than come to enjoy all the good things we can offer you for dinner; hence, I offer my tempting bait. We have also, just now, great numbers of widgeon and some grebe and teal. *"Hoc scripsi, non otii abundantio, sed amoris erga te."* I have written this, not from having an abundance of leisure, but of love for you.

'Ever sincerely,
'CHARLES WATERTON.'

But indeed, the exploits, the adventures of this chivalrous, wise, loving and gay saint were so many, and his bravery so extraordinary, that it is impossible to do justice to them in the space at my command. Thackeray, in *The Newcomes*, writes of that saintliness which must have irradiated all who knew this beautiful character. 'A friend who belongs to the old religion took me, last week, into a church where the Virgin lately appeared to a Jewish gentleman, flashed down upon him from heaven in light and splendour celestial, and of course, straightway, converted him. My friend made me look at the picture, and, kneeling down beside me, I know prayed with all his honest heart that the truth might shine down upon me, too. But I saw no glimpse of heaven at all, I saw but a poor picture, an altar with blinking candles, a church hung with tawdry strips of red and white calico. The good kind W. went away, humbly saying that such might have happened again if heaven so willed it. I could not but feel a kindness and admiration for the good man. I know that his works are made to square with his faith, that he dines on a crust, lives as chastely as a hermit, and gives his all to the poor.'

Saintliness came to him as a heritage, for through his grandmother he was ninth in descent from Sir Thomas More, and numbered amongst his other ancestors Saint Matilda Queen of Germany, Saint Margaret Queen of Scotland, Saint Humbert of Savoy, Saint Louis of France, Saint Vladimir of Russia, and Saint Anne of Russia.

His life was one long record of saintliness, faithful love to the young and lovely girl of seventeen who was his wife, and who died after only a year of marriage, leaving him broken-hearted – a long record of high ideals, the maddest tricks and escapades, and of hair-raising adventure. Who but Mr Waterton, for instance, could have survived the Black Vomit, in the Plague of Malaga, of which he gives an account, which to me at least is more terrible than Defoe's history of the Plague of London. I give it in its entirety, for it shows that Charles Waterton was, at his best, a great writer.

'There began', he wrote, 'to be reports spread up and down the city that the black vomit had made its appearance; and every succeeding day brought testimony that things were not as they ought to be. I myself, in an alley, near my uncle's house, saw a mattress of most suspicious appearance hung out to dry. A Maltese Captain, who had dined with us in good health at one o'clock, lay dead in his cabin before sunrise the next morning. A few days after this I was seized with vomiting and fever during the night. I had the most dreadful spasms, and it was supposed that I could not last out till noon the next day. However, my strength of constitution got me through it. In 3 weeks more, multitudes were seen to leave the city, which shortly after this was declared to be in a state of pestilence. Some apprised that the disorder had come from the Levant; others said that it had been imported from the Havana; but I think it probable that nobody could tell in what quarter it had originated.

'We had now all retired to the country house on my eldest uncle's estate. Returning to Malaga, from time to time, according as the pressure of business demanded his presence in the city, he left us on Sunday evening, and said that he would be back again some time on Monday; but that was my poor uncle's last day's ride. On arriving at his house in Malaga, there was a messenger waiting to inform him that Father Bustamente had fallen sick, and wished to see him. Father Bustamente was an aged priest, who had been particularly kind to my uncle on his first arrival in Malaga. My uncle went immediately to Father Bustamente, gave him every consolation in his power, and then returned to his own house very unwell, there to die a martyr to his charity. Father Bustamente breathed his last before daylight; my uncle took to his bed and never rose more. As soon as we had received information of his sickness I immediately set out on foot for the city. His friend Mr Power, now of Gibraltar, was already in his room doing everything that friendship could suggest or prudence dictate. My uncle's athletic constitution bore up against the disease much longer than we thought it possible. He struggled with it for 5 days, and sank at last about the hour of sunset. He stood 6 feet 7 in. high, and was of so kind and generous a disposition, that he was beloved by all who knew him. Many a Spanish tear flowed when it was known that he had ceased to be. We got him a kind of coffin made, in which he was conveyed at midnight to the outskirts of the town, there to be put into one of the pits which the galley slaves had dug during the day for the reception of the dead. But they could not spare room for the coffin; so the body was taken out of it, and thrown upon the heap which already occupied the pit. A Spanish marquis lay just below him.

'Thousands died as though they had been seized with the black vomit, and others of decided yellow fever. There were a few who departed this life with very little pain or bad symptoms; they felt unwell, they went to bed, they had an idea that they would not get better – and they expired in a kind of slumber. It was sad in the extreme to see the bodies placed in the streets at the close of day, to be ready for the dead carts as they passed along.

' *"Plurima perque vias sternuntur mortua passim Corpora."*

'The dogs howled fearfully during the night. All was gloom and horror in every street; and you might see the vultures on the strand tugging at the bodies which were washed ashore by the eastern wind. It was said that 50,000 people left the city at the commencement of the pestilence; and that 14,000 of those who remained in it fell victims to the disease.

'There was an intrigue going on at court, for the interest of certain powerful people to keep the port of Malaga closed long after the city had been declared free from the disorder; so that none of the vessels in the mole could obtain permission to depart for their destination.

'In the meantime, the city was shaken with earthquakes, shock succeeding shock, till we all imagined that a catastrophe awaited us similar to that which had taken place at Lisbon. The pestilence killed you by degrees; and the approaches were sufficiently slow, in general, to enable you to submit to it with firmness and resignation. But the idea of being swallowed up alive by the yawning earth at a moment's notice made you sick at heart, and rendered you almost fearful of your own shadow. The first shock took place at six in the evening, with a noise as though a thousand carriages had dashed against each other. This terrified many people to such a degree that they paced all night long up and down the Alamada, or up the walks, rather than retire to their houses.'

This was Charles Waterton's earliest and most terrible adventure. The whole life of this noble, brave, and beloved old man was the life of a denizen of another planet.

He was a great gentleman, one of a long race of untitled nobles, and showed the pride and splendour of his race in every action of his long life. He comes into this book because his very bravery is born of such an irrepressible sense of fun that it is impossible to exclude him. He was an eccentric only as all great gentlemen are eccentric, by which I mean that their gestures are not born to fit the conventions or the cowardice of the crowd. His biographer, Father J. Wood, says, very rightly: 'It was perhaps eccentric to have a strong religious faith, and act up to it. It was eccentric, as Thackeray said, to "dine on a crust, live as cheaply as a hermit, and give his all to the poor". It was eccentric to come into a large estate as a young man, and to have come to extreme old age without having wasted an hour or a shilling. It was eccentric to give bountifully and never allow his name to appear in a subscription list. It was eccentric to be saturated with the love of nature. It might be eccentric never to give dinner-parties, preferring to keep an open house for his friends; but it was a very agreeable kind of eccentricity. It was eccentric to be childlike, but never childish. We might multiply instances of his eccentricity to any extent, and we may safely say that the world would be much better than it is if such eccentricity were more common.'

11

The God of this World

'THE news from St John Street', said Mercurius Fumingosus, published in 1654, 'is that the Turk danced so high in capering on the upper rope, discovered a myne of gold in the ayre, which hangs in an island right over Cheapside Cross, which gold, the old philosophers are of opinion, was attracted by the heat of the sun into a cloud, where it became sperme or seed of gold, which hath since engendered and become a mountain of gold, as big if not bigger than Highgate Hill, hanging about 35 miles in the sky.'

This can be but the partial history, since I cannot read the hearts of such men, of those who devoted their days to the service of gold. Some worshipped it alone, and lived for it like the alchemists, while others starved and died for it – like the misers.

The story of the alchemists is too well known to be repeated here, but this is a dimmed and rubbed-out portrait, with all the gold worn away, of one of the last of the alchemists. I found it among the portraits in Mr Timbs' book of English Eccentrics:

'The last true believer in alchemy was not Dr Price, but Peter Woulfe, the eminent chemist, and Fellow of the Royal Society, who made experiments to show the nature of mosaic gold,' Mr Brande says. 'It is to be regretted that no biographical memoir has been preserved of Woulfe. I have picked up a few anecdotes respecting him from two or three friends who were his acquaintances. He occupied chambers in Barnard's Inn, Holborn (the older buildings), while residing in London, and usually spent the summer in Paris. His rooms, which were extensive, were so filled with furnaces and apparatus that it was difficult to reach his fireside. A friend told me that he once put down his hat, and never could find it again, such was the confusion of boxes, packages, and parcels that lay about the chamber. His breakfast was at four in the morning; a few of his select friends were occasionally invited to this repast to whom a secret signal was given by which they gained entrance, knocking a certain number of times at the inner door of his apartment. He had long vainly searched for the Elixir, and attributed his repeated failures to the want of due preparation by pious and charitable acts. I understand that some of his apparatus is still extant, upon which are supplications for success and for the welfare of the adepts. Whenever he wished to break an acquaintance, or felt himself offended, he resented the supposed injury by sending a present to the offender, and never seeing him afterwards. These presents were sometimes of a curious description, and consisted usually of some expensive chemical product or preparation. He had an heroic remedy for illness – when he felt himself seriously indisposed, he took a place in the Edinburgh mail and, having reached that city, immediately came back in the returning coach to London.'

A cold taken in one of these expeditions terminated in inflammation of the lungs, of which Woulfe died in the year 1805. Of his last moments we received the following account from his executor, then Treasurer of Barnard's Inn. 'By Woulfe's desire, his laundress shut up his chambers, and left him, but returned at midnight, when Woulfe was still alive. Next morning, however, *she found him dead*. His countenance was calm and serene, and apparently he had not moved from the position in his chair in which she had last left him.'

Here come the old spiders running, spinning their webs behind their darkened windows, accumulating dirt for the giant dust-heap. Here comes horrible, mad John Ward of

Hackney, who, when in prison for committing forgery and for a mistake with respect to a name in a deed in which the interest of the Duchess of Buckingham was implicated (1727), 'amused himself by giving poison to dogs and cats and seeing them expire by slower or quicker torments'. A thin ragged paper is clutched in his bony hands, white like a fish's belly. The paper contains Mr Ward's prayer to the God he has made in his own image:

'O Lord ,Thou knowest that I have nine estates in the City of London; and likewise that I have lately purchased one estate in fee simple in the county of Essex; I beseech Thee to preserve the two counties of Middlesex and Essex from fire and earthquakes; and as I have a mortgage in Hertfordshire, I beg of Thee likewise to have an eye of compassion on that county; and for the rest of the counties Thou mayst deal with them as Thou art pleased. O Lord, enable the Bank to answer their bills, and make all my debtors good men. Give a prosperous voyage and return to the *Mermaid* ship, because I have insured it; and as Thou hast said the days of the wicked are but short, I trust in Thee, that Thou wilt not forget Thy promise, as I have purchased an estate in reversion, which will be mine on the death of that profligate young man, Sir J. L. Keep my friends from sinking, and preserve me from thieves and housebreakers, and make all my servants so honest and faithful that they may attend to my interests, and never cheat me out of my property, night or day.'

'The miser', said Cyrus Redding in his *Memoirs of Remarkable Misers*, 'is not a character to be seen in the noonday sun; he rather resembles his own accumulated hoards, abiding in the gloom that he creates around him, in the unsocial estate in which he vegetates rather than lives.'

One of the humbler of these unpleasant forms of vegetation, so sapless, so untouched by the sun, was the Reverend

Mr Jones, who was curate of Blewberry in Berkshire. This arid and joyless old person, who died at the age of eighty, wore for an everyday dress the same hat and coat throughout his curacy of forty-three years; after about thirty-five years, however, the brim of the hat in question having been worn off to the very crown, he was observed hovering about an equally miserable scarecrow in the field, with a view to stealing the hat which protected it from the rain. Having succeeded in this enterprise, he bound the brim of the scarecrow's hat to the crown of his own, by means of some tar-twine, and appeared for the rest of time in this peculiar millinery, which was remarkable for the variegation of its colour, the crown being brown, and the brim jet-black.

Another clerical person of the same kind was the Reverend Mr Trueman, of Daventry. Happy in the possession of more than one rectorship, among these being Bilton, where Addison had lived at one time, this parsimonious old body, whose yearly income had been £400, left £50,000 behind him when he died. His position as rector was a great help to him, for, when visiting farms in order to administer spiritual aid, he was enabled to steal turnips in the fields as he walked to this work of righteousness. The aid having been administered, he would then beg for a piece of bacon to boil with them. This request was never denied, and if the farmer's wife turned her back for a moment, leaving the bacon in his vicinity, he would take out his pocket-knife and steal a second piece. The next recipient of spiritual grace would then be asked for greens to cook with the present he had just received; the third for potatoes. When Mr Trueman's clothes or stockings were in need of mending, he would contrive to get benighted in one of the richer farmhouses of his parish, on such a night that it would be impossible for him to return home, so that the farmer would be obliged to ask the rector to spend the night in his best bedroom. This would give him the opportunity of stealing the red or white worsted out of the corners of the blankets, and with these variegated pickings he mended his clothes and his stockings. This scarecrow in parson's clothes actually fell in love with the daughter of a farmer in his parish, and recollecting that he had heard, from those more experienced than himself, that presents of some sort of finery to the beloved might cancel out in some degree the absence of beauty in the lover, he remembered that he had a brother in Daventry who kept a haberdasher's shop. He exhibited, therefore, signs of great affection towards this brother and, whilst visiting him, stole and hid a large piece of ribbon. What was the surprise of the unclerical Mr Trueman, when buying butter shortly afterwards, on market day, to find the piece of ribbon decorating the person of his reverend brother's parishioner. Even this gift however, as far as I know, did not soften the heart of the lady, and the Reverend Mr Trueman seems to have died unmarried, between the years 1780 and 1790, and to have been buried, at his own request, under a summer-house in the garden.

The life of Mr John Elwes is so well known that I shall not expatiate upon it at any length. But this passion which made him remarkable, if anything so cold, so bleak and thin as miserliness can be called a passion, seems to have been inherited from his mother, who starved herself to death, though she was in possession of nearly a hundred thousand pounds.

'While in the Genevese capital', we are told by Mr Redding, Mr Elwes 'was introduced to Voltaire, but that man of genius made no impression upon Elwes.' The uncle of Mr Elwes was more fortunate in this respect, and the nephew, who had stopped at an inn at Chelmsford on his way to visit his relative, dressed in a manner calculated to please him, wearing a worn-out coat, darned worsted stockings, and rusty iron buckles. Sir Harvey Elwes was satisfied by these evidences of a virtuous life, and these two exemplary characters sat by a fire which had been lighted with one stick, sharing a glass of wine between them, and complaining about the extravagance of the times, till it was time to go to bed, when they found their way upstairs without the help of a candle, and put themselves to bed in the dark.

Mr Elwes had had the foresight to dine at the inn before visiting his uncle, for he was a hearty eater; what, therefore, can have been the pride of the old gentleman on finding that his heir, that worthy scion of his race, would do no more than share one partridge and one potato with him, whilst the thin fire flickered and went out. Sir Harvey, indeed, lived on partridges from the estate, since these cost him nothing; and he insisted that the manservant and two maids, who were the only inhabitants of his house, should do the same. Lean and starved in appearance, clad in an old grey coat and worsted stockings, and wearing a black velvet cap, Sir Harvey rode a horse as miserable as himself. When the bleak weather made it impossible for him to go out, he walked up and down in the hall, so as to save firing, and, when it was necessary to have fires, he would light them with a single stick.

Mr Redding tells us that when, between the ages of eighty and ninety, Sir Harvey died, and his nephew came into the estate and the old house attached to it, 'the beds were ghostly, antique, a prey to devastating insects and the roof let in both rain and air at numerous interstices'.

Mr Elwes, when in possession of his fortune, would walk from one end of London to another, in the pelting rain, rather than pay the fare of a shilling for a coach; he would eat putrid meat in order to avoid buying a fresh joint, and he would sit in wet clothes throughout an afternoon and evening rather than pay for a fire with which to dry them.

He wore the cast-off wig of a beggar, which he had picked up out of a wet ditch, and, when he had worn his only coat to rags, sat down to dinner in one belonging to a long-dead ancestor, a coat made of green velvet with slashed sleeves, which, with the beggar's wig from the ditch toppling over his straggling white hair, made a strange impression.

It is a curious fact that this thin old miser was also a great gambler, staking thousands of pounds at a sitting, in the company of men of his own social standing, for, in spite of his habits, he had remained on speaking terms with the world into which he was born.

I do not know if Mr Elwes lamented the 'wasteful habits' of the gentlemen in whose company he would gamble, when in London, but he certainly lamented those of the common crow – that bleak and boring bird. For, having the custom of picking up stray chips, bones, wool, etc., with which to light his fire, he was found, on one occasion, demolishing an old crow's nest. The interested observers asked him why he should give himself so much trouble, whereupon the old gentleman replied: 'Oh, sir, it is really a shame that these creatures should do so – do but see what a waste they make.'

'The miser Claude', said Mr Redding, 'was a man whose appetite was at one time voracious, while at another it would seem as if air were sufficient for his sustenance.' And this cold, universal, uncaring air, indeed, seems to be the only food of all misers. They are not of the human race; their passions are not ours, for they have no warmth; they devour their own flesh when the unsatisfying air is not enough. Foscue, a farmer-general of France, existing in Languedoc about 1762, descending, spiderlike, by means of a ladder to count the money he had hidden in a vault, found himself walled in that grave by the falling of the trap door. Those in the free and open world outside searched for him, night and day, dragging the pools of his estate, and offering rewards from his own gold for the recovery of his being. At last, giving him over for lost, the property he had accumulated with such diligence was sold, together with his house and all that it contained. But it happened that the newcomer to the house wished some alterations to be made in the cellar, and the workmen found that living grave which had held, nightly, the man who for so long was both living and dead, and which now held him for ever. Here he sat, surrounded by his treasures, so enormous and glittering that they dazzled the eyes, though seen by the light of one candle alone. Beside the high priest of the god of this world lay a candlestick, but in it was no candle, for the priest had eaten it. In the pangs of famine, this saint of Mammon, deserted by his god, had gnawed the flesh from both his arms.

These true and faithful worshippers of the god would, without a qualm, give their flesh and their blood upon this monstrous altar. A miser named Vaudille, when it became necessary to bleed him, as was the custom in the century in which he lived, bargained thus with the barber whom he had called in, for cheapness' sake. The barber agreed to open a vein for the sum of three sous for each operation. 'How often will the operation be necessary?' inquired the miser. 'Three times,' the barber answered. 'How much blood would you take altogether?' 'About twenty-five ounces, and that, you know, will be nine sous.' 'It is too expensive,' replied the high priest of Mammon. 'Take all the blood at once. You want to operate three times. Take away all the blood in one operation. I must save my six sous.'

Vaudille gave, therefore, twenty-five ounces of his frozen blood at one stroke upon the altar. The quantity was too great, and he died of exhaustion, unlamented even by his god.

In his death, at least, he produced a great and significant gesture.

Many of these acolytes died of inanition, from the pangs, hardly felt by their chilled blood, of hunger and of cold; but others lived to be ninety years of age or more, because life and death could exhibit no noticeable difference to them. Skeletons they were since early youth; skeletons they remained.

Mr Daniel Dancer and his sister were two remarkable anatomies of this sort. Though possessed of £3,000 a year, this precious pair, who lived at Harrow Weald Common, near Harrow on the Hill, on one occasion found a sheep that had died of disease and was rotting into decay. They skinned it and made what was left of the rot into pies, living entirely upon these until they were finished.

Miss Dancer, on the heap of rags which was her death-bed, was allowed no medical assistance, for, as her pious brother said: 'Why should I waste my money on wickedly endeavouring to counteract the will of Providence? If the old girl's time is come, the nostrums of all the quacks in Christendom cannot save her – she may as well die now as at any future period.'

During this probation for the future state, he administered to her the usual cold dumpling, with the usual piece of 'sticking beef' with, for consolation, the remark, 'If you don't like it, you may go without it.'

This bundle made of rags, bones, and a decaying heart, possessed one object, apart from his money, on which he lavished affection, and this was poor Bob, his dog, whom he would address as 'Bob, my child', and to whom he would devote a pint of milk a day although, rather than spend a penny on himself, he would drink the pot liquor in Lady Tempest's kitchen, and drink so enormously as to be obliged to roll himself on the floor before he could go to sleep. Yet when Bob was accused of chasing sheep, he took his friend to a blacksmith's shop, and had the poor animal's teeth broken short, committing this beastly act of cruelty for fear that Bob might chase and worry sheep and that he might have to pay damages.

This amiable old person was so economical in all things that he manured his fields in this manner: he would stuff the pockets of his ragged clothes with cattle dung from the road and common, whilst at the same time he would forage for old bones, using the scraps of any meat which he found upon these for his own food, then breaking up the bones for the broken-toothed Bob. With any dung that was left over, when he had manured his land, he formed a kind of cupboard in which to hide his money.

The home life of Mr Dancer was certainly remarkable, and his fancy led him to heights – or depths – undreamed of before or since. Free and wandering, it roamed at will, and this freedom was shown particularly in Mr Dancer's preparation of food. His benefactor, Lady Tempest, knowing that he was fond of trout stewed in claret, sent him some as a present. But the weather was hard and wintry. So Mr Dancer, afraid of contracting toothache from the unwarmed trout and claret, and unwilling to go to the expense of a fire by which to thaw these, sat, henlike, upon this pleasant mixture until it was thawed by the warmth of his body.

Mr Cyrus Redding, his biographer, did not approve of him, and tells us, without comment, that 'Never after a shirt came into his hands was it known to have been washed, or even mended. It generally fell from his back in rags. Hence, it may be supposed that notwithstanding his solitary tendencies as a miser, he was never without a colony of insect friends attached to his person, that affected for his body the most lively interest.' Mr Redding adds, gloomily, that 'Mr

Dancer's shoes had been mended, by himself, so often that they became out of shape and heavy, and were more like hogs' troughs than shoes.' As for his state upon his death-bed, we are told that 'During the illness in 1794, which terminated the life of this miserable creature in the seventy-eighth year of his age, Lady Tempest accidentally called upon him, and found him lying in an old sack, which came up to his neck. On her remonstrating with him against the impropriety of such a proceeding, he replied that he came into the world without a shirt, and he was determined to go out in the same manner.'

Naked he lived, and naked he died, and was gone. . . . And now, blown along the street like a black and filthy cobweb waving in the draught of some dusty window, comes the ghost of old 'Lady' Lewson, who lived in Coldbath Square, Clerkenwell, for ninety years. Her likeness to a cobweb is produced by the fact that she wears the 'ruffs, and cuffs and fardingales' of her youth (she was born in 1700), and that she never washed herself for fear of catching cold, and so laying the foundation of a disease. She does, however, besmear herself with hog's lard, to which she adds rose-pink over the cheeks. Now, as the cobweb is blown towards us, we can see that it bore, once, the likeness of a flimsy silk gown with a long train, a deep flounce, and sleeves coming to below the elbow with many frills attached.

This strange antique trumpery, at the age of eighty-seven, cut two new teeth, which were a source of pride to her and of wonder to her neighbours.

Her large house in Coldbath Square contains only four other beings, ghosts like herself, two old lap-dogs, an aged cat, and an old man whose occupation had been that of wandering from house to house in the district, earning pieces of food by running errands and cleaning boots. But now that 'Lady' Lewson's only servant has married, she has taken

him into her house, where he acts as steward, butler, cook
and housemaid.

The cobweb has blown away again, back to those incrusted
lightless windows of the house in Coldbath Square, and Mr
Pinks, author of the *History of Clerkenwell*, is gossiping to
us, telling us the history of the cobweb, the history of the
house. The latter was large, it seems, and elegantly furnished. The beds were made every day, as if visitors were
expected, though nobody ever came. As for 'Lady' Lewson's
room, it was never washed, and only swept very occasionally,
whilst 'the windows were so crusted with dirt that they
hardly admitted a ray of light'. For 'Lady' Lewson believed
that a drop of water in her room would be dangerous as the
sea, and that, if the windows were washed, they would be
broken, the person washing them would be injured, and so
the expense would fall upon her.

The aged cobweb enjoyed the open air, however, in the
large garden at the back of the house, and might have been
seen, on warm days, suspended from a chair placed under
the dark trees. Here she would sit and read, or talk of the
events of the last hundred years to the few acquaintances
whom she permitted to visit her. Her life was managed
according to rules, for she would never drink tea excepting
from a favourite teacup, nor sit down excepting in a
favourite chair. The immortality of this old lady seemed
assured, until the sudden death of an ancient neighbour
caused her to tremble – to doubt in her own immortality. She
weakened, took to her bed, and on Tuesday, the twenty-
eighth of May, died at the age of 116 years. A Mr Warner,
wandering over the house after her death, 'was struck with
astonishment at the number of bars, bolts, etc., to the whole
of the doors and windows'. The ceilings of the upper floor
were completely lined with strong boards, braced together

with iron bars, to prevent anyone getting into the house from the roof.

This old lady, though wealthy, hoarded not so much gold as useless memories. No piece of fluff, no small possession, was allowed to slip from her grasp, during the space of the ninety years in which she lived in Coldbath Square.

The sky darkens, and in this strange 'Goose-Weather' when even the snow and the black-fringed clouds seem like old theatrical properties, dead players' cast-off rags, 'the complexion of a murderer in a bandbox, consisting of a large piece of burnt cork, and a coal-black Peruke', and the wind is like an empty theatre's 'Sea, consisting of a dozen large waves, the tenth a little bigger than ordinary, and a little damaged', I will arrange the Profits of this Dust-sifting.

'Zero', says Lorenz Oken, in his *Elements of Physiophilosophy*, 'must be endlessly positing itself, for in every respect it is indefinite or unlimited, eternal. . . . The whole of Arithmetic is nothing but the endless repetition of Nothing, endless positing and suppressing of nothing.' So here they fall, these units, these gestures, arising from nothing, drifting into nothing, melting like the snow, sifting and falling on to the giant dust-heap.

'Charon in Lucian, as he wittily feigns, was conducted by Mercury to such a place, where he might see all the world at once; after he had sufficiently viewed and looked about, Mercury would needs know of him what he had observed. He told them that he saw a vast multitude and a promiscuous, their habitations like molehills, the men as emmets . . . he could discern cities like so many hives of bees, wherein every bee had a sting, and they did naught else but sting one another, some domineering like hornets bigger than the rest, some like filching wasps, others as drones. Over their heads were hovering a confused company of perturbations –

hope, fear, anger, avarice, ignorance, etc.; and a multitude of diseases hanging, which they still pulled on their pates. Some were brawling, some fighting, riding, running, *sollicite ambulantes, callide litigantes* (earnestly suing or cunningly disputing) for toys and trifles, and such momentary things; their towns and provinces were factions, rich against poor, poor against rich, nobles against artificers, they against nobles, and so the rest. In conclusion, he condensed them all for madmen, fools, idiots, asses, *O stulti, quaenam haec est amentia*? O fools, O madmen! he exclaims, insane *studia*, insane *labores*, etc., mad endeavours, mad actions, mad, mad, mad, *O seculum insipiens et infacetum*, a giddy-headed age.'

Appendix I

12

Of the Benefits
of Posthumous Fame

'PHYSIOGNOMY', wrote Sir Thomas Browne, 'outlives ourselves, and ends not in our graves.

'Severe contemplators, observing these lasting reliques,
may think them good monuments of persons past, little advantage to future beings, and considering that power which
subdueth all things unto itself, that can resume the scattered
atomes, or identifie out of anything conceive it superfluous
to expect a resurrection out of Reliques. But the soul sub-
sisting, other matter, clothed with due accidents, may salve
the individuality.'

This, then, is the history of the bones of one John Milton,
who was paid the sum of £20 for the poem *Paradise Lost*,
who was 'not in affluence, expired in an emaciated state, in
a cold month', or, alternatively, it may be the history of the
bones of the youngest Miss Smith. In any case, a grateful
country was eager to harbour them.[1]

'In the first series of *Notes and Queries*, vol. v, p. 369
(April 17, 1852), is a note from which the following is an ex-
tract: "In vol. v, p. 275, mention is made of Cromwell's
skull; so it may not be out of place to tell you that I have
handled one of Milton's ribs. Cowper speaks indignantly of
the desecration of our divine poet's grave, on which shameful
occurrence some of the bones were clandestinely distributed.
One fell to the lot of an old and esteemed friend, and between

1. All that follows is reprinted from John Ashton's *Eighteenth-
Century Waifs*, by kind permission of Messrs Hurst and Blackett
Ltd, the publishers.

forty-five and fifty years ago, at his house, not many miles from London, I have often examined the said rib-bone."

'The lines of Cowper's to which he refers were written in August, 1790, and are entitled

STANZAS

On the late indecent Liberties taken with the remains of the great Milton. Anno 1790

Me too, perchance, in future days,
The sculptured stone shall show,
With Paphian myrtle or with bays
Parnassian on my brow.

But I, or ere that season come,
Escaped from every care,
Shall reach my refuge in the tomb,
And sleep securely there.

So sang, in Roman tone and style,
The youthful bard, ere long
Ordain'd to grace his native isle
With her sublimest song.

Who then but must conceive disdain,
Hearing the deed unblest,
Of wretches who have dared profane
His dread sepulchral rest?

Ill fare the hands that heaved the stones
Where Milton's ashes lay,
That trembled not to grasp his bones
And steal his dust away!

O ill-requited bard! neglect
Thy living worth repaid,
And blind idolatrous respect
As much affronts thee dead.

'Leigh Hunt possessed a lock of Milton's hair which had been given to him by a physician – and over which he went into such rhapsodies that he composed no less than three sonnets addressed to the donor – which may be found in his *Foliage*, ed. 1818, pp. 131, 132, 133. The following is the best:

TO — M.D.
On his giving me a lock of Milton's hair.

It lies before me there, and my own breath
Stirs its thin outer threads, as though beside
The living head I stood in honoured pride,
Talking of lovely things that conquered death.
Perhaps he pressed it once, or underneath,
Ran his fine fingers, when he leant, blank-eyed,
And saw, in fancy, Adam and his bride
With their heaped locks, or his own Delphic wreath.
There seems a love in hair, though it be dead.
It is the gentlest, yet the strongest thread
Of our frail plant – a blossom from the tree
Surviving the proud trunk – as if it said,
Patience and Gentleness is Power. In me
Behold affectionate eternity.

'How were these personal relics obtained? By rifling his tomb. Shakespeare solemnly cursed anyone who should dare to meddle with his dead body, and his remains are believed to be intact.

Good friend, for Jesus' sake, forbear
To dig the dust inclosed here;
Blest be the man who spares these stones,
And cursed be he who moves my bones.

'But Milton laid no such interdict upon his poor dead body – and it was not very long after his burial, which took place in 1674, that the stone which covered it, and indicated his resting-place, was removed, as Aubrey tells us in his *Lives* (vol. iii, p. 450). "His stone is now removed. About two

years since (1681) the two steppes to the communion-table
were raysed, Ighesse, Jo. Speed, and he lie together." And
so it came to pass that, in the church of St Giles', Cripplegate, where he was buried, there was no memorial of the
place where he was laid, nor, indeed, anything to mark the
fact of his burial in that church until, in 1793, Samuel Whitbread set up a fine marble bust of the poet, by Bacon, with
an inscription giving the dates of his birth and death, and
recording the fact that his father was also interred there.

'It is probable that Mr Whitbread was moved thereto by
the alleged desecration of Milton's tomb in 1790, of which
there is a good account writting by Philip Neve, of Furnival's Inn, which is entitled, "A Narrative of the Disinterment of Milton's coffin, in the Parish-Church of St Giles,
Cripplegate, on Wednesday, August 4th, 1790; and the
Treatment of the Corpse during that and the following
day".

'As this narrative is not long, I propose to give it in its
entirety, because to condense it would be to spoil it, and, by
giving it *in extenso*, the reader will be better able to judge
whether it was really Milton's body which was exhumed.

' "A NARRATIVE, ETC.

' "Having read in the *Public Advertiser*, on Saturday the
seventh of August, 1790, that Milton's coffin had been dug
up in the parish church of St Giles, Cripplegate, and was
there to be seen, I went immediately to the church, and
found the latter part of the information to be untrue; but,
from conversations on that day, on Monday, the ninth, and
on Tuesday, the tenth of August, with Mr Thomas Strong,
Solicitor and F.A.S., Red Cross Street, Vestry-Clerk; Mr
John Cole, Barbican, Silversmith, Churchwarden; Mr John
Laming, Barbican, Pawnbroker; and Mr Fountain, Beech
Lane, Publican, Overseers; Mr Taylor, of Stanton, Derby-

shire, Surgeon; a friend of Mr Laming, and a visitor in his house; Mr William Ascough, Coffin-maker, Fore Street, Parish Clerk; Benjamin Holmes and Thomas Hawkesworth, journeyman to Mr Ascough; Mrs Hoppey, Fore Street, Sexton; Mr Ellis, No. 9 Lamb's Chapel, comedian of the Royalty Theatre; and John Poole (son of Rowland Poole), Watch-spring maker, Jacob's Passage, Barbican, the following facts are established:

' "It being in the contemplation of some persons to bestow a considerable sum of money in erecting a monument, in the parish church of St Giles, Cripplegate, to the memory of Milton, and the particular spot of his interment in that church having for many years past been ascertained only by tradition, several of the principal parishioners have, at their meetings, frequently expressed a wish that his coffin should be dug for, that incontestable evidence of its exact situation might be established, before the said monument should be erected. The entry, among the burials, in the register-book, twelfth of November, 1674, is 'John Milton, Gentleman, consumption, chancell'. The church of St Giles, Cripplegate, was built in 1030, was burnt down (except the steeple) and rebuilt in 1545; was repaired in 1682; and again in 1710. In the repair of 1782, an alteration took place in the disposition of the inside of the church; the pulpit was removed from the second pillar, against which it stood, north of the chancel, to the south side of the present chancel, which was then formed, and pews were built over the old chancel. The tradition has always been that Milton was buried in the chancel, under the clerk's desk; but the circumstance of the alteration in the church, not having, of late years, been attended to, the clerk, sexton, and other officers of the parish have misguided inquirers, by showing the spot under the clerk's desk, in the present chancel, as the place of Milton's interment. I have twice, at different periods, been shown that spot as the place where Milton lay. Even Mr Baskerville, who died a few years ago, and who had requested, in his will, to be buried by Milton, was deposited in the above-mentioned spot of the present chancel, in pious intention of compliance with his request. The church is now, August, 1790, under a general repair, by contract, for £1350, and Mr Strong, Mr Cole, and other parishioners, having very prudently judged that the search would be made with much less inconvenience to the parish at this time, when the church is under repair, than at any period after the said repair should be completed, Mr Cole, in the last days of July, ordered the workmen to dig in search of the coffin. Mr Ascough, his father, and grandfather, have been parish clerks of St Giles for upwards of ninety years past. His grandfather, who died in February 1759–60, aged eighty-four, used often to say that Milton had been buried under the clerk's desk in the chancel. John Poole, aged seventy, used to hear his father talk of Milton's person, from those who had seen him; and also, that he lay under the common-councilmen's pew. The common-councilmen's pew is built over that very part of the old chancel, where the former clerk's desk stood. These traditions in the parish reported to Mr Strong and Mr Cole readily directed them to dig from the present chancel, northwards, towards the pillar, against which the former pulpit and desk had stood. On Tuesday afternoon, August 3rd, notice was brought to Messrs Strong and Cole that the coffin was discovered. They went immediately to the church, and, by help of a candle, proceeded under the common-councilmen's pew to the place where the coffin lay. It was in a chalky soil, and directly over a wooden coffin, supposed to be that of Milton's father; tradition having always reported that Milton was buried next to his father. The registry of the father of Milton, among the burials, in the parish-book, is 'John Melton, Gentleman, 15th of March 1646–7'. In digging through the whole space from the present chancel, where the ground was opened, to the situation of the former clerk's desk, there was not found any other coffin, which could raise the smallest doubt of this being Milton's. The two oldest found in the ground had inscriptions, which Mr Strong copied; they were of as late dates as 1727 and 1739. When he and Mr Cole had examined the coffin, they ordered water and a brush to be brought, that they might wash it, in search of an inscription, or initials, or date; but, upon its being carefully cleansed, none was found.

' "The following particulars were given me in writing by Mr Strong, and they contain the admeasurement of the coffin, as taken by him, with a rule. 'A leaden coffin, found under the common-councilmen's pew, on the north side of the chancel, nearly under the place where the old pulpit and clerk's desk stood. The coffin appeared to be old, much corroded, and without any inscription or plate upon it. It was, in length, five feet ten inches, and in width, at the broadest part, over the shoulders, one foot four inches.' Conjecture naturally pointed out, both to Mr Strong and Mr Cole, that, by moving the leaden coffin, there would be a great chance of finding some inscription on the wooden one underneath; but, with a just and laudable piety, they disdained to disturb the sacred ashes, after a requiem of one hundred and sixteen years; and having satisfied their curiosity, and ascertained the fact, which was the subject of it, Mr Cole ordered the ground to be closed. This was on the afternoon of Tuesday, August the 3rd; and, when I waited on Mr Strong, on Saturday morning, the 7th, he informed me that the coffin had been found on the Tuesday, had been examined, washed, and measured by him and Mr Cole; but that the ground had been immediately closed, when they left the church – not doubting that Mr Cole's order had been punctually obeyed. But the direct contrary appears to have been the fact.

' "On Tuesday evening the 3rd, Mr Cole, Messrs Laming & Taylor, Holmes, &c., had a merry meeting, as Mr Cole expresses himself, at Fountain's house; the conversation there turned upon Milton's coffin having been discovered; and, in the course of the evening, several of those present expressing a desire to see it, Mr Cole assented that, if the ground was not already closed, the closing of it should be deferred until they should have satisfied their curiosity. Between eight and nine on Wednesday morning, the 4th, the two overseers (Laming and Fountain) and Mr Taylor, went to the house of Ascough, the clerk, which leads into the church-yard, and asked for Holmes; they then went with Holmes into the church, and pulled the coffin, which lay deep in the ground, from its original station to the edge of the excavation, into daylight. Mr Laming told me that, to assist in thus removing it, he put his hand into a corroded hole, which he saw in the lead, at the coffin foot. When they had thus removed it, the overseers asked Holmes if he could open it, that they might see the body. Holmes immediately fetched a mallet and a chisel, and cut open the top of the coffin, slantwise from the head, as low as the breast; so that the top, being doubled backward, they could see the corpse; he cut it open also at the foot. Upon first view of the body, it appeared perfect, and completely enveloped in the shroud, which was of many folds; the ribs standing up regularly. When they disturbed the shroud, the ribs fell. Mr Fountain told me that he pulled hard at the teeth, which resisted, until some one hit them a knock with a stone, when they easily came out. There were but five in the upper jaw, which were all perfectly sound and white, and all taken by Mr Fountain; he gave one of them to Mr Laming; Mr Laming also took one from the lower jaw; and Mr Taylor took two from it. Mr Laming told me that he had, at one time, a mind to bring away the whole underjaw, with the teeth in it; he had it in his hand, but tossed it back again. Also that he lifted up the head, and saw a great quantity of hair, which lay straight and even behind the head, and in the state of hair which had been combed and tied together before interment; but it was wet, the coffin having considerable corroded holes, both at the head and foot, and a great part of the water with which it had been washed on the Tuesday afternoon having run into it. The overseers and Mr Taylor went away soon afterwards, and Messrs Laming and Taylor went home to get scissors to cut off some of the hair: they returned about ten, when Mr Laming poked his stick against the head, and brought some of the hair over the forehead; but, as they saw the scissors were not necessary, Mr Taylor took up the hair, as it lay on the forehead, and carried it home. The water, which had got into the coffin on the Tuesday afternoon, had made a sludge at the bottom of it, emitting a nauseous smell, which occasioned Mr Laming to use his stick to procure the hair, and not to lift up the head a second time. Mr Laming also took out one of the leg-bones, but threw it in again. Holmes went out of church, whilst Messrs Laming, Taylor, and Fountain were there the first time, and he returned when the two former were come the second time. When Messrs Laming and Taylor had finally quitted the church, the coffin was removed from the edge of the excavation back to its original station; but was no otherwise closed than by the lid, where it had been cut and reversed, being bent down again. Mr Ascough, the clerk, was from home the greater part of that day, and Mrs Hoppey, the sexton, was from home the whole day. Elizabeth Grant, the grave-digger, who is servant to Mrs Hoppey, therefore now took possession of the coffin; and, as its situation under the common-councilmen's pew would not admit of its being seen without the help of a candle, she kept a tinder-box in the excavation, and, when any persons came, struck a light, and conducted them under the pew, where, by reversing the part of the lid which had been cut, she exhibited the body, at first for sixpence, and afterwards for threepence and twopence each person. The workers in the church kept the doors locked to all those who would not pay the price of a pot of beer for entrance, and many, to avoid that payment, got in at a window at the west end of the church, near to Mr Ascough's counting-house.

' "I went on Saturday, the 7th, to Mr Laming's house, to request a lock of the hair; but, not meeting with Mr Taylor at home, went again on Monday, the 9th, when Mr Taylor gave me part of what hair he had reserved for himself. Hawkesworth having informed me, on the Saturday, that Mr Ellis, the player, had taken some hair, and that he had seen him take a rib-bone, and carry it away in paper under his coat, I went from Mr Laming's on Monday to Mr Ellis, who told me that he had paid 6d. to Elizabeth Grant for seeing the body; and that he had lifted up the head, and taken from the sludge under it a small quantity of hair, with which was a piece of the shroud, and, adhering to the hair, a bit of the skin of the skull, of about the size of a shilling. He then put them all into my hands, with the rib-bone, which appeared to be one of the upper ribs. The piece of the shroud was of coarse linen. The hair which he had taken was short; a small part of it he had washed, and the remainder was in the clotted state in which he had taken it. He told me that he had tried to reach down as low as the hands of the corpse, but had not been able to effect it. The washed hair corresponded exactly with that in my possession, and which I had just received from Mr Taylor. Ellis is a very ingenious worker in hair, and he said that, thinking it would be of great advantage to him to possess a quantity of Milton's hair, he had returned to the church on Thursday, and had made his endeavours to get access a second time to the body; but had been refused admittance. Hawkesworth took a tooth, and broke a bit off the coffin; of which I was informed by Mr Ascough. I purchased them both of Hawkesworth, on Saturday the 7th for 2/-; and he told me that, when he took the tooth out, there were but two more remaining; one of which was afterwards taken by another of Mr Ascough's men. And Ellis informed me that, at the time when he was there, on Wednesday, the teeth were all gone; but the overseers say they think that all the teeth were not taken out of the coffin, though displaced from the jaws, but that some of them must have fallen among the other bones as they very readily came out, after the first were drawn. Haslib, son of William Haslib, of Jewin Street, undertaker, took one of the small bones, which I purchased of him, on Monday the 9th, for 2/-.

' "With respect to the identity of the person; anyone must be a skeptic against violent presumptions to entertain a doubt of its being that of Milton. The parish traditions of the spot; the age of the coffin – none other found in the ground which can at all contest with it, or render it suspicious – Poole's tradition that those who had conversed with his father about Milton's person always described him to have been thin, with long hair; the entry in the register-book that Milton died of consumption, are all strong confirmations, with the size of the coffin, or the identity of the person. If it be objected that, against the pillar where the pulpit formerly stood, and immediately over the common-councilmen's pew, is a monument to the family of Smith, which shows that 'near that place' were buried, in 1653, Richard Smith, aged 17; in 1655, John Smith, aged 32; and in 1664, Elizabeth Smith, the mother, aged 64; and in 1675, Richard Smith, the father, aged 85; it may be answered that, if the coffin in question be one of these, the others should be there also. The corpse is certainly not that of a man of 85; and, if it be supposed one of the first named males of the Smith family, certainly the two later coffins should appear; but none such were found, nor could that monument have been erected until many years after the death of the last person mentioned in the inscription; and it was then placed there, as it expresses, not by any of the family, but at the expense of friends. The flatness of the pillar, after the pulpit had been removed, offered an advantageous situation for it; and '*near this place*', upon a mural monument, will always admit of a liberal construction. Holmes, who is much respected in that parish, and very ingenious and intelligent in his business, says that a leaden coffin, when the inner wooden case is perished, must, from pressure and its own weight, shrink in breadth, and that, therefore, more than the present admeasurement of this coffin across the shoulders must have been its original breadth. There is evidence, also, that it was incurvated, both on the top and at the sides, at the time when it was discovered. But the strongest of all confirmations is the hair, both in its length and colour. Behold Fairthorne's quarto-print of Milton, taken *ad vivum* in 1760, five years before Milton's death. Observe the short locks growing towards the forehead, and the long ones flowing from the same place down the sides of the face. The whole quantity of hair which Mr Taylor took was from the forehead, and all taken at one grasp. I measured on Monday morning, the 9th, that lock of it which he had given to Mr Laming, six inches and a half by a rule; and the lock of it which he gave to me, taken at the same time, and from the same place, measures only two inches and a half. In the reign of Charles II how few, besides Milton, wore their own hair! Wood says Milton had light-brown hair, the very description of that which we possess; and, what may seem extraordinary, it is yet so strong that

Mr Laming, to cleanse it from its clotted state, let the cistern-cock run on it for near a minute, and then rubbed it between his fingers without injury.

' "Milton's coffin lay open from Wednesday morning, the 4th, at 9 o'clock, until 4 o'clock in the afternoon of the following day, when the ground was closed.

' "With respect to there being no inscriptions on the coffin, Holmes says that inscription-plates were not used, nor invented at the time when Milton was buried; that the practice then was to paint the inscription on the outside wooden coffin, which in this case was entirely perished.

' "It has never been pretended that any hair was taken except by Mr Taylor and by Ellis the player; and all which the latter took would, when cleansed, easily lie in a small locket. Mr Taylor has divided his share into many small parcels; and the lock which I saw in Mr Laming's hands on Saturday morning, the 7th, and which then measured six inches and a half, had been so cut and reduced by divisions among Mr Laming's friends, at noon, on Monday, the 9th, that he thus possessed only a small bit, from two to three inches in length.

' "All the teeth are remarkably short, below the gums. The five which were in the upper jaw, and the middle teeth of the lower, are perfect and white. Mr Fountain took the five upper jaw teeth; Mr Laming one from the lower jaw, Mr Taylor two from it; Hawkesworth one; and another of Mr Ascough's men one; besides these, I have not been able to trace any, nor have I heard that any more were taken. It is not probable that more than ten should have been brought away, if the conjecture of the overseers, that some dropped among the other bones, be founded.

' "In recording a transaction which will strike every liberal mind with horror and disgust, I cannot omit to declare that I have procured those relics which I possess, only in hope of bearing part in a pious and honourable restitution of all that has been taken; the sole atonement which can now be made to the violated rights of the dead, to the insulted parishioners at large; and to the feelings of all good men. During the present repair of the church, the mode is obvious and easy. Unless that be done, in vain will the parish hereafter boast a sumptuous monument to the memory of Milton; it will but display their shame in proportion to its magnificence.

'"I collected this account from the mouths of those who were immediate actors in this most sacrilegious scene; and before the voice of charity had reproached them with their impiety. By it those are exculpated whose just and liberal sentiments restrained their hands from an act of violation, and the blood of the lamb is dashed against the doorposts of the perpetrators, not to save, but to mark them to posterity.

PHILIP NEVE.

Furnival's Inn,
14th of August, 1790."'

Mr Ashton adds: 'This Mr Neve, whose pious horror at the sacrilegious desecration of the poet's tomb seems only to have been awakened at the eleventh hour, and whose restitution of the relics he obtained does not appear, was probably the P.N. who was the author, in 1789, of *Cursory Remarks on some of the Ancient English Poets, particularly Milton*. It is a work of some erudition, but the hero of the book, as its title plainly shows, was Milton. Neve places him in the first rank, and can hardly find words with which to extol his genius and intellect, so that, probably, some hero-worship was interwoven in the foregoing relation of the discovery of Milton's body; and it may be as well if the other side were heard, although the attempt at refutation is by no means as well authenticated as Neve's narrative. It is anonymous, and appeared in *St James's Chronicle*, September 4–7th, 1790, and in the *European Magazine*, vol. xviii, pp. 206–7, for September, 1790, and is as follows:

' "MILTON

' "*Reasons why it is impossible that the Coffin lately dug up in the Parish Church of St Giles, Cripplegate, should contain the reliques of* MILTON.

' "*First*. BECAUSE Milton was buried in 1674, and this coffin was found in a situation previously allotted to a wealthy family, unconnected with his own – See the mural monument of the Smiths, dated 1653, etc., immediately over the place of the supposed MILTON's interment. – In the time that the fragments of several other sarcophagi were found; together with two skulls, many bones, and a leaden coffin, which was left untouched because it lay farther to the north, and (for some reason, or no reason at all) was unsuspected of being the Miltonic reservoir.

' "*Secondly*. The hair of MILTON is uniformly described and represented as of a light hue; but far the greater part of the ornament of his pretended skull is of the darkest brown, without any mixture of gray.[2] This difference is irreconcilable to probability. Our hair, after childhood, is rarely found to undergo a total change of colour, and MILTON was 66 years old when he died, a period at which human locks, in a greater or less degree, are interspersed with white. Why did the Overseers, &c, bring away only such hair as corresponded with the description of Milton's? Of the light hair there was little; of the dark a considerable quantity. But this circumstance would have been wholly suppressed, had not a second scrutiny taken place.

' "*Thirdly*. Because the skull in question is remarkably flat

2. The few hairs, of a lighter colour, are supposed to have been such as had grown on the sides of the cheeks after the corpse had been interred.

and small, and with the lowest of all possible foreheads; whereas the head of MILTON was large, and his brow conspicuously high. See his portrait so often engraved by the accurate Vertue, who was completely satisfied with the authenticity of his original. We are assured that the surgeon who attended at the second disinterment of the corpse only remarked, 'that the little forehead there was, was prominent'.

' "*Fourthly*. Because the hands of MILTON were full of chalk stones. Now it chances that his substitute's left hand had been undisturbed, and therefore was in a condition to be properly examined. No vestige, however, of cretaceous substances was visible in it, although they are of a lasting nature, and have been found on the fingers of a dead person almost coeval with MILTON.

' "*Fifthly*. Because there is reason to believe that the aforesaid remains are those of a young female (one of the three Miss Smiths); for the bones are delicate, the teeth small, slightly inserted in the jaw, and perfectly white, even, and sound. From the corroded state of the pelvis, nothing could, with certainty, be inferred; nor would the surgeon already mentioned pronounce *absolutely* on the sex of the deceased. Admitting, however, that the body was a male one, its very situation points it out to be a male of the Smith family; perhaps the favourite son, John, whom Richard Smith, Esq., his father, so feelingly laments. (See Peck's *Desiderata Curiosa*, p. 536.)[3] To this darling child a receptacle of lead might have been allotted, though many other relatives of the same house were left to putrefy in wood.

' "*Sixthly*. Because MILTON was not in affluence[4] – ex-

3. MDCLV, May VI, died my (now) only and eldest son, John Smith (Proh Dolor, beloved of all men) at Mitcham in Surrey. Buried May IX in St Giles, Cripplegate.

4. Edward Philips or Phillips, in his life of Milton, attached to

pired in an emaciated state, in a cold month, and was interred by direction of his widow. An expensive outward coffin of lead, therefore, was needless, and unlikely to have been provided by a rapacious woman who oppressed her husband's children while he was living, and cheated them after he was dead.

' *"Seventhly.* Because it is improbable that the circumstance of MILTON's having been deposited under the desk should, if true, have been so effectually concealed from the whole train of his biographers. It was, nevertheless, produced as an ancient and well-known tradition, as soon as the parishioners of Cripplegate were aware that such an incident was gaped for by antiquarian appetence, and would be swallowed by antiquarian credulity. How happened it that Bishop Newton, who urged similar inquiries concerning MILTON above forty years ago in the same parish, could obtain no such information?[5]

Letters of State, written by Mr John Milton, etc., London, 1964 (p. 43), says: 'He is said to have dyed worth £1500 in Money (a considerable Estate, all things considered), besides Household Goods; for he sustained such losses as might well have broke any person less frugal and temperate than himself; no less than £2,000 which he had put for Security and Improvement into the Excise Office, but, neglecting to recall it in time, could never after get it out, with all the Power and Interest he had in the Great ones of those Times; besides another great Sum by mismanagement and for want of good advice.'

5. Thomas Newton, Bishop of Bristol, thus writes in his life of Milton, prefixed to his edition of *Paradise Lost*, London, 1749: 'His body was decently interred near that of his father (who had died very aged about the year 1647) in the chancel of the church of St Giles, Cripplegate; and all his great and learned friends in London, not without a friendly concourse of the common people, paid their last respects in attending it to the grave. Mr Fenton, in his short but elegant account of the life of Milton, speaking of our author's having no monument, says that "he desired a friend to inquire at St Giles's Church, where the sexton showed him a small monument, which he

' "*Eighthly*. Because Mr Laming (see Mr Neve's pamphlet, second edition, p. 19) observes that the 'sludge' at the bottom of the coffin 'emitted a nauseous smell'. But, had this corpse been as old as that of MILTON, it must have been disarmed of its power to offend, nor would have supplied the least effluvium to disgust the nostrils of our delicate inquirer into the secrets of the grave. The last remark will seem to militate against a foregoing one. The whole difficulty, however, may be solved by a resolution not to believe a single word said on such an occasion by any of those who invaded the presumptive sepulchre of MILTON. The man who can handle pawned stays, breeches and petticoats without disgust may be supposed to have his organs of smelling in no very high state of perfection.

' "*Ninthly*. Because we have not been told by Wood, Philips, Richardson, Toland, etc., that Nature, among her other partialities to MILTON, had indulged him with an uncommon share of teeth. And yet above a hundred have been

---

said was supposed to be Milton's; but the inscription had never been legible since he was employed in that office, which he has possessed about forty years." This sure could never have happened in so short a space of time, unless the epitaph had been industriously erased; and that supposition, says Mr Fenton, "carries with it so much inhumanity that I think we ought to believe it was not erected to his memory". It is evident that it was not erected to his memory and that the sexton was mistaken. For Mr Toland, in his account of the life of Milton, says that he was buried in the chancel of St Giles's Church, "where the piety of his admirers will shortly erect a monument becoming his worth, and the encouragement of letters in King William's reign". This plainly implies that no monument was erected to him at that time, and this was written in 1698, and Mr Fenton's account was first published, I think, in 1725; so that not above twenty-seven years intervened from the one account to the other, and consequently the sexton, who it is said was possessed of his office about forty years, must have been mistaken, and the monument must have been designed for some other person, and not for Milton.'

sold as the furniture of his mouth by the conscientious worthies who assisted in the plunder of his supposed carcase, and finally submitted it to every insult that brutal vulgarity could devise and express. Thanks to fortune, however, his corpse has hitherto been violated but by proxy! May his genuine reliques (if aught of him remains unmingled with common earth) continue to elude research, at least while the present overseers of the poor of Cripplegate are in office. Hard, indeed, would have been the fate of the author of *Paradise Lost* to have received shelter in a chancel, that a hundred and sixteen years after his interment his *domus ultima* might be ransacked by two of the lowest human beings, a retailer of spirituous liquors, and a man who lends sixpences to beggars on such despicable securities as tattered bedgowns, cankered porridge-pots, and rusty gridirons.[6] *Cape saxa manu, cape robora, pastor!* But an Ecclesiastical Court may yet have cognizance of this more than savage transaction. It will then be determined whether our tombs are our own, or may be robbed with impunity by the little tyrants of a workhouse.

> If charnel-houses, and our graves, must send
> Those that we bury back, our monuments
> Shall be the maws of kites.

It should be added that our Pawnbroker, Gin-seller, and Company, by deranging the contents of their ideal MILTON's coffin, by carrying away his lower jaw, ribs, and right hand – and by employing one bone as an instrument to batter the rest – by tearing the shroud and winding-sheet to pieces, &c.,

6. Between the creditable trades of pawnbroker and dram-seller there is a strict alliance. As Hogarth observes, the money lent by Mr Gripe is immediately conveyed to the shop of Mr Killman, who, in return for the produce of rags, distributes poison under the specious name of cordials. See Hogarth's celebrated print called 'Gin Lane'.

&c., had annihilated all such further evidence as might have been collected from a skilful and complete examination of these nameless fragments of mortality. So far, indeed, were they mutilated that, had they been genuine, we could not have said with Horace:

Invenies etiam disjecti membra Poetae.

' "Who, after a perusal of the foregoing remarks (which are founded on circumstantial truth), will congratulate the parishioners of St Giles, Cripplegate, on their discovery and treatment of the imaginary dust of MILTON? His favourite, Shakespeare, most fortunately reposes at a secure distance from the paws of Messieurs Laming and Fountain, who, otherwise, might have provoked the vengeance imprecated by our great dramatic poet on the remover of his bones.

'From the preceding censures, however, Mr Cole (Church-warden), and Messrs Strong and Ascough (Vestry and Parish Clerks), should, in the most distinguished manner, be exempted. Throughout the whole of this extraordinary business, they conducted themselves with the strictest decency and propriety. It should also be confessed, by those whom curiosity has since attracted to the place of MILTON's supposed disinterment, that the politeness of the same parish officers could only be exceeded by their respect for our illustrious author's memory, and their concern at the complicated indignity which his nominal ashes have sustained."

'Now it was hardly likely that Mr Neve, with the extremely plausible case that he had, would sit still and see his pet theory knocked on the head, so he issued a second edition of his pamphlet with this

' "POSTSCRIPT

' "As some reports have been circulated, and some anonymous papers have appeared, since the publication of this pamphlet, with intent to induce a belief that the corpse mentioned in it is that of a woman, and as the curiosity of the public now calls for a second impression of it, an opportunity is offered of relating a few circumstances which have happened since the 14th of August, and which, in some degree, may confirm the opinion that the corpse is that of Milton.

' "On Monday, the 16th I called upon the overseer, Mr Fountain, when he told me that the parish officers had then seen a surgeon who, on Wednesday the 4th, had got through a window into the church, and who had, upon inspection, pronounced the corpse to be that of a woman. I thought it very improbable that a surgeon should creep through a window, who could go through a door for a few half-pence; but I no otherwise expressed my doubts of the truth of the information than by asking for the surgeon's address. I was answered 'that the gentleman begged not to have it known, that he might not be interrupted by inquiries'. A trifling relic was, nevertheless, at the same time withholden, which I had expected to receive through Mr Fountain's hands; by which it appeared that those in possession of them were still tenacious of the spoils of the coffin, although they affected to be convinced they were not those of Milton. These contradictions, however, I reserved for the test of an inquiry elsewhere.

' "In the course of that week I was informed that some gentlemen had, on Tuesday, the 17th, prevailed on the churchwardens to suffer a second disinterment of the coffin, which had taken place on that day. On Saturday, the 21st, I waited on Mr Strong, who told me that he had been present at such second disinterment, and that he had then sent for an experienced surgeon of the neighbourhood, who, upon inspection and examination of the corpse, had pronounced it to be that of a man. I was also informed, on that day, the

21st, by a principal person of the parish, whose information cannot be suspected, that the parish officers had agreed among themselves that, from my frequent visits and inquiries, I must have an intention of delivering some account of the transaction to the world; and that, therefore, to stop the narrative from going forth, they must invent some story of a surgeon's inspection on the 4th, and of this declaration that the corpse was that of a woman. From this information it was easy to judge what would be the fate of any personal application to the parish officers, with intent to obtain a restitution of what had been taken from the coffin. I, therefore, on Wednesday, the 25th, addressed the following letter to Mr Strong:

' " 'Dear Sir,

' " 'The reflection of a few moments, after I left you on Saturday, clearly showed me that the probability of the coffin in question being Milton's was not at all weakened, either by the dates, or the number of persons on the Smiths' monument; but that it was rather confirmed by the latter circumstance. By the evidence which you told me was given by the surgeon, called in on Tuesday, the 17th, the corpse is that of a male; it is certainly not that of a man of eighty-five; if, therefore, it be one of the earlier buried Smiths, all the later coffins of that family should appear, but not one of them is found. I, then, suppose the monument to have been put there because the flat pillar, after the pulpit was removed, offered a convenient situation for it, and '*near this place*' to be open, as it is in almost every case where it appears, to very liberal interpretation.

' " 'It is, therefore, to be believed, that the unworthy treatment, on the 4th, was offered to the corpse of Milton. Knowing what I know, I must not be silent. It it a very unpleasant story to relate; but, as it has fallen to my task, I will not shrink from it. I respect nothing in this world more than truth, and the memory of Milton; and to swerve in a tittle from the first would offend the latter. I shall give the plain and simple narrative, as delivered by the parties themselves. If it sit heavy on any of their shoulders, it is a burthen of their own taking up, and their own backs must bear it. They are all, as I find, very fond of deriving honour to themselves from Milton, as their parishioner; perhaps the mode, which I have hinted, is the only one which they have now left themselves of proving an equal desire to do honour to him. If I had thought that, in personally proposing to the parish officers a general search for, and collection of, all the spoils, and to put them, together with the mangled corpse and old coffin, into a new leaden one, I should have been attended to, I would have taken that method; but, when I found such impertinent inventions as setting up a fabulous surgeon to creep in at a window practised, I felt that so low an attempt at derision would ensure that, whatever I should afterwards propose, would be equally derided, and I had then left no other means than to call in the public opinion in aid of my own, and to hope that we should, at length, see the bones of an honest man, and the first scholar and poet our country can boast, restored to their sepulchre.

' " 'The narrative will appear, I believe, either tomorrow or on Friday; whenever it does, your withers are unwrung, and Mr Cole has shown himself an upright churchwarden.

' " 'I cannot conclude without returning you many thanks for your great civilities, and am, &c.'

' "The corpse was found entirely mutilated by those who disinterred it on the 17th; almost all the ribs, the lower jaw, and one of the hands gone. Of all those who saw the body on

Wednesday, the 4th, and on Thursday the 5th, there is not one person who discovered a single hair of any other colour than light brown, although Mr Laming and Mr Ellis lifted up the head, and although the considerable quantity of hair which Mr Taylor took was from the top of the head, and that which Ellis took was from behind it; yet, from the accounts of those who saw it on the 17th, it appears that the hair on the back of the head was found of dark brown, nearly approaching to black, although all the front hair remaining was of the same light brown as that taken on the 4th. It does not belong to me either to account for or to prove the fact.

' "On Wednesday, September the 1st, I waited on Mr Dyson, who was the gentleman sent for on the 17th, to examine the corpse. I asked him simply, whether, from what had then appeared before him, he judged it to be male or female? His answer was that, having examined the pelvis and the skull, he judged the corpse to be that of a man. I asked what was the shape of the head? He said that the forehead was high and erect, though the top of the head was flat; and added that the skull was of that shape and flatness at the top which, differing from those of blacks, is observed to be common and almost peculiar to persons of very comprehensive intellects. I am a stranger to this sort of knowledge, but the opinion is a strong confirmation that, from all the premises before him, he judged the head to be that of Milton. On a paper, which he showed me, enclosing a bit of the hair, he had written 'Milton's hair'.

' "Mr Dyson is a surgeon, who received his professional education under the late Dr Hunter, is in partnership with Mr Price, in Fore Street, where the church stands, is of easy access, and his affability can be exceeded only by his skill in an extensive line of practice.

' "Mr Taylor, too, who is a surgeon of considerable practice and eminence in his county, judged the corpse, on the 4th, to be that of a male.

' "A man, also, who has for many years acted as grave-digger in that parish, and who was present on the 17th, decided, upon first sight of the skull, that it was male; with as little hesitation, he pronounced another, which had been thrown out of the ground in digging, to be that of a woman. Decisions obviously the result of practical, rather than of scientific knowledge; for, being asked his reasons, he could give none, but that observation had taught him to distinguish such subjects. Yet this latter sort of evidence is not to be too hastily rejected; it may not be understood by everybody, but to anyone acquainted with those who are eminently skilled in judging of the genuineness of ancient coins, it will be perfectly intelligible. In that difficult and useful art, the eye of a proficient decides at once; a novice, however, who should inquire for the reasons of such decision, would seldom receive a further answer than that the decision itself is the result of experience and observation, and that the eye can be instructed only by long familiarity with the subject; yet all numismatic knowledge rests upon this sort of judgment.

' "After these evidences, what proofs are there, or what probable presumptions, that the corpse is that of a woman?

' "It was necessary to relate these facts, not only as they belonged to the subject, but lest, from the reports and papers above mentioned, I might, otherwise, seem to have given either an unfaithful or a partial statement of the evidences before me; whereas now it will clearly be seen what facts appeared on the first disinterment, which preceded, and what are to be attributed to the second, which succeeded the date of the narrative.

' "I have now added every circumstance which has hitherto come to my knowledge relative to this extraordinary transaction, and conclude with this declaration, that I should be very glad if any person would, from facts, give me reason to believe that the corpse in question is rather that of Elizabeth Smith, whose name I know only from her monument, than that of JOHN MILTON.

P.N."'

8th of September, 1790

Appendix II

13

More Pliant Beings

Foreword

THESE beings, following the main procession of this book, move a little apart from it. The shadows they cast are less gigantic; though they, like those cast by the main procession, 'do not lie in their proper geometrical proportions'.

Some of the beings portrayed in the earlier part of the book seem to exist in a 'universe reigned over by any deformation whatsoever – in accordance with any laws, as complicated as we liked' – 'these laws ruling over our bodies also, and the rays of light emanating from the various bodies'.[1]

At moments they had the 'rigid and even splendid attitude of Death'; at others, 'some exaggeration of the attitudes common to Life'. In the chapters to follow, we find those attitudes are a little more pliant; and it is for that reason that I have placed them apart from the main body of the book.

But we find, however, in the chapter 'Of Revelations, courteous and otherwise, and of admirable Removals,' an 'exaggeration of the attitudes common to Life', or, rather, to the world, inasmuch as the Spirits in whom the chapter abounds, showed a most peculiar persistence, believing themselves, as do many of those who still walk the earth, to be alive – and an equal persistence in the habits in which they clothed themselves before their transformation. The spirits of old Mr and Mrs Furze, for instance, enjoyed frightening and bullying their son's young servant, poor nettle-dull Mr Fry,

1. Henri Poincaré, *Science and Method*, translated by Francis Maitland.

after their death as during their lifetime, reducing his in-comprehension and rustic fears into chaos. Persistence, too, was the characteristic of certain pretended scholiasts, such as Mr Bray and Mr Combe, for whom the world existed, mainly, in order to prove their theories were right.

'I am afraid, sir,' said a young writer in Borrow's *Laven-gro*, 'it was very wrong to write such trash, and yet more to allow it to be published.'

'Trash! Not at all,' was the reply, 'a very pretty piece of speculative philosophy. Of course you were wrong in saying there is no world. The world must exist, to have the shape of a pear; and that the world is shaped like a pear and not like an apple, as the fools of Oxford say, I have satisfactorily proved in my book. Now, if there were no world, what would become of my system?'

Dr Kettle had many of the characteristics of what Mr de la Mare called 'poor gay Mr Punch', hitting a head whenever he saw it and screaming in a highly ghostly voice. He seemed always to be outside the world, but descending on it to punish it for existing.

The adventurers, the Pious Pirates, were inspired, first, we think, by the certainty that every action they might take was right; secondly, by the same spirit that inspired the 'silly country fellow' of whom Robert Burton quotes 'Lod: Vives' as saying that he 'killed his ass for drinking up the moon, *ut lunam mundo redderet*' (that he might restore the moon to the world). (The lost and unknown world that had fallen under the dominion of a heaven they did not under-stand.)

The troubles of the ordinary man are as nothing to those of the man of science, the learned, the wholly conscious – such men, let us say, as Thomas Carlyle.

'I am standing on the threshold about to enter a room,' wrote Sir Arthur Eddington, in *The Nature of the Physical*

World.[2] 'It is a complicated business. In the first place, I must shove against an atmosphere pressing with a force of fourteen pounds on every square inch of my body, I must make sure of landing on a plank travelling at twenty miles a second round the sun – a fraction of a second too early or too late, the plank would be miles away. I must do this while hanging from a round planet – head outward into space, and with a wind of aether blowing at no one knows how many miles a second through every interstice of my body. The plank has no solidity of substance. To step on it is like stepping on a swarm of flies. Shall I not slip through? No, if I make the venture, one of the flies hits me and gives me a boost up again; I fall again and am knocked upwards by another fly; and so on. I may hope that the net result will be that I remain about steady; but if unfortunately I should slip through the floor or be boosted too violently up to the ceiling, the occurrence would be, not a violation of the laws of Nature, but a rare coincidence. These are some of the minor difficulties. I ought really to look at the problem four-dimensionally as concerning the intersection of my world-line with that of the plank. Then again, it is necessary to determine in which direction the entropy of the world is increasing in order to make sure that my passage over the threshold is an entrance, not an exit.

'Verily it is easier for a camel to pass through the eye of a needle than for a scientific man to pass through a door. And whether the door be barn door or church door, it might be wiser that he should consent to be an ordinary man and walk in rather than wait till all the difficulties involved in a really scientific ingress are resolved.'

The inhabitants of this world might be divided into two classes, the first, and infinitely the largest, preferring the

2. Published by The Macmillan Company, New York, N.Y. Reprinted with their kind permission.

existence of the child of Mary Clark, in whom 'there was not the least indication of either cerebrum, cerebellum, or any medullary substance whatever'. The second, like myself, preferring the life endured by the man of science – sans flies, however.

14

Of Revelations, Courteous and Otherwise, and of Admirable Removals

THERE are spirits (according to Sir Thomas Browne) who, being 'noble essences' (having a friendly regard for us), will make us 'courteous revelations', and there are Spirits (but Sir Thomas does not mention these) whose revelations are anything but courteous!

The behaviour of some – whether noble or otherwise – was so peculiar as to bring them within the scope of this book.

'Bodine', said Robert Burton in *The Anatomy of Melancholy*, 'will have these ... genii, spirits, devils ... to be of some shape, and that absolutely round, like sun and moon, because that is the most perfect form, which has no rough edges, no corners, no twists, no projections, but is the most perfect of shapes ... that they can assume other aerial bodies, all manner of shapes at their pleasures, appear in what likeness they will themselves, that they are most swift in motion, can pass many miles in an instant, and so likewise transform bodies of others into what shape they please, and with admirable celerity remove them from place to place ... most writers of this subject credibly believe; and that they can foretell future events, and do many strange miracles ...'

And Leo Suavius, a Frenchman (out of some Platonists), will have the air to be as full of them as snow falling in the skies, and that they may be seen, and withal sets down the means how men may see them ...

Carden in his *Hyperchen*, out of the doctrine of Stoicks, will have some of these genii (for so he calls them) 'to be desirous of men's company, being affable and familiar with them, as dogs are'.

Whether absolutely round, like sun and moon, with no rough edges, or otherwise, the ghost of Lady Hoby (sister to Lady Burleigh, she married Sir Thomas Hoby, Ambassador to France, in 1533, and, after his death, Lord Russell) must cause a certain amount of alarm, since, according to Miss Christina Hole's *Haunted England*, she has the disconcerting habit of appearing 'in reverse colouring, like a photographic negative, her face and hands being black and her dress white'. Nor is this all. The door of a bedroom opens, and the phantom issues, a basin floating before her, with no visible means of support, and in this she washes her hands, ceaselessly.

The reason for this alarming manifestation is that, according to a legend, she had a little son named William who was slow with his lessons, and whom she (one of the most learned women of the time) beat unmercifully until one day she beat him too long and too hard, and he died.

And yet – no mention of a child of that time named William is to be found. In Bisham Church the names of four Hoby children are preserved – Edward, Thomas Posthumous, (whom she persecuted unremittingly in minor ways), Elizabeth, and Ann (who died within a few days of each other in 1570). And Francis was the name of the only son of her marriage with Lord Russell. But it is said (again in *Haunted England*) that when some alterations were being made in Bisham Abbey, some old, dusty copybooks were found that had once been wet with a little boy's tears, and that these 'bore the name of William Hoby, written in a childish hand'.

If those copybooks existed, the tears of them have long since turned to dust, like the short, unhappy life of the little boy who shed them – if he was real and not, like Lady Hoby in her present manifestation, a ghost.

During her lifetime, the appearance of Lady Hoby must have caused almost as much alarm as that of her ghost. She was, when living, a pest of an outstanding quality, and her nephew, Sir Robert Cecil, then in office, can scarcely have known an instant's peace. A Dean wished to be a Bishop, a neighbour to be a Knight. A Judge of the Common Pleas had to be rebuked for having given an adverse judgement against her, and 'my being your Aunt, my place had deserved more regard of justice'. Sir Robert must 'yield your best service to a doughty, honest, and honourable nobleman, the Earl of Kent, to be in the Earl of Huntington's place'. But then comes a note of caution : 'I would not have it known to proceed from me, because he is a widower and I a widow.'

Lady Russell was quite willing to come to Court to make up the quarrel between Sir Robert and Sir William Knollys, Comptroller of the Royal Household – but only on condition that Her Majesty 'ordered my Lord Chamberlain that I may have a convenient lodging within the house … otherwise, upon the least wet of my feet or legs by long clothes or cold, my pate is so subject to rheum that my hearing is so bad as that I am fit for no company, or other place but my own cell.

'Your Aunt that ever deserved the best.

E. R. Dowager'

According to Miss Violet Wilson – from whose entertaining book, *Society Women of Shakespeare's Time*, I culled these details of Lady Russell's manifestations when alive – the afflicted Sir Robert must have known, from one look at the signature of these letters, what was in store for him, in the way of reproaches or grievances: 'Your honest, plain-dealing Aunt', 'Your desolate wronged Aunt', 'Your loving Aunt, poor but proud'.

As for Sir Posthumous Hoby, his life was spent in captivity. At one moment of his boyhood he ran away to sea. But her Ladyship 'overtook the fugitive in the Isle of Stepney', and brought him back, captive, to her house in Stepney. Lord Burleigh was then pestered into taking him into his household, and his mother, with commendable firmness, married him to an heiress.

As for the 'translation with admirable celerity', or, as Mr John Aubrey expressed it, 'Transportation by an Invisible Power', it seems to have been actuated solely by a wish to bewilder.

A certain Lord Duffus, we are told by Aubrey, walking in the fields near his house, heard 'the noise of a whirlwind, and of voices crying "Horse and Hattock" [these are the words the fairies are said to use when they remove from any place]'. Whereupon he cried 'Horse and Hattock' also, and was immediately caught up and transported through the air by the fairies, far away over the bright fields of summer, 'to the French King's cellar in Paris, where, next day, after having "drunk heartily" and fallen asleep, he found himself with a silver cup in his hand'. Brought into the King's presence, and 'questioned by him, who he was, and how he came thither, he told his name, his Countrey, and the place of his residence'. His Majesty, apparently, showed great understanding of the situation.

The gentleman who told Aubrey this tale was the tutor to his Lordship's eldest son, and seems to have been addicted to the idea of transportation of this kind, for he himself, when a schoolboy, 'whipping his top with his schoolfellows, heard the noise of a wind, and at some distance saw small dust begin to arise and turn around, which motion continued, advancing till it came the place where they were; whereupon they began to bless themselves: but one of their number [being, it seems, a little more bold and confident than his companions] said "Horse and Hattock with my top", and immediately they all saw the top lifted from the ground'. Translated in a cloud of dust, this enchanted plaything, whirling high in the air, was carried away – away.

A gentleman of John Aubrey's acquaintance, Mr A. M., 'was in Portugal, *anno* 1655, when one was burnt by the Inquisition for being brought thither from Goa, in East Indies, in the air, in an incredible short time'.

Francis Fry, 'aged twenty-one next August, 1683', was, according to a letter from the Reverend Andrew Paschal, Rector of Chedzoy in Somersetshire to Mr Aubrey, an outstanding sufferer from translations and apparitions.

First, he was accosted in a field by the Apparition of an aged gentleman with a pole in his hand, 'like that he was wont to carry about with him when living, to kill moles withal', who warned Mr Fry not to be afraid of him but to give his master, son to the Apparition, the message that several legacies he had bequeathed, were unpaid.

After that, the sufferings of Mr Fry were acute. The ghost of an old lady mounted his horse behind him, and caused that quadruped ('a mean beast') to spring at least twenty-five feet, in the presence of Mr Fry's master, Mr Furze.

'The Spectrum' then appeared once more to the afflicted youth, and caused the Spectre of his wife (denounced by him as 'that wicked woman' although the clerical author of the letter knew her to be a very good woman) to manifest herself not only to Fry, but to Mrs Thomasin Gridley, Anne Langdon, and to a little child who shrieked so persistently that she was forced to be removed from the house. Sometimes the old lady would manifest herself in her own shape, sometimes in shapes even more alarming, such as that of a dog belching fire, or of a horse, appearing suddenly in the house, and flying out of the window.

But worse was to come. The Spectres seem to have succeeded in wedging Mr Fry's face into the framework of a chair; and the 'entangling of Fry's face and legs about his neck, and about the frame of the chair' was such that they were 'with great difficulty disentangled'.

Mr Fry was careful to shut his periwig in a box and lock the latter at night. But the Spectres got at it and tore it to flitters. As for his shoe-strings, a maid assured the Rector that she saw one of these walk out of his shoe and fly to the other side of the room, without any visible means of locomotion. The other was about to follow suit, but the maid put a stop to this, and, instead, helped it out, whereupon it 'crisped and curled about her hand like a living eel'.

A barrel full of salt marched from one room into another; an andiron placed itself over a pan of milk scalding on the fire. Nor was this all. The Spectrum of Mrs Furze, senior, had the trying habit of appearing dressed, to the last detail, in the same manner as her daughter-in-law.

Then came the day when Mr Fry, returning from work, was seized by old Mrs Furze by the skirts of his doublet, and carried into the air. And there he remained, between heaven and earth, for the space of half an hour!

At the end of this time, a whistling and singing was heard coming from a quagmire, and, on inquiry being made, there, sure enough, was Mr Fry.

This phenomenon was ascribed, unsympathetically, to Mr Fry's fits. But on coming to himself, an hour after, he protested solemnly that Mrs Furze had carried him so high that he 'saw his master's house underneath him, no bigger than a haycock', that he was in perfect sense, and prayed God not to suffer him to be destroyed.

His periwig was sighted next morning at the top of a tall tree.

As for Anne Langdon, the Rector reported that, excepting for the 'aerial journey', she had been as grievously treated. He added gloomily, that 'her fits and obsessions seem to be greater, for she screeches in a most hellish tone'.

'Thomasin Gridley (though removed) is in trouble as I hear.'

It is agreeable to turn from these dark hauntings to the contemplation of two pleasant ghosts.

John Aubrey tells the story of the friendship lasting beyond the death of one of the friends, between Lord Middleton and the Laird Bocconi. Lord Middleton, then General Middleton, went into the Highlands to try to raise an army for King Charles I. Warned, while there, by an old gentleman with second sight that he was in danger, he yet persisted. He was taken prisoner 'at Worcester fight, and was prisoner in the Tower of London, under three locks'. One night, the Laird Bocconi appeared to him. Lord Middleton asked him if he were dead or alive. He said that he was dead, and a ghost, and told him that he would escape, in three days; and this he did: Having spoken thus, the Laird 'gave a frisk, and said:

> Givenni Givanni 'tis very strange,
> In the world to see so sudden a change.

and then gathered up and vanished'.

As for the other pleasant ghost: '*Anno* 1670, not far from Cirencester, was an apparition; being demanded, whether a good spirit, or a bad? returned no answer, he disappeared with a curious perfume and most melodious twang. Mr W. Lilly believes it was a fairy.'

15

Weathercock Wits

'THE days spent at school', ancient persons of a short memory are in the habit of telling schoolboys, 'are the happiest in a man's life.'

It cannot be said that under the rule of the Reverend Dr Ralph Kettle (who was born in 1553 and died in 1643) the life of the undergraduate at Trinity College, Oxford, was an unmixed pleasure. They were young – in those days undergraduates were of the age of public-school boys – and they were mischievous.

'One of the Fellowes', John Aubrey, from whom I have culled this account, tells us, 'was wont to say that Dr Kettle's braine was like a Hasty-Pudding, where there was Memorie, Judgment, and Phancy all stirred together. He had all these Faculties in Great Measure, but they were all just so jumbled together. If you had to doe with him, taking him for a Foole, you would have found in him great Subtilty and reach; è contra, if you treated him as a wise man, you would have mistaken him for a Foole.'

In short, you never knew where you had him.

'One of his maximes of governing', said Aubrey, 'was to keepe downe the *Juvenilis Impetus*.'

In pursuit of this ideal, 'He'd have at any him that had a white Cap on; for he concluded him to have been drunk, and his head to ake.'

He was exceedingly irascible, and was 'irreconcileable to long haire; called them hairy Scalpes, and as for Periwigges (which were then very rarely worne), he beleeved them to be the Scalpes of men cutte off after they were hang'd, and so tann'd and dressed for use. When he observ'd the Scholars haire longer than ordinary (especially if they were Scholars of the House), he would bring a paire of Cizers in his Muffe (which he commonly wore) and woe be to them that sat on the outside of the Table. I remember he cutt Mr Radford's haire with the knife that chipps the bread on the Buttery Hatch, and then he sang (this is in the old play, *Gammer Gurton's Needle*):

> And was not Grim the Collier finely trimmd?
> Tonedi, Tonedi.

"Mr Lydall," said he, "how do you decline *tondeo? Tondeo? tondes, tonedi?*" '

The Doctor was in the habit of wandering about the College, looking through keyholes to 'see whether the Boyes did follow their books or no'. But, luckily, 'he dragg'd with one foot a little, by which he gave warning (like a rattle-snake) of his comeing'.

He would scold 'idle young boies', calling them 'Turds, Tarrarags (these were the worst sort), rude Rakills, Rascall-Jacks, Blindcinques, Slobberlotchers (these did no hurt, were sober, but went idleing about the Grove)'.

But the boys would laugh at him in Chapel, 'for he had a thin shrill high Treble'; but there was one impudent young jackanapes who had one still higher, and he was wont to raise this as far as it would go, in order to inspire the Doctor to still greater heights.

He was in the habit of divulging the faults of the under-graduates from the pulpit, and when young Mr Ettrick and some other boys were in trouble for frightening a poor simple young freshman of Magdalen by pretending to 'conjure' – that is, raise up spirits – the old Doctor denounced Mr Ettrick, who was of small stature, in these terms: 'Mr Ettrick will conjure up a Jackanapes to be his great-grand-father.'

Indeed, Dr Kettle's sermons were by no means devoid of surprises. A neighbour of Mr Aubrey heard him conclude a sermon with these words: *'But now I see it is time for me to shutt up my Booke; for I see the Doctor's men come in wiping of their beardes from the Ale-house.'* For he had seen, from the pulpit, these unfortunates steal out at the beginning of the sermon and, hoping to be undetected, creep in at the end.

Nor can it be said that his instruction was dull. 'I will show you,' he told his pupils, 'how to inscribe a Triangle in a Quadrangle. Bring a pig into the quadrangle, and I will sett the colledge dog at him, and he will take the pig by the eare, then come I and take the Dog by the tayle and the hog by the tayle, and so there you have a Triangle in a quadrangle, *quod erat faciendum*.' But he would take his hourglass to lectures, and would threaten 'the Boyes ... that if they did not doe their exercise better he would bring an Hower-glasse two howers long'.

If his irascibility was great, so was his charity. And often, if he guessed an industrious young boy was poor, he would slip money through the boy's window and on to his windowsill. And if one of his parishioners at Garsington was in want, he would let his parsonage to him for a year – two years – three years – at forty pounds a year (then a large sum) less than its value.

But it was dangerous to toy with him, and when Lady Isabella Thynne and her friend Mrs Fenshawe visited him 'as a frolick', the Doctor, addressing Mrs Fenshawe, said, 'Madam, your husband and father I bred up here, and I knew your grandfather. I know you to be a gentlewoman, I will not say you are a whore, but gette you gonne for a very (true) woman.'

He lived to be very old. And John Aubrey thought he would have 'finished his century' 'had not those civill warres come on; which much grieved him, that was wont to be absolute in the colledge, to be affronted and disrespected by rude soldiers'.

Indeed, one went so far as to break the dreaded hour-glass.

And, too, he was shocked that Mrs Fenshawe and Lady Isabella Thynne came 'to our Chapell, mornings, halfe dressd, like Angells'. He was grieved by the dissoluteness of the age, and so 'his dayes were shortened, and he dyed and was buried at Garsington'.

'How would the good old Doctor have raunted and beate-up his Kettle Drum', if he should have seen such Luxury in the College as there is now! *Tempora mutantur!*

16

Serious Circles

In the summer of the year 1841, 'a queer, three-cornered, awkward girl, sallow and dark' – to quote a description of her as a schoolgirl – might have been seen making her way into Mr Bray's garden on the outskirts of Coventry and approaching a group of people who were lying, sprawling, or sitting on a bearskin spread on the grass.

The group in question provided the twenty-two-year-old Miss Marian Evans with her first experience of intellectual society.

Marian Evans can scarcely, at that time, have shown signs of greatness. Nor does she seem to have been in any way striking to look at. But in later years the great novelist who was known as George Eliot had, in spite of her ugliness, a monolithic, mysterious, primeval grandeur of countenance, like that of an Easter Island statue, washed by oceans of light.

She was, at the time of her visits to Mr and Mrs Bray, a positive glutton for boredom – devouring, with apparent enthusiasm, such works as Scrope's *Deer-stalking in the Highlands*, Mrs Jameson's *Winter Scenes and Summer Rambles in Canada* (although this book aroused in her grave doubts of Mrs Jameson's religious principles), Professor Hopper's work on the subject of Schism, Milner's *Church History*, and W. Gresley's *Portrait of an English Churchman*.

When her brother Isaac took her to London in the summer of the year 1838 (she was then aged nineteen), she was 'not at all delighted with the stir of the Great Babel'; and, having unwisely allowed some flippant friends, a little later in the same summer, to take her to an Oratorio, she could not help asking herself, 'Can it be desirable and would it be consistent with millennial holiness for a human being to devote the time and energies that are barely sufficient for real exigencies, in acquiring trills, cadences, etc. etc.?'

But in after years, it must be admitted that she was so weak as to be seduced by Handel's Oratorio 'The Messiah'; and it is recorded of her that even in girlhood she was so overcome by the religious feeling of some Oratorio to which, again, she had allowed herself to be taken, that she burst into a loud howling, the bassoon-like notes of which persisted throughout the work, gravely disturbing the rest of the audience.

However, irresponsible pleasures of this kind were far from the intellectual pleasures to be found in Mr and Mrs Bray's garden.

At first, the owner of the garden and the bearskin had been extremely loath to pursue Miss Evans' acquaintance, which he had made at the house of his sister, Mrs Pears. She reminded him but too vividly of his seven rigidly Evangelical sisters. For Mr Bray was, at one time, a convinced Unitarian. But this resemblance, strangely enough, while it formed, at first, an insuperable barrier between Mr Bray and Miss Evans, was to lead to their ultimate friendship. For Mrs Pears saw, in this serious-minded girl, a possible influence for good, and after some months during which Mr Bray seems to have resisted strongly, a new meeting was arranged – this time in the home of Mr and Mrs Bray.

They were immediately captivated by her, and not only Mrs Bray, but her husband, found her a most desirable visitor.

This serious-minded man, a ribbon-manufacturer by profession, was, by now, incurably addicted to the study of Phrenology. Having sent to a London bookseller's for Andrew Combe's *Physiology*, he received, instead, a copy of

George Combe's *Phrenology*, and, on opening it, was at once 'seized [wrote Mr Laurence and Mrs Elizabeth Hanson, in their life of George Eliot, *Marion Evans and George Eliot*] with wild excitement', for 'in this science he could clearly see physical confirmation of the mental demonstration of Philosophical Necessity he had just read in Freedom of Will' (Jonathan Edwards' *Enquiry into the Freedom of Will*).

A prey to this ungovernable excitement, he dashed up to London and into the first hairdresser's shop he saw, and demanded that his head should be shaved completely bare. A cast of his head was then made, and Mr Bray rushed back to Coventry to inquire, from Mr Combe's book, if his mind was of the order that he supposed.

It was. But alas! The sacrifice of his hair had been unnecessary, for it would have been possible, he discovered, for the cast to have been made with his hair intact. However, he was now assured that 'the laws of mind were equally fixed or determined with those of matter', and, regarding himself as a missionary, he rode through the countryside, distributing casts to the villagers, who, attracted by the sight of his gleaming cranium, gathered round him.

The sacrifice of his hair had by no means impeded his courtship, and, the year after the sacrifice in question, he married a Miss Sara Hennell, the daughter of another ribbon-manufacturer, and on their honeymoon made the breath-taking announcement to her that he had renounced Unitarianism for ever. Then, producing from his luggage Holbach's *System of Nature* and Volnay's *Ruin of Empires*, he called upon his bride to read these and to follow his example.

He was, in time, to become the author of a work called *The Philosophy of Necessity*, as well as of an *Address to the Working Class on the Education of the Body and the Education of the Feelings*.

The guests who sprawled upon the bearskin were as serious-minded as their host. George Dyson, who was much influenced by Carlyle, would insist on delivering, in a horizontal position, interminable lectures on whatever subject was at the time occupying his attention. Mesmerism was to Mr Lafontaine what Phrenology was to Mr Bray, and Mr Bray financed a meeting in which it was hoped that Mr Lafontaine would make evident his powers. Unfortunately, the meeting was a fiasco, because, although he succeeded in mesmerizing a young lady, he could not induce her to divulge the contents of a book she had not read, and on which she was sitting, and this led to Mr Lafontaine being denounced as an impostor, and to the audience yelling for their money to be returned to them.

But most cherished of all Mr Bray's guests was the great George Combe, the author of the work that had excited Mr Bray on the subject of Phrenology. Mr Combe had, for some years, been married to Mrs Siddons' daughter Cecilia. But before suggesting marriage to her, he, following his tenets, insisted on his doctor examining him from the top of his head to the soles of his feet. The doctor assured him that he might marry with propriety, but warned him against choosing a young wife. As far as age went, Cecilia was a satisfactory choice, for she was thirty-nine. But she must yet pass a further test. Were the lobes of her brain satisfactory? This must be inquired into! Mr Combe therefore made a thorough examination of her head, and discovered, to his relief, that 'her anterior lobe is large; her Benevolence, Conscientiousness, Firmness, Self-Esteem [by which I suppose he meant self-respect] and Love of Approbation are amply developed, while Veneration and Wonder are equally moderate with my own'. But he was still undecided. However, in the end, having consulted his brother and his niece, who approved the match, he went over her letters and found that they 'undoubtedly show very superior business talents and thorough rationality'. But still a doubt remained. Might she not have a mistaken idea as to his financial situation and his ideas on the spending of money? He wrote to her, explaining these. Her answer was all for which he could have hoped. No longer able to suppress his ardour, he proposed to her, she accepted him, and they were married.

Mr Combe was given the place of honour on the bearskin, and from that position would discourse for hours on end – Mr Bray placing it on record that these monologues 'made his presence a wholesome sedative to our spirits. It did not surprise us, sometimes', he continued, 'when his devoted wife dropped asleep in the middle of his discourses, her head inclined towards him in a reverent attitude of attention.'

Sleep, 'in a reverent attitude of attention', was the keynote of life with the Brays. . . . But in another circle, more exalted intellectually, sleep seemed out of the question.

The man of genius and the aristocrat are frequently regarded as eccentrics by the ordinary, because both genius and aristocrat are entirely uninfluenced by the opinions and vagaries of the crowd. The giant will forgive the diminutive; the diminutive will never pardon the giant; 'I remember when I was at Lilliput', said Gulliver, 'the complexions of those diminutive people appeared to me the fairest in the world: and talking upon this subject with ... a friend of mine, he said that my face appeared much fairer and smoother when he looked on me from the ground than it did upon a nearer view when I took him up in my hand, and brought him close; which he confessed was at first a very shocking sight. He said, he could discover great holes in my skin; that the stumps of my beard were ten times stronger than the bristles of a boar; and my complexion made up of several colours altogether disagreeable ...'

The present writer does not intend to exhibit to the crowd

the 'great holes in the skin' of the giant Thomas Carlyle. She intends, rather, to prove that, just as those holes appear of immense size to the Lilliputian, so is the ceaseless meaningless flurry in the dust caused by the Lilliputians as they rush about their unimportant business, arising from nothing and dying away to nothing, magnified in the hearing and sight of the giant, until it becomes a torment.

Considering the household of Mr and Mrs Thomas Carlyle, one might almost quote these words from Mr Carlyle's *The French Revolution*: 'Insurrectionary Chaos lies slumbering round the Palace, like Ocean round a Diving Bell.'

The pair showed marked differences of temperament. 'Excitement', said Jane Carlyle, 'is my rest.' Whereas, according to Geraldine Jewsbury, Thomas was 'much too grand for everyday life. A sphinx does not fit in comfortably in our parlour-life arrangements, but seen from a proper point of view is a supernaturally grand object.'

In spite of being a sphinx, Mr Carlyle had always been exceedingly restless, and during his wife's first acquaintance with him, 'scratched the fender dreadfully. I must', said Jane, 'have a pair of carpet shoes and handcuffs prepared for him. . . . His tongue only should be left at liberty – his other members are most fantastically awkward.'

'London', declared Mr Carlyle, although it had 'a boiling uproar', yet 'amid its huge deafening hubbub of a Death-song, are to be heard tones of a Birth-song.'

The Birth-song, however, was not always popular; for in the 'Insurrectionary Chaos' that surrounded and filled the house in Cheyne Row, Chelsea, and indeed every house that the Carlyles inhabited or visited, dogs barked (had the whole world, Jane wondered, changed into a huge dog-kennel?), parrots yelled, servants played quoits with all the dishes and plates.

When the Carlyles took a holiday at Ramsgate, a 'brass

band', wrote Jane, 'plays all through our breakfast, and the brass band is succeeded by a band of Ethiopians, and that again by a band of female fiddlers! And interspersed with these are individual barrel organs, individual Scotch bagpipes and individual French horns.'

Even this was better than what must be endured in London, where the neighbours' cocks 'must either withdraw or must die'.

They did not die. Therefore, owing to Mr Carlyle's ceaseless flight from the Birth-song, the house was in a constant state of upheaval. Fresh rooms had to be built, exoduses planned.

In 1853, a sound-proof room had to be constructed, stretching from end to end of the top floor. In consequence, 'In rushed [a] troop of incarnate demons – bricklayers, whitewashers', etc. There was constant racket as Mr John Chorley (who, in his character of Carlyle's friend, was superintending the building operations) galloped ceaselessly up and down ladders. One workman fell through the ceiling into Mr Carlyle's bedroom, bringing a good deal of the building material with him. Another crashed into Mrs Carlyle's room, narrowly missing her head. The tables and chairs all had 'their legs in the air as if in convulsions'. Things got lost. Mr Carlyle 'kicked up a considerable of a row about a book he had mislaid' – and which was, of course, found where he had left it.

At last the building operations were finished and Mr Carlyle was installed in his new study. But no sooner was he installed than the young lady in the next house began practising the piano. The cocks heralded the dawn; the macaws screamed. All had been in vain.

What should be done? Should they rent the house next door? 'What is forty or forty-five pounds a year, to saving one's life and sanity?' Jane inquired. In the end, Mrs Carlyle paid the next-door neighbour five pounds on condition that nothing that barked, screamed, or crowed should ever disturb their peace again. She then retired to bed with a headache.

Not only the worlds of fur and feather seemed to be against them, but also the whole of the insect world. One morning, on their return from a visit to Scotland, in 'a room where everything is enveloped in dark yellow fog', Mr Carlyle said, across the breakfast table, 'My dear, I have to inform you that my bed is full of bugs, or fleas, or some sort of animals that crawl over me all night.'

The insect world, indeed, seems to have been tireless in its invasions – these, at times, being of a most peculiar order. One night, the maid dashed into the drawing-room, shrieking that a black-beetle had insisted on intruding into her ear, and was now making its way into her brain.

She was rushed to the surgery at the end of Cheyne Row, and part of the black-beetle was expelled, but the doctor thought that 'a leg or two' remained in this unusual mortuary chamber.

This, however, does not seem to have incommoded the maid; but Mrs Carlyle narrowly escaped catching a cold through venturing into the night air.

Mrs Carlyle was of great delicacy, though nothing prevented the lively, enchanting creature from enjoying any innocent pleasure that was to be found. But she was much addicted to influenza, colds, and headache. A friend – Mrs Brookfield – heard her say, 'The very least attention from Carlyle just glorifies me. When I have one of my headaches, and the sensation of red-hot knitting needles darting into my brain, Carlyle's way of expressing sympathy is to lay a heavy hand on the top of my head and keep it there in perfect silence for several seconds, so that although I could scream with nervous agony, I sit like a martyr smiling with joy at such a proof of profound pity from him.'

Mr Carlyle, as may be imagined, was much given to the praise of Silence. But the exiled Mazzini was driven by his constant monologues on the subject – lasting, sometimes, for over half an hour – to the conclusion that 'he loved silence somewhat platonically'.

Francis Espinasse, described by Mrs Carlyle as 'a painful youth whose "conversation" does not promise to be a treat', was, according to Mr Julian Symons' admirable biography of Carlyle, subjected to a long monologue dealing with the origin of the Arabic numerals from 2 to 9 'by the addition of strokes and curves to the perpendicular straight line which denotes the primitive numeral 1'.

Mr Carlyle disliked poetry, for 'empty as other folks' kettles are, artists' kettles are emptier, and good for nothing but tying to the tails of mad dogs'. (Milnes' Biography of Keats was, according to him, 'an attempt to make us eat dead dog by exquisite currying and cooking! Won't eat it. . . . The kind of man that Keats was gets ever more horrible to me. Force of hunger for pleasure of every kind and what of all other force – that is a combination'. He would therefore, as a rebuke to bores, 'recite in impressive monotone', to anyone who bored him, long stretches of poetry in which he frequently, quite deliberately, misquoted a word or a phrase.

It must have been terrifying to be subjected to the scrutiny of either Thomas or Jane – for, although they were often merciless in their judgements, they were also nearly always right – excepting in their criticism of poetry or the other arts.

Alfred Tennyson, however, was forgiven for being a poet. And Leigh Hunt was a frequent guest in the evenings. 'He enjoyed much,' said his host, 'and with a kind of chivalrous silence and respect, her [Jane's] Scottish tunes on the piano, most of which he knew already, and their Burns or other accompaniment; this was commonly enough the wind-up of the evening; "supper" being ordered (uniformly porridge of Scotch oatmeal), most likely the piano, on some hint, would be opened, and continue till the porridge came – a tiny basin of which Hunt always took, and ate with a teaspoon of sugar, and many praises of the excellent frugal and noble article.'

How different was such an evening as this from that endured by Jane at a dinner party given by the Kay-Shuttleworths. 'It was a very locked-jaw sort of business,' she told her husband; 'Little Helps was there, but even I could not animate him; he looked pale and as if he had a pain in his stomach. Milnes was there, and affable enough, but evidently overcome with a feeling that weighed on all of us – the feeling of having been dropped into a vacuum. ... Mrs — was an insupportable bore; she surely has the air of a retired unfortunate female; her neck and arms were naked, as if she had never eaten of the Tree of the Knowledge of Good and Evil! She reminded me of the Princess Huncamunca, as I once saw her represented in a barn. She ate and drank with a certain voracity; sneez'd once during the dinner, just like a hale old man, and altogether nothing could be more ungraceful, more unfeminine than her whole bearing.'

Miss Harriet Martineau was a constant visitor. According to Mrs Carlyle, she 'presented Mr Carlyle with her ear-trumpet with a pretty air of coquetry'. But after a time Mr Carlyle came to the conclusion that, although 'her very considerable talent would have made her a quite shining Matron of some big Female Establishment', yet she was 'totally inadequate to grapple with deep spiritual and social questions'. Also, she was 'too happy and too noisy', and when she arrived one day 'with an ear-trumpet, muff, and cloak' for a visit that lasted for an hour and a half, Mr Carlyle was so wearied by the noise of her happiness that he wrote in his

Journal, 'I wish this good Harriet would be happy by her-self.'

Worse still was the visit from Emerson – a visit that lasted not only for an hour and a half, but for the whole time he was in London.

The two sages had met, and been delighted with each other, in Scotland about fifteen years before, and now Car-lyle invited Emerson to be his guest in London: 'Know then, my friend,' he wrote, 'that in verity, your Home while in England is here. . . .'

But circumstances had changed since those happy meetings in Scotland. Each of the friends was now famous; each was accustomed to having his own way, and each enjoyed talking but not listening. Also, Mr Carlyle would brook no con-tradiction.

At first, the visit went moderately well. But life under the same roof was an ordeal. 'For two days,' wrote Jane, 'I have lived on the manna of his [Emerson's] speech, and I have escaped to my bedroom, to *bathe my head in cold water*, and report progress ... they do not hate each other *yet* C. still calls Emerson "a most polite and gentle creature! a man of a really Seraphic nature! tho' on certain sides of him overlaid with really mad rubbish" – and Emerson still (in confidence to me) calls C. "a good child!" in spite of all his deification of the *Positive*, the *Practical* – most astonishing for those who first made acquaintance with him in his Books! . . . he avoids, with a laudable tact, all occasions of dispute, and when dragged into it by the hair of his head (morally speaking) he *gives*, under the most provoking contradictions, with the softness of a feather bed.' But as against this, 'although he is genial, it seems to be with his head, rather than with his heart – a sort of theoretic geniality'.

Jane and Thomas had 'literally, not five minutes alone to-gether since Emerson arrived'. 'He [Emerson] sits up after me at nights,' said Jane, 'and is down before me in the mornings, till I begin to feel as if I had the measles or some such thing.'

As for Carlyle, he told Lady Harriet Baring (Lady Ashburton), 'I was torn to pieces, talking with him; for his sad Yankee rule seemed to be, that talk should go on incessantly except when sleep interrupted it: a frightful rule.'

But worst of all the visitors was Miss Geraldine Jewsbury. This young lady had written Mr Carlyle an enthusiastic letter, and, rather against Mrs Carlyle's wish, she was invited 'in a sort of way' to come to Cheyne Row for two or three weeks.

She came, and was pronounced by Carlyle to be 'one of the most interesting young women I have seen for years'.

Alas! Within a very short time: 'That girl', he remarked, 'is an absolute fool, and it is a mercy she is so ill-looking.'

The visit was an unqualified fiasco. Miss Jewsbury maddened Carlyle by (literally) lying at his feet and staring up adoringly at him, or else falling asleep and remaining on the floor for hours – with the result that he took to 'sitting upstairs in the evenings as well as in the forenoons', according to his wife; and 'of other people she has seen very few – and all of these decline talking with her'.

This was as well; for when she *did* succeed in forcing someone to converse with her, 'doctrines flew like bats'.

'I wish,' said Carlyle, 'she could once get it firmly into her head that neither woman nor man was born for the exclusive, or even for the chief, purpose of falling in love or being fallen in love with.' For 'Geraldine', Mrs Carlyle wrote, years afterwards, 'has one besetting weakness: she is never happy unless she has a *grande passion* on hand; and, as unmarried men take flight at her impulsive, demonstrative ways, her grande passions have been all expended on *married* men, who felt themselves safe.'

She pursued, in a remorseless manner, all the men who visited Cheyne Row – to the great annoyance of Mrs Carlyle, and to the considerable embarrassment of the men, who refused to be left alone in the room with her.

She developed an exaggerated, unconsciously unwholesome affection for Mrs Carlyle, to whom she said, 'I feel much more like a lover towards you than a female friend.' And 'I am as jealous as a Turk, and don't, besides, care half a straw for seeing my friends except *tête à tête* when I feel strongly disposed to assassinate everybody who does not keep out of reach.'

Both Mr and Mrs Carlyle were thoroughly bored by her and wished the three weeks of her visit would end. But five weeks passed – and only then did she go. The acquaintance, however, continued.

Carlyle, quite unconsciously, gave his wife cause for pain by his entirely innocent friendship with Lady Harriet Baring (who, when her husband succeeded to the peerage, became Lady Ashburton). A friendship that could allow her husband to write such phrases, in letters to his friend, as 'You are indeed the best and beautifullest, bountiful as the summer and the sun' and 'Oh best and beautifullest of Heaven's creatures, I kiss the hem of your garment' must have been very hard to bear. And so must the taunts to which it laid her open. The odious Samuel Rogers, described by Carlyle as 'a half-frozen Whig gentleman! no hair at all, but one of the whitest bald scalps, blue eyes shrewd, sad, and cruel; toothless horse-shoe mouth drawn up to the very nose; slow-croaking, sarcastic insight, perfect breeding', showed that perfect breeding at a dinner party given by Dickens, by inquiring ' "Is your husband as much infatuated as ever with Lady Ashburton?" "Oh, of course" I' [Jane] 'said *laughing* – "why shouldn't he?" – "Now – do you like her – tell me honestly is she kind to *you* – as kind as she is to your husband?" "Why, you know it is impossible for *me* to know how kind she is to *my* husband; but I can say she is extremely kind to *me*, and I should be stupid and ungrateful if I did not like her." "Humph!" (disappointedly). "Well! it is very good of you to like her when she takes away all your husband's company from you – he is always there, isn't he?" "Oh, good gracious no!" (still laughing *admirably*). "He writes and reads a good deal in his own study." "But he spends all his evenings with her, I am told?" – "No, not all – for example, you see he is *here* this evening." "Yes," he said in a tone of vexation, "I *see* he is here *this* evening – and hear him, too – for he has done nothing but talk across the room since he came in!" '

Lady Harriet died in the spring of the year 1857, but though she had gone, her shadow remained, dimming the colours of Mrs Carlyle's life.

In August and early September 1863, Mr and Mrs Carlyle had spent, according to Carlyle, 'six weeks of beautiful green solitude'. But to Jane they were a red fire of constant pain, day and night; and, owing to neuralgia, she was not able even to comb her hair, 'or do anything in which a left arm is needed as well as a right one'.

On a day towards the end of September, as she walked towards St Martin's-le-Grand, to take an omnibus, she slipped and crashed to the ground, lying there in agony. A crowd collected; a policeman appeared; and she was lifted into a cab and returned to Cheyne Row. 'Do get me up to my room,' she implored a neighbour and the maid, 'before Mr Carlyle knows anything about it. He'll drive me mad if he comes in now.'

But Carlyle had heard her arrive.

Her martyrdom reached its height: 'such a deluge', wrote her husband, 'of intolerable pain, indescribable, unaidable pain, as I have never seen or dreamt of, and which drained

six or eight months of my poor darling's life as in the blackness of very death.' 'Oh, I have seen such expressions in those
dear and beautiful eyes as exceeded all tragedy! (One night
in particular, when she rushed desperately out to me, without speech, got laid and wrapped by me on the sofa, and
gazed silently on all the old familiar objects and me.) Her
pain she would seldom speak of, but when she did, it was in
terms as if there were no language for it; "any honest pain,
mere pain, if it were of cutting my flesh with knives, or saw-
ing my bones, I could hail that as a luxury in comparison."'

At times she thought she was going insane, and implored
her husband not to put her in an asylum. At others, she
begged the doctor to take pity on her and kill her.

In the new year of 1864, 'she has', her husband wrote 'no
sleep, can get none; one sound sleep in 7 weeks, that has
been her allowance'.

In October of the following year, whilst she was, once
more, having a protracted fit of sleeplessness, Mr Carlyle 'has
been off his sleep again, listening for "railway whistles"
which have been just audible – nothing more – for years . . .'
'the bad nights I have had lately were not my own fault but
produced by listening to Mr C. jumping up to smoke, to
thump at his bed and so on'.

And then: 'Imagine the situation', she wrote to the new
Lady Ashburton, her dearest friend. 'You have heard, I
think, of our troubles in long past years from neighbouring
Cocks. How I had to rush about to one and other House-
holder, going down on my knees, and tearing my hair
(figuratively speaking); to obtain the silence of those
feathered Demons, that broke Mr C.'s sleep with their least
croupy crow; when you might have fired a *Pistol* at his ear
without waking him! Thro efforts that I still shudder at the
recollections of, the neighbouring gardens were quite cleared
of Cocks, and Mr C. forgetting all the woe they brought him

had been free, latterly, to devote his exclusive attention to – *Railway Whistles!* Bearing this in mind, be so good as to imagine my sensations, one morning about a month ago, on being startled awake, before daylight, with the loud crowing of a full-grown Cock, from under my very bed (as it seemed in the bewilderment of the first moment!) . . .'

Mrs Carlyle kept 'the bad secret in her breast' for a full week, during which, 'Thanks to the prepossession of *Railway Whistles*, Mr C. never heard the *crowing* under his nose! But night after night I expected to hear his foot descend on the floor overhead, with the old frantic stamp – precluding much.'

In the end, however, Mrs Carlyle had the cock silenced, 'to the raptures of Mr C., who had just discovered his Enemy, the very day that he was delivered from him, when he was "just going off to Tyndall to beg him to supply him privately with some Strychnine".'

So Mr Carlyle clasped his wife in his arms, and assured her over and over again that she was his Guardian Angel. 'Humph!' wrote Mrs Carlyle. 'It is no sinecure.'

She had still two more years to live. At moments, it seemed as if she would recover. Then again she would drown in a red sea of pain, a grey sea of sleeplessness. She tried to hide these deaths from her husband, and he, only too willingly, often allowed her to do so. . . . He was occupied with his own 'new depths of stupefaction and dull misery of body and mind'. 'He is just now', wrote Geraldine Jewsbury, in the new year of 1865, 'what in a mere mortal would be called "cross," *very* cross; but as he is a hero and demigod, I suppose the proper formula would be that he sees keenly and feels acutely the unsatisfactory nature of all human and domestic sayings and doings, and he expresses his sentiments very forcibly.'

In 1866, the prophet was honoured in his own country. On

the 2nd of April, Carlyle succeeded Gladstone as Rector of Edinburgh University. He left for Scotland on the 29th of March.

His wife did not accompany him, for 'the frost and snow of the last day or two have chilled my spirit of enterprise into one lump of ice'. But she was in a state of hysterical excitement and joy, and was 'only', she wrote, 'kept in her skin by a constant supply of telegrams and letters'.

As he left the house, she kissed him twice, standing watching him as he walked through the door.

He was never to feel that warm kiss again.

His home-coming was a little delayed because he had sprained his ankle. But two days before he was, at last, to return to her, she, happy and peaceful in mind, went for her usual afternoon drive in the brougham, her little dog Tiny sitting on her lap. The brougham took her through Kensington Gardens; she got out of the carriage, walked for a little, then returned to the brougham. As the carriage approached Victoria Gate, she told the coachman, Sylvester, to stop, and let the dog out; he ran for a little, beside the carriage, until a brougham, crossing the road, knocked the dog over. Jane rushed from the carriage to the side of the dog, which lay on its back, howling. Some women came up to Jane, and together they examined the dog, whose only hurt was a bruise on his paw. Jane returned to the brougham with the dog in her arms.

The drive was continued – past Hyde Park Corner, past the Serpentine, past the place where the dog had been knocked over, then back to Hyde Park Corner again.

Sylvester turned and looked at Jane. She did not speak.

He drove once more towards the Serpentine. Still no word came from her. She had not moved, and her hands were still lying in her lap. Her eyes were closed.

The sleepless had found sleep at last.

'For forty years,' wrote her husband, in his agony of mind, 'she was the true and ever-loving helpmate of her husband, and by act and word unweariedly forwarded him, as none else could, in all of worthy that he did or attempted. She died in London, 21st April, 1866; suddenly snatched away from him, and the light of his life as if gone out.'

'Oh, if you could look into my heart of hearts,' he had written to her, at the height of her pain about his friendship with Lady Harriet Baring, 'I do not think you could be angry with me, or sorry for yourself either.'

She would never know, now, how much he had loved her.

17

Marine Adventurers
(Piracy and Piety)

'For almost two thousand years,' wrote John Livingston Lowes in that great book, *The Road to Xanadu*, 'a vast and mysterious austral continent beckoned through the mists of terrible and haunted seas.

'The Antipodes lay, enveloped in mystery, in the oceans about the austral pole . . .

'But between were fire and ice and the terrors of impenetrable mists. . . . One word, and only one, stretches in dim capitals across the whole southern hemisphere. . . . It is BRUMAE: fogs . . . Frigida and Perusta: frozen and burned – the icy breath of polar seas and the fiery noon of equatorial calms – front each other across the huge trough of the ocean. . . . The ocean which no mortal sees by reason of that zone in which the elements melt with fervent heat. . . . And like sea, like land. "*Dixerto dexabitado per caldo*" (a desert uninhabited on account of heat) stands in red along the sides of the South of a fifteenth-century planosphere. But beyond the ocean lies another barrier: "*circulus autralis qui est ex frugore inhabitabilis*", as a map of the twelfth century has it – the austral zone where nobody can live by reason of the cold.'

Such were the wastes to be invaded and conquered by the Pygmean empire of Man, in its later days, and to these came a certain Captain Simon Hatley for the adventure that was to be the subject of one of the greatest poems in the English language.

But in his time, a large part of the world was no longer a mystery.

An earlier traveller, Sir John Mandeville (who, it seems, existed only in imagination, and never took on flesh and blood) although, according to his biographer, Mr Malcolm Letts, 'he had no doubt that the world was round' – was, at the same time, 'concerned about the Antipodes, because of the suggestion by the supporters of the flat-earth theory that, if the earth were, in fact, a sphere, the men on the sides and lower surface would be living sideways or upside down, even if they did not fall off into space.' However, he comforted himself by the reflection that 'if a man thinks he is walking upright, he is, in fact, walking the right way up, as God meant him to do, and that is all that matters'.

The mariners of whom I am about to speak were not concerned about the roundness or flatness of the earth, but they were undoubtedly under the impression that, whatever their actual attitude might be, they were walking upright, as God meant them to do.

Many of these later travellers were in business as Pirates, and, when we think of the careers of such foreigners as Captain Yallers and Captain Cauchemar, it is a surprise to learn that there were English and American pirates who were men of exemplary piety. Captain Halsey, for instance, was born at Boston in 1670, and, according to Captain Philip Gosse's *The Pirates' Who's Who*, having received a commission from the Governor of Massachusetts to cruise as a privateer on the Banks, turned pirate as soon as he was out of sight of the land. Virtuous and merciful (he never killed a prisoner excepting under the strictest necessity), he was much beloved by his men, and when he died, in 1716, of some tropical fever, he was buried with full honours, 'with great solemnity, the prayers of the Church of England being read over him and his sword and pistols laid on his coffin, which was covered with a ship's Jack. As many minute guns were fired over him as he was old – viz. 46.' 'His grave was made in a garden of water-melons and fenced in to prevent his being rooted up by wild pigs.'

Captain Bartholomew Roberts (1682–1722) of the *Royal Fortune*, captured, among other treasures, in the year before his death, a clergyman. The virtuous Captain Roberts was desperately anxious to secure the services of a minister of religion to superintend the spiritual life of his crew and to keep them in the way of sanctity, and he begged the captive to sign on, swearing that nothing should be asked of him but to conduct the services and to make rum punch. But the cleric remained obdurate, and at last, in despair, Captain Roberts let him go, restoring to him all his possessions excepting a corkscrew and three prayer-books, which, said Dr Gosse, 'were sorely needed aboard the *Royal Fortune*'.

It is true that no English pirate could compete, as to piety, with the French pirate Captain Misson, who was so grieved by the bad language imported by some Dutch pirates on to his ship, that he addressed his crew as follows:

'Before he had the Misfortune of having them on Board, his Ears were never grated with hearing the Name of the great Creator profan'd, tho' he, to his Sorrow, had often since heard his own Men guilty of that Sin, which administer'd neither Profit nor Pleasure, and might draw upon them a severe Punishment: That if they had a just Idea of that great Being, they wou'd never mention him, but they wou'd immediately reflect on his Purity, and their own Vileness.'

Finally, 'he gave the Dutch Notice, that the first whom he catch'd either with an Oath in his Mouth or Liquor in his Head should be brought to the Geers, whipped and pickled, for an Example to the rest of his Nation.'

Still, as I have hinted, many English pirates were men of exemplary piety, regarding their vocation as a religious duty. In pursuit of this, they braved the terrors of the deep, and the monsters to be found there – such as 'The Physeter, which in English, we are told, is called The Whirlpool' (Lowes, op. cit.) – 'the ill-omened creature with a human face and a monkish cowl, whose German name is Wasserman; the delicate monster seen off Poland in 1531, whose scaly skin assumed the likeness of a Bishop's garb, the bat-winged demon worthily named the Satyr of the Sea; the grisly Ziphius, the Rosmarus, an elephant in size, which lumberingly scales the mountains bordering on the sea; the Scolopendra, with face of flame and eyes which measure twenty feet around; the formidable Monoceros'.

These monsters, for some reason best known to themselves, seem never to have appeared to any Englishman; nor has any member of our race recorded having beheld the land of the Farici, whose food consists of raw gibbets of lions and panthers (Santorem, *Histoire*, III.2) or that of the Manoculi, a race that though endowed with only one leg could run like the wind, and that would lie lazily under the sun, using their one huge foot (some said that this was blue) as a parasol.

For the English are notoriously addicted to incredulity. But this does not prevent some members of the race from having customs – personal habits – as strange as that of the races above mentioned.

In the year 1708, financed by some merchants of Bristol, and also by Dr Thomas Dover – an eminent physician of that city, who accompanied the expedition as second Captain of *The Duke* – two pirate ships, *The Duke* and *The Dutchess*, set out for the South Seas. Their crews, filled with religious enthusiasm, were interested neither in Physeter, Wasserman, Ziphius, nor Rosmarus, but in the Spaniards, to them far greater monsters whom they intended to harry and despoil – for were not the Portuguese and the Spaniard Roman Catholics, and was it not therefore a pious duty to deprive them of their possessions?

Not only Dr Dover (the inventor of the famous Dover Powders, the terror of infants in the late seventeenth, eighteenth and early nineteenth centuries), but also other members of the expedition were to become famous: the Chief Pilot, William Dampier (afterwards Captain Dampier), the author of *New Voyage Round the World* – 'old Dampier, a rough sailor, but a man of exquisite mind', according to Coleridge; Captain Woodes Rogers, and Simon Hatley, third mate of *The Dutchess*. I do know that Captain Dampier was particularly eccentric – apart from his excessive friendliness with the harried and plundered Portuguese; and Hatley's only eccentricity, as far as we know, was his extreme addiction to superstition. But this was to lead Mr Hatley to an act that made him famous throughout the poetry-reading world – though not under his own name.

But the adventures of these pirates – if not their characters – had that exaggeration of gesture that may be called eccentricity.

Dr Dover had this peculiarity: a fondness for inflicting the internal remedy of vitriol and quicksilver on his patients. However, these remedies were to stand the crews of two ships in good stead.

Arrived at the two cities of Guaiaquil, under the Line, in the South Seas, the adventurers took these by storm, burning and plundering. But the dead inhabitants of the cities, slain by a more terrible enemy than the English, were to be revenged on them. By night, the pirates lay down to sleep in the Cathedral.

The silence surged about them like a sea.

Then a strange air – an odour only half perceptible, but that seemed a part of the silence – came to them.

It was some time before they realised who were their bedfellows . . . 'Enough semi-mummified corpses, dead of that epidemic of Plague that had invaded the two cities, lay, unburied, on the floors of the Cathedral to form a world of mummies made medicine.' ('That mummye', according to Peter Treveris' *The Grete Herbal* 'is to be chosen that is bright blacke, stynkynge and styffe. And that is whyt and draweth to a dunne colour and that is not stynkyng nor styffe and that poudreth lightly is naught.')

Dr Dover, however, did not make medicine of these mummies; but, when one hundred and eight of his men were seized with the Plague, he had them bled, then gave them 'Large Quantities of Water, acidulated by Oil or Spirit of Vitriol; and by this method, no more than seven or eight of the men were lost.'

The rest of the company continued, for several nights, to share the Cathedral, with their long-sleeping bedfellows. . . . This was in 1709 . . .

But let us leave these cold shadows for the memory of the heat and violence of the tropical sun, and the consequent discomforts.

The year before Dr Dover's triumphant victory over the Plague, the mariners had had trouble with 'very large spiders', which, according to Woodes Rogers, 'weave their webs so strong that 'tis difficult to get thro 'em'; also 'the heats are excessive to us who come newly from Europe, so that several of our men began to be sick and were blooded'.

But the religious devotions of the crew were undisturbed. 'We began to read prayers in both ships, mornings and evenings, as opportunity would permit, according to the Church of England; designing to continue it the term of the voyage.'

Dr Dover and others went shooting, and brought back with them, as their only prize, 'a monstrous creature, which they had kill'd, having prickles like a hedgehog, with fur between them, and a head and tail like a monkey's. It stunk' (Mr Rogers assures us) 'intolerably, which the Portuguese told us was only the skin, that the meat of it is very delicious and that they often kill'd them for the table. But our men, being not yet at very short allowance, none of 'em had stomach good enough to try the experiment, so that we were forc'd to throw it overboard to make a sweet ship.'

But there were gayer interludes. At the Isle de Grande, says Rogers, 'assisting with both ships' musick' at a great religious ceremony, 'we waited on the Governour, Signior Raphael de Silva Lagos, in a body, being ten of us, with two trumpets and a hautboy, which he desir'd might play us to church, where our musick did the office of an organ, but separate from the singing, which was by the fathers well perform'd. Our musick played "Hey, boys, up we go!" and all manner of noisy paltry tunes. And after service, our musicians, who were by that time more than half drunk, march'd at the head of the company; next to them an old father and two fryars carrying lamps of incense, then an image dressed with flowers and wax candles, then about forty priests, fryars, etc., followed by the Governour of the town, myself, and Captain Courtney, with each of us a long wax candle lighted. The ceremony held about two hours; after which we were splendidly entertained by the fathers of the convent, and then by the Governour. They unanimously told us they expected nothing from us but our Company, and they had no more but our musick.'

Next day, before he sailed, Rogers entertained the Governor, priests and friars on board *The Duke*, 'where they were very merry, and in their cups propos'd the Pope's health to us. But we were quits with 'em by proposing the Archbishop of Canterbury; and to keep up the humour, we also propos'd William Penn's health, and they liked the liquor so well, that they refused neither.'

It was thought advisable that the Governor and the rest of the guests should spend the night on board. As they left next morning, said Rogers, 'we saluted 'em with a huzza from each ship . . .'

'Our musick . . .'

The expedition was accompanied by fiddlers, hautboy players, trumpeters and mountebanks, their hats gaily beribboned with streamers of Drake colour, gozelinge colour, marigold, Popinjay blue, lusty gallant, Judas colour, Devil in the hedge, and Dead Spaniard.

I do not know what, with the exception of 'Hey, boys, up go we', the musicians played, but I feel the tunes were more likely to be such country music as 'Bonnets so Blue', 'None so Pretty', 'Jenny Pluck Pears', 'Rufty Hufty', 'Trunkles', 'Dargason', 'Bonny Green Garters', and 'Lumps of Plum Pudding' – tunes reminding them of their native Devonshire lanes and Bristol haunts – than more material airs.

I imagine, too, that the seas, though tropical waters, would have been less haunted, for these gay sailors, by the Physeter and other terrors, than by such marine creatures as 'the Hat Slime-fish', which 'hath a blew Button or Knob, that . . . may also be compared unto such a Straw Hat as our Women wear', and the 'Rose-like-shaped Slime-fish', that Martens saw on his Journey to Greenland – and that might, indeed, have swum from the Arctic circles to the Tropics, to greet them.

At the turn of the year, had Captain Dampier but known it, he was to be brought face to face with an old shipmate who was by no means pleased to see him.

In 1703, five years or so before the religious feast at the Isle de Grande, another expedition, consisting of two ships, had sailed to the South Seas, and amongst the crew was a pirate named Alexander Selkirk – in his turn to become famous. The captain of one ship was William Dampier, that of the other, Captain Stradling. Both captains seem, at that time, to have been in the habit of marooning, or, in any case, of deserting, their followers. Mr Selkirk, it is true, brought his fate upon himself, since, after a violent quarrel with Captain Stradling, he deserted the ship and swam to the deserted island of Juan Fernandez—about one hundred and ten leagues from the coast of Chile.

Then, as the sound of the ships' oars retreated, the horror of his situation overcame him, and, rushing into the water, he screamed to the departing ships, imploring his shipmates to return. From the deck of one ship, Stradling mocked his despair. The ships drifted farther and farther away. He was alone.

'Day after day', said Mr de la Mare in *Desert Islands and Robinson Crusoe*,[1] 'he sat in watch, his face towards the sea, until his eyes and the light failed him and he could watch no more. By night he had lain shivering with terror at the howlings of sea-monsters on the shore . . .'

But, 'as time went on . . . he vanquished his blues, he set to work, kept tally of his days, and, like Orlando, cut his name in the trees. He fed plentifully on turtle until he could no more stomach it except in jellies. . . .' 'Seals . . . in November came ashore to whelp and engender, their bleating and howling so loud that the noise of them could be heard inland a mile from the shore. Another creature strange to Selkirk was the sea-lion, the hair of whose whiskers is "stiff enough to make tooth-pickers!"'

But there were other living beings. Mr Selkirk was, according to one biographer, 'much annoyed by multitudes of rats' which, while he was asleep, persisted in gnawing his feet and other parts of his person.

But, rats or no rats, this virtuous pirate 'kept up that simple but beautiful form of family worship he had been accustomed

1. Published by Farrar and Rinehart, New York, N.Y. Reprinted with their kind permission.

to in his father's house. . . . His devotions and frequent study of the scriptures soothed and elevated his mind.'

No doubt this strengthened his determination to thwart the rats, and, according to the same authority, John Howell, he 'caught and tamed wild cats and amused himself by teaching them to dance'.

Cheered by these exercises in the Terpsichorean art, and also, perhaps, by the art of song (for it was believed by some that Mr Selkirk, also, taught the cats to sing), he whiled away the tedious hours.

'He caught, as well, goats,' Mr Howell continued, 'and taught them, as well as his cats, to dance; and he often afterwards declared, that he never danced with a lighter heart or greater spirit anywhere to the best of music. . . .' 'He was, perhaps, as happy a man, nay happier, than the gayest ballroom could have presented, in the most civilised country upon earth.'

This happy state was interrupted by the arrival of *The Duke* and *The Dutchess*, which, surprised by the appearance of a fire on an apparently deserted island, determined to investigate the cause.

At first, hearing that Captain Dampier, his former commander, was on board, Mr Selkirk utterly refused to be rescued. But he was, at last, persuaded to join one of the ships as mate, and gradually, Mr Howell tells us, 'resumed his old habits as a seaman, but without the vices which sometimes attach to the profession. He rigidly refrained from profane oaths. . . .' Indeed, 'religion obtained command over all the actions' of this pious pirate.

His adventures were by no means over. He was, of course, a witness to Dr Dover's victory over the Plague, and he was sent in search of his shipmate Mr Hatley, who, having been sent on an expedition from the ship with a handful of companions, had vanished, and had been captured by a barbarous people, who flogged them and tied them to trees by the neck, from which precarious situation they were rescued by a priest.

Mr Hatley's shipmate, Alexander Selkirk – or Robinson Crusoe, as Defoe called him – on his return to England was on the verge of becoming an Ornamental Hermit (though unpaid). For, 'on the top of an eminence, in his father's garden at Largo, he constructed a sort of cave, in which he would meditate, frequently in tears'.

Perhaps he missed his dancing partners.

As for Captain Hatley: 'he arrived safe in London in the year 1723', Mr Howell tells us, 'after which period there is no further account of him'.

. . . And yet . . .

In Captain George Shelvocke's *Voyage Round the World by the Way of the Great South Sea* (pages 72, 73) we read 'We had continual squals of sleet, snow, and rain, and the heavens were perpetually hid from us by gloomy dismal clouds. In short, one would think it impossible that any living thing could subsist in so rigid a climate; and indeed we all observed that we had not the sight of one fish of any kind, since we were come to the southward of the streights of *le Mair*, nor one seabird, except a disconsolate black *Albitross*, who accompanied us for several days, hovering about us as if he had lost himself, till *Hatley*, my second Captain, observing, in one of his melancholy fits, that this bird was always hovering near us, imagined, from his colour, that it might be some ill omen. That which, I suppose, induced him the more to encourage this superstition, was the continued series of contrary tempestuous winds, which had oppressed us ever since we had got into this sea. Be that as it would, he, after some fruitless attempts, at length shot the *Albitross*, not (perhaps), doubting that we should have a fair wind after it.'

John Livingstone Lowes says (op. cit.), 'this may be the so-called "sooty albatross" (once *Diomedea fuliginosa*, now, in scientific parlance, *Phoebetria palpebrata antarctica*), which haunts the same latitudes; and this albatross, as its name in the vernacular implies, may quite properly be called black'.

For Mr Howell was wrong in saying there was no further account of Simon Hatley.

He was the original of the Ancient Mariner.

Index

343

MORE ABOUT PENGUINS

Penguinews, which appears every month, contains details of all the new books issued by Penguins as they are published. From time to time it is supplemented by *Penguins in Print*, which is a complete list of all books published by Penguins which are in print. (There are well over three thousand of these.)

A specimen copy of *Penguinews* will be sent to you free on request, and you can become a subscriber for the price of the postage. For a year's issues (including the complete lists) please send 30p if you live in the United Kingdom, or 60p if you live elsewhere. Just write to Dept EP, Penguin Books Ltd, Harmondsworth, Middlesex, enclosing a cheque or postal order, and your name will be added to the mailing list.

Some other books published by Penguins are described on the following pages.

Note: *Penguinews* and *Penguins in Print* are not available in the U.S.A. or Canada

Men and Dinosaurs

Edwin H. Colbert

The dinosaur has always enjoyed better public relations than his competitors. Like Penguin or Hoover his brand-name, for many of us, serves to describe the whole range of extinct monsters.

In *Men and Dinosaurs* a Professor of Vertebrate Palaeontology tells of the men involved, during the last 150 years, in the gradual reconstruction of the dinosaur. In a pageant of personalities he introduces Gideon Mantell, who discovered the iguanadon in Tilgate forest and filled his house so full of fossils that there was no room for his family, who left; William Buckland (who first described the Megalosaurus in 1824), the man who pointed out to the church authorities of Palermo that the remains of St Rosalia must be the bones of a defunct goat; and Franz Baron Noposa von Felsö-Szilvás, a character as colourful as he was learned about dinosaurs and who once applied for a job as King of Albania.

Boasting less flesh and blood but no less fascination, the story (which goes back some 200 million years) of the extinct herbivorous reptile itself emerges from Dr Colbert's delightful account.

'An enjoyable book, telling a story which is full of interest' – *Nature*

1066 and All That

W. C. Sellar and R. J. Yeatman

All the history you can remember . . . 40 years later.
   A historical harlequinade of howlers, jests, and jibes, which has been a best-seller for over thirty years.

'It is possibly the best thing of its kind ever done. Indeed it is the *only* thing of its precise kind . . . quotation is hopeless; every sentence clamours for it' – *Observer*

Not for sale in the U.S.A. or Canada

Eminent Victorians

Lytton Strachey

'*Eminent Victorians* is the work of a great anarch, a revolutionary textbook on bourgeois society written in the language through which the bourgeois ear could be lulled and beguiled, the Mandarin style' – Cyril Connolly in *Enemies of Promise*

Lytton Strachey's desire 'to lay bare the facts . . . as I understand them, dispassionately, impartially, and without ulterior intentions' gave him, in an age of panegyric, the reputation of an iconoclast. In his famous study of four Victorian figures, in fact, only the essays on Cardinal Manning and Dr Arnold are consistently severe: his portrait of Florence Nightingale, though it exploded the fable of the Lady of the Lamp, is often admiring, and the tragedy of General Gordon is retailed with a note of tenderness.

If these studies, with their free and expressive lines, can be seen as, in the best sense, caricatures, yet (as Michael Holroyd has written in his major biography of Strachey): '*Eminent Victorians* marked . . . the initial stage in a more benign treatment of the Victorian age'.

Also available

QUEEN VICTORIA

Not for sale in the U.S.A.

The Queens and the Hive

Edith Sitwell

No hive can tolerate two Queens.

In the fatal clash between the Protestant Queen of England and the Catholic Queen of Scots, men were determined that 'The death of Mary is the life of Elizabeth'.

In this moving chronicle a modern poet magnificently recaptures the splendid colour and sordid intrigue of the most spectacular period of history in Britain.

Not for sale in the U.S.A.